TOW
PAR
BY W. HARDING.
1839.
CW00968863

VICTORIAN FARNHAM

RICHARD MASON
solicitor and public servant, 1866-1910

VICTORIAN FARNHAM

The story of a Surrey Town
1837 - 1901

by
EWBANK SMITH

PHILLIMORE
London and Chichester

1971

Published by

PHILLIMORE & CO. LTD.
Shopwyke Hall, Chichester, Sussex, England

SBN 900592 30 3

Thanks are due to the generous help of the Marc Fitch Fund in enabling this volume to be published

Text set by Phillimore in 11/12 pt. Press roman
Printed by Eyre & Spottiswoode (Portsmouth) Ltd., at the Grosvenor Press

CONTENTS

Contents *(continued)*

LIST OF ILLUSTRATIONS

PREFACE

NO HISTORY, if it is to be detailed and comprehensive, can be contained in one single book; it can only be told in a number of correlative volumes, each dealing with one of the many different aspects which together make up the whole. This notebook on Farnham is one piece of the jigsaw. Its period is that of Queen Victoria (with a brief recapitulation); also it presents the town from one viewpoint only—that of its public administrators. Moreover it does not set out to be a municipal lawyer's *vade mecum.* The prolific legislation of Victoria's reign is admirably taken care of in other pieces of the jigsaw—Pratt & Mackenzie, Lumley, Ryde and other massive tomes, which deal individually and exhaustively with local government statutes and case law. This book undertakes to be nothing more than a chronicle of the reactions of local people to these laws and of how they were implemented in Farnham.

It has been compiled from records kept by the authorities that governed Farnham during the Queen's reign—the Vestry Meetings, and *ad hoc* bodies elected to control the individual services, the Local Board and, finally, the Urban District Council. Though it had its beginnings several centuries earlier, local government grew in Victoria's reign in range and stature to the form we know today. It was during these important years that Britain not only reached her zenith in world affairs but also put her own house in order with a series of social reforms. In the 19th century, the coterie of men in a small country town who were able and willing to devote their energies and time to the public welfare—the landowners, professional men, prosperous tradesmen, (in Farnham) the hopgrowers and brewers, and the suchlike–was limited. From its ranks were chosen those who sat on the various Boards and Committees, with the few solicitors in the town acting as their paid officials. Being in short supply, they often sat on more than one body and it was not unknown, in times of differences of opinion, for spirited correspondence to pass between a member of one such body and himself, as member of another. Having discovered a source of humour, one looks for and finds others. If I have highlighted these, then I have done so as a means of rendering the somewhat clinical jargon of the minute-books in a more palatable form with a view to making it attractive to a wider circle of readers. There is no thought of scoffing at the characters in this book, for whom I have a deep respect and admiration.

ACKNOWLEDGEMENTS

THIS BOOK would not have been possible without reference to records of the 19th century in the custody of the Farnham Urban District Council. I am indebted to the Chairman and Members of the Council and their staff for allowing me unrestricted access to such documents and for helping in many other ways. I am especially grateful to Sir John Verney Bt. M.C. for his interest and encouragement and for an introduction to a publisher. My thanks are also offered to the following ladies and gentlemen who have so kindly entrusted me with photographs and other forms of illustrations, or who have contributed in various ways to my knowledge of events of the period–Mrs. M.J. Bide, Mrs. B.I. Bilcliffe, H.G. Ashton Booth Esq., A.T.D., A.M.A. (Curator of the Farnham Museum), Mrs. N.G. Cass, Mrs. E.H. Crundwell, Miss B.E. Falkner, J.E. Goddard Esq., B.W. Hawkes Esq., Mrs. S.A. Johnson, R.C.R. Mason Esq., R.J. Parker Esq., F.L.A. (Chief Librarian, Farnham Public Library), Mrs. W.F. Rankine, E.R. Robins Esq., F.W. Simmonds Esq., Nigel Temple Esq.

I am deeply indebted to the Trustees of the Marc Fitch Fund and to the Farnham Urban District Council for their generous contributions towards the cost of publication, which grants have enabled the book to be offered to the public at a reduced price.

E.S.

KEY TO AREAS AND AUTHORITIES

FARNHAM PARISH. This was the original ecclesiastical parish adopted for the purposes of civil administration. It comprised the town and outlying districts of Dippenhall, Hoghatch, Hale, Heath End, Weybourne, Badshot Lea, Runfold, Waverley, Tilford, Bourne (Lower and Upper), Wrecclesham and Rowledge. Over the centuries control had passed out of the hands of the vicar and magistrates to various *ad hoc* bodies of townspeople elected annually in the vestry.

THE OVERSEERS were responsible for the levying of rates, the administration of charities and parochial matters of minor importance. Their paid officer was the Assistant Overseer.

THE BOARD OF GUARDIANS–responsible for the relief of the poor, a duty once that of the Overseers. The Guardians operated in a union of neighbouring parishes called the Farnham Union and comprising the parishes of Farnham, Aldershot (until 1897), Dockenfield, Frensham and Frimley. Their functions finally passed to the Surrey County Council.

BOARD OF SURVEYORS OF HIGHWAYS. Maintenance of roads, footways and bridges in the parish. Precepted on the Overseers for funds. Salaried officers, Clerk and Assistant Surveyor.

INSPECTORS OF LIGHTING AND WATCHING. Provision of street-lighting and maintenance of the Watch. Operated in the town area only, in which a special rate was levied by the Overseers for the purpose. Paid staff, the Clerk and Serjeant of the Watch.

FARNHAM BURIAL BOARD. Set up in 1855 for the provision

of cemeteries. Officer, Clerk and Registrar of Burials (combined appointment).

FARNHAM LOCAL BOARD. Set up in 1866 with the object of establishing a sanitary authority capable of introducing drainage to the urban area of the parish. It took over all local government services save those of the Overseers, Guardians and Burial Board. The remainder of the parish remained unchanged. Given power to levy a general district rate to meet expenses. Salaried officers, Clerk and combined posts of Surveyor, Inspector of Nuisances and Rate Collector.

FARNHAM URBAN DISTRICT COUNCIL. Formed in 1895 under the Local Government Act 1894, which also inaugurated the Farnham Rural District Council in the Farnham Parish area. The district was that of the former Local Board. Chief officers, Clerk and Surveyor/Inspector of Nuisances; minor posts were created as the functions of local government grew.

I

THE STORY SO FAR

ENGLISHMEN HAVE put up with some form of local government, in an official sense, ever since there were enough of them around to form a quorum. From that time, any upward trend has been marked, not so much by an awareness of personal benefit to the ratepayer, if any, as by the higher rate demand-note he has received. There is a limit even to the bottomless purse and the aspirations of those who would improve the standard of living have throughout been geared to the willingness, and to a large extent the ability, of those who have been called upon to foot the bills. More than any other factor, this has impeded the growth and quality of social services, and their development over the course of history has been a long, tortuous and often contested process that has needed the occasional shot in the arm from a watchful central government to halt paralysis and to regenerate interest.

In recording the history of a particular reign, it is advisable to begin retrospectively, with a résumé of related events, so that, on starting what is after all an instalment of a serial story, the reader may be in possession of at least some of the facts that led up to the opening chapter.

The Lighting and Watching Act, 1830 (11 Geo. 4 c.27) was aimed at the Inspectors of Lighting and Watching, whose oil lamps and eyes, as things go, were no doubt dimming. As an adoptive act it was entirely at the discretion of the townspeople whether they adopted it or not. And to demonstrate their democratic independence in the matter, the townspeople went to it with gusto.

Requisition to Churchwardens–Notice of Meeting and Proceedings in Vestry.
To the Churchwardens of and for the Market Town of Farnham in the County of Surrey.

We the undersigned being rated Inhabitants of the Market Town of Farnham aforesaid do hereby make application to you and by virtue of the Act of Parliament hereinafter referred to you are required within ten days after the receipt of this application to appoint and notify a time and place for a public Meeting in Vestry of the Inhabitants of the said Market Town for the purpose of determining whether the Provisions contained in an Act made and passed in the Eleventh year of the reign of His late Majesty King George the Fourth entitled 'An Act to make provision for the lighting and watching of Parishes in England and Wales' shall be adopted and carried into execution in the said Market Town.

Dated this Second day of August 1830

Jas. Stevens
Geo. Trimmer
Thos. Eyre
Geo. Miller
R. Shurlock
R. Drinkwater
C.J. Hume
Jas. Shotter
W. Newnham
Saml. Andrews
Robert Clark
W. Crump

We being the Churchwardens to whom the above Application is made and directed do hereby appoint and notify that a public Meeting in Vestry of the Inhabitants of this Market Town will be holden in the Parish Church on Wednesday the Eighteenth Instant at twelve o'clock at noon for the purpose of determining whether the provisions contained in the Act referred to by the above application shall be adopted and carried into Execution in the said Market Town.

Witness our Hands this Seventh day of August 1830

Geo. Miller)
John Knight) Churchwardens

At a Vestry Meeting assembled in Farnham Church this 18th day of August 1830 pursuant to the above Notice affixed on the principal outer door of such Church and also by publication of the same therein during Divine Service on Sunday Morning last.

The Revd. C.J. Hume in the Chair–

RESOLVED and determined at this Meeting by a Majority of three fourths of Votes ascertained and taken in the manner pointed out by the third section of the Act of Parliament referred to in the above Requisition that the Provisions of the said Act shall be adopted and shall henceforth take effect and come into operation within the liberty and precincts of this Township or Market Town and that Nine Inspectors shall be elected to carry such purposes into effect.

RESOLVED also that the highest Amount of Rate in the Pound which the said Inspectors shall have power to call for in any one year in order to carry into effect the provisions of the said Act shall not exceed the sum of One shilling and Four pence.

The following persons having been proposed and seconded and being qualified, as required by the ninth section of the above mentioned Act are elected Inspectors for the purposes of the said Act, viz.

ROBERT CLARK
WILLIAM CRUMP
JOHN KNIGHT
GEORGE MILLER
HENRY NICHOLS
WILLIAM PINKE PAINE
JAMES STEVENS
GEORGE TRIMMER
JOSEPH WILLIAMS

Six of the inspectors got down to business the same evening at their meeting room at the Savings Bank and resolved that William Beagley and Thomas Cole be appointed as Watchmen and Night Patrol 'for the proper protection of the Inhabitants, Houses and Property, Streets and other places within the limits of this Market Town at the weekly wages of Twelve shillings each', and that James Steer be also appointed and employed in the same capacity and at the same wages during any emergency or in the case of illness or absence of either Beagley or Cole. It was also ordered that the Watchmen's duties should be to patrol the Town of Farnham every hour from the 25th March to the 29th September from eleven o'clock at night till four in the morning and from 29th September to the 25th March from eleven at night till five in the morning.

> That one of them shall patrol once at least in every hour, West Street and through the Church Yard by Captain Prescott's to Longbridge, over the Bridge to Sir George Barlow's gate and into Red Lion Lane, and back by Longbridge to the Borough—occasionally to go from West Street by Miss Willmer's through the Meadows to the Church Yard and occasionally from Longbridge by the Meadows to the end of Dogflood, and to cry the hour in an audible voice.
>
> And that the other Watchman shall in like manner patrol Dogflood and Bear Lane to Castle Street, from thence through the Borough to the end of Longbridge and back to the Borough—occasionally to go from the end of Dogflood through the Hop Ground into Castle Street and thence behind the Lion and Lamb to the end of West Street.

Mr. Thomas Eyre was made Treasurer and Mr. William Mason the Secretary during pleasure. It was to be made known by Notice posted in the town that persons willing to contract 'for lighting about sixty lamps with good oil in the Town of Farnham from dusk in the evening of the first of September 1830 and continue every night until the thirty-first of March 1831 inclusive, except the night of each full Moon and three nights before and three after' should submit tenders.

At the next meeting on 23 August 1830, at which all nine Inspectors were present, William Moorton, plumber, was invited to sign the contract. Robert Elliott and George Smith, farriers, were ordered to make new lamps as required and to repair the old ones. A half-yearly rate of 8d. in the pound, to raise £114 5s. 1d., was levied on that part of the area within the beat of the Watchmen and limits of lighting, and a precept issued on the Overseers of the Poor, those long-suffering parish officers who, with over 200 years' experience of collecting rates, were the people most suited to carry out the disagreeable but necessary chore of raising funds.

James Steer was added to the rota of Watchmen during the emergency of the hop-picking season. Hats were ordered for the Watchmen at 5s. 6d. each. At a special meeting on 8 October 1830, the Inspectors investigated the conduct of Watchman Beagley in not having apprehended two loose characters whom he had seen in the street just before one o'clock that morning and who had been into Mr. James Lamport's garden. Beagley was suspended for one month, to be reinstated only on the production of a strong recommendation from the inhabitants in his favour. A William Hughes was appointed for a month to fill the gap—labour in those days was cheap and easy to come by. But all ended well, for Beagley had a lot of friends and got his job back, moreover Hughes was kept on as supernumerary watchman. All four men were put on special duty on Guy Fawkes night 'to prevent any tumult or riot in the Town'.

The rejuvenising effect of 11 Geo. 4 c.27 had begun to wear off and the Inspectors were settling down to the old familiar pattern of safeguarding during the dark hours a small and reasonably crime-free town, renewing Moorton's contract for lighting the oil lamps with good oil, keeping the Watchmen vigilant, staving off their creditors and harassing the Overseers for funds. The Watchmen came and went—Beagley, Hughes and Steer resigned in 1832 and were replaced with William Stannard and William Roe. The town was quiet—perhaps too quiet in the Churchyard at night. They were instructed to report all public houses and beer shops found open after hours; as Milton had put it two hundred years earlier:

> When night
> Darkens the streets, then wander forth the sons
> Of Belial, flown with insolence and wine.

And then in 1833, as if Westminster sensed that the time was ripe—as it probably was—for another booster, a Bill went through Parliament, namely the Lighting and Watching Act, 1833 (3 & 4 Will. 4 c.90), which repealed the Act of 1830 and the bumbledom started all over again. After the usual formalities, the public meeting on 27 September 1833, chaired by James Shotter, solicitor of 88 West Street, could not make up its mind whether or not to adopt the new Act. It scraped through by a two-thirds majority at a poll held the following month.

The area of the Parish to receive lighting was defined as:

> West Street extending from the western lamp to the Borough; the Borough extending from West Street to Dogflood; Dogflood Street extending from the eastern lamp to the Borough; the whole of Castle Street including the Castle; the whole of Downing Street including Longbridge to the extremity of the Pocket of Hops Public House and the Lanes or Streets leading from Downing Street to the Church.

The *Pocket of Hops* was the old name for the *Hop Bag Inn.* East Street was then known as Dogflood Street; a movement to restore this ancient name to the Woolmead development in 1964 met with canine-inspired opposition.

At a Vestry held on 1 November 1833, John Hollest of Leigh House (now the G.P.O.), West Street, in the chair, nine new Inspectors of Lighting and Watching were elected under the new Act. They were the same mixture as before, except that Joseph Williams was replaced by George Smith, innkeeper. They met at the Savings Bank on 4 November and the old order of things was resumed. John Newell, a constable, was employed to patrol the streets on 5 November 'for the purpose of preventing mischief by fire'. One must be fair about this. In the 1830s, there was no theatre, cinema, evening institute, youth club or way of escape. To be sure, there were many pubs—making beer and drinking it were the prevailing occupations of the inhabitants. But alternative outlets were the crying need of the younger set and Guy Fawkes Night provided one.

Sir George Barlow of Firgrove House wrote asking for the resumption of watching and lighting as far as his house (by some inadvertence these services had been discontinued). One-time Governor of India, Sir George had come to Firgrove House in 1828. His niece, Hilaire Barlow, married the Rev. William Nelson, brother of the late Lord Nelson, in 1828. As Farnham's Nelsonian link, albeit *post-obit*, Barlow ranked high. He got his light and, presumably, a Watchman to call round at hourly intervals during the night to tell him the time and report that all was well.

Then came the enlightened pronouncement (7 July 1834) that the Inspectors proposed to sound the recently formed Farnham Gas Company on the likely terms of lighting the town with gas. A pilot light was agreed upon for the period from 30 August to 5

November 1834, the arrangement being for the setting up of 40 gas lamps, having batswing burners, and for the lighting thereof during the said period for the sum of £25. In the event of the Gas Company not being in a state of readiness in time, the Company was to maintain the existing oil lamps at 8s. 4d. each. Negotiators for the Gas Company were Doctor William Newnham of West Street, Andrew Collyer, junior, of Collyer's Coaches, Henry Gosden Gray, grocer and William Kingham's predecessor at 18 West Street, and Robert Sampson, brewer of Red Lion Lane.

On 6 October 1834, the Inspectors burnt their oil lamps by offering them for sale to the public, but the cult of collecting antiques was not then fashionable and the lamps were removed into safe-keeping at Mr. Mason's shop. And so Farnham passed from the oil age into the gas era with a contract dated 6 January 1835 for the lighting of 38 lamps in the town part of the Parish. It cost the ratepayers another £100 a year and an example was set by the Inspectors themselves in ceasing to rent their room at the Savings Bank and meeting at each other's houses (they later held their meetings at the offices of the Gas Company). They also touched the Trustees of the Turnpike Road (East Street, Borough and West Street) for a sub and won £15 a winter from them.

The Watchmen, who missed no opportunity of persuading their employers that a Watchman's lot was not a happy one, reported any incident which happened in the streets at the dead of night. One concerned Watchman Stannard on the night of 6 September 1835 as he was making his rounds between eleven and twelve o'clock. He saw Richard Young, George Young and Charles Hack near the Market House in Castle Street. George Young had a ferret in his hand which he (Stannard) endeavoured to gain a sight of, believing it to have been stolen, when he was thrown down by Richard Young. On getting up, Richard Young attempted to strike him again but the Watchman defended himself with his staff and knocked Young down. At the subsequent Bench, the culprits apologised and promised never to assault William Stannard again. As if to signify their appreciation, the Inspectors bought Stannard a new coat and cape from Stovolds, the outfitter, costing three guineas. At the same meeting, the Watchmen were admonished for not having cried the hour (they pleaded hoarseness) and were commanded to do so every hour in future.

It is difficult nowadays to understand the wish of the inhabitants to be informed of the time at hourly intervals throughout the night, even with the added assurance that all was well. Was it due to an instinctive fear, in this still partly civilized age, that could be allayed by a repeated reminder of the presence of law and order?

Henry Downes and Stephen Scarlett joined as Watchmen in place of Roe. In March 1837, John Newell was appointed Superintendent of the Watch at £5 a year 'to have an eye of the Watchmen at least twice a week and keep a report book regarding the regularity or otherwise of the Watchmen'. The Treasurer was authorised in the event of any neglect or supposed impropriety of conduct on the part of the Watchmen to suspend them and withhold their wages. They were an unreliable lot and yet it was these men, dressed in Mr. Bumble uniforms, armed with staves and patrolling their lonely beats in the ill-lit, awesome streets through the long hours of the night, who are the real players in this tragicomedy. Beside them, their masters, the Inspectors, do not really matter much.

. . . . .

The Board of Surveyors of Highways of the Parish of Farnham, to give it its full title, was reinvigorated with the Highway Act, 1835 (5 & 6 Will. 4 c.50). This was one of those immensely long-winded 'principal Acts' which, from time to time, consolidate and bring up to date all the piecemeal legislation that has erupted from Parliament since the date of the last principal Act.

The need to keep the escape routes open in the event of civil wars had always been of prime importance. From the Magna Carta onwards, successive monarchs had enforced laws in the first instance for the bridging of rivers, which would prove embarrassing to a retreating army or a convenient spot for an ambush, and later, when wheeled vehicles came, for the upkeep of roads. The onus for this was thrust upon the inhabitants who, having no particular cause themselves to travel beyond the confines of their parishes, begrudged the considerable expense and labour of providing roads and bridges for the benefit of strangers they had no particular desire to meet. But, by the 19th century, the parishioners had accepted the situation so that the 1835 Act, instead of being compulsory, was an adoptive act. The citizens of Farnham again used their democratic privilege with a full dress *tour de force,* of which–a sample having already been narrated word for word–only the concluding resolution of the Vestry Meeting on 25 March 1836 need be recited.

> It was determined unanimously to form a Board for the superintendence of the Highways of the Parish and the following Persons being respectively Householders and residing in and assessed to the rate for the relief of the Poor of the Parish and also liable to be rated to the repair of the Highways therein were nominated and elected to serve the office of Surveyors of the Highways for the year ensuing and act as a Board to be called The Board for repair of the Highways in the Parish of Farnham, viz.

JAMES AVENELL
JOHN BARRETT
RICHARD CRUMP
DANIEL EDWARDS
CHARLES FALKNER
HENRY GOSDEN GRAY
HENRY HARRIS
CHARLES KNIGHT
JOHN KNIGHT
GEORGE KNIGHT
JOHN LIDBETTER
GEORGE MILLER
CHARLES MAY
WILLIAM PINKE PAINE
SAMUEL STEVENS
GEORGE SMALL
GEORGE SMITH
JAMES STIDSTON
JAMES STEVENS
EDMUND STEVENS

which made fairly heavy demands on the pool of local statesmen. They held their first meeting under the new Act in the *Bush Hotel* three days later. George Miller, of Castle Hill House, was voted as Chairman. The Assistant Surveyor-cum-Rate Collector who in view of subsequent events might have preferred to remain anonymous, was appointed to superintend the work done on the roads, to account for all tools, materials, implements and other things provided for the repairs of the said roads and to collect the Highway Rates and pay the bills. Richard Andrews, solicitor of West Street, was appointed Clerk of the Board at £6 per annum and Knights Bank the Treasurers. A rate of 3d. in the pound was levied.

Theirs was no mean task; unlike the limited area of the Inspectors of Lighting and Watching, the Board's district covered the whole of the Farnham Parish, larger in area than the present Urban District. A contemporary account of the beating of the bounds in the north-eastern sector of the Parish on 21 November 1823 describes how jealously this frontier with Aldershot was guarded.

At half past seven o'clock commenced walking or perambulating the Bounds of this Parish and went from the *Goats Head,* kept by Mr. R. Robinson, having waited till this time for the Rev. Mr. Austin who then took the lead, supported on right and left by the Churchwardens and Overseers (Mr. T. Eyre, Mr. Cowdrey, Mr. P. Smith–Churchwardens then present), Mr. P. Trimmer soon afterwards overtook us on horseback, Mr. Robert Sampson and George Falkner, the only Overseers present all the time, Mr. Thos. Clark, High Constable, John Newall, Constable, Thos. Pisley, the only tything man then present, George Mason, junr, Acting Overseer, and a numerous train of followers with white wands proceeded to the first Bound mark (which will be described by "X"), which is on the Hill near a gate and called Bishops Bank and was then dug out by George Young, being the third time by him, and several boys were here bumped to make them remember, as also several ludicrous circumstances, as that of painting the faces which was carried to too great an excess to the annoyance, and am sorry to say disgrace, but the body of young men were so numerous that it was impossible then to prevent it and it continued on until everyone was disfigured more or less. At this the first X were all as before stated and John Nichols junr at 20, Wm. Moorton 14, Walter Moorton 13, Charles Harding, Thos. Piper junr. Mr. T. Avenell and Mr. Geo. Trimmer on horseback who assisted in giving direction. We here waited some considerable time for a Drum and Fife, during which time we recognised Mr. Jas. Darwell with two sons etc. etc. Here we left at 9 o'clock with a pipe playing to the 2nd X ... chains from first, having the first on our right hand and continued so to do all round the Parish, and hence 3rd X, head of Boreley Bottom, 4th X ... chain, to next bearing eastward, here the Hampshire map was opened at this X to prove the division of the counties of Hampshire and Surrey, as we were coming into some ground that was claimed by Aldershot Parish which is in the County of Hampshire, as also a plan of the Parish of Farnham taken from the map on a large scale. 5th X .. chains.

Here Mr. Lunn was present on the behalf of Crondal, on a grey horse, which was very soon blacked on the near hind leg, and a notice was read to him respecting meeting to see that we were not infringing on the Parish of Crondal. He seemed quite satisfied on that head, but was offended at having his horse marked. 6th X chains continuing on ridge of Boreley Bottom to 7th X, we here turned round very crooked as described on plan round the Hill, crossing the path leading to Boreley Bottom to 8th X under the Hill opposite a Holly Bush .. chains. Here G. Young declared this the third time he had opened it, west of Brickesbury Hill to 9th X between a valley on left but still keeping Farnham to our right. New 10th X but also found the old one which was left, at which 2 boys were bumped and Mr. T. Avenell marked himself for fear others should as it here became very bad and joined by a Bugal and Drum. Following close to the edge of the Hill to 11th X–here J. Young said the stones taken out of this X had been in 45 years, and as we were on the disputed ground near this X Mr. Nicholls was seize with a fit etc. etc. From hence .. chains came to a X supposed to be done by Aldershot, where Mr. Clement junr of Alton attended professionally on behalf of Aldershot and protested against the right of our enclosing that within our perambulations. It must be here remarked that the whole of the compy. old and young was marked more or less, when on crossing up to hear Mr. Clements protest, several saw Mr. C. with a penknife open and heard him say he would rip up the first man that dare mark his face, and after that said to the High Constable for Farnham in the County of Surrey (he Mr. C. protesting that the ground belonged to Aldershot in the County of Hants) to give orders and see that men kept order. Mr. C sitting then on horseback with his penknife open in his hand, which he afterwards said at

Farnham what is said above, altho on the disputed ground said he met their to do "business" on behalf of the Aldershot Parish. This occurred on what is called Jockeys Ring. 12th X on the left side of the path under the Hill, here Farmer Tice was marked and he was very angry etc. From thence to 13th X west corner of Brixbury Moor, about .. chains on left of old X, leaving this road on our left about 6 feet. 14th X in the Bottom, from hence to a small hill. Here Mr. Clements again protested over Right, when a boy was bumped, thence along a ditch, crossed the road and left it on our right to 15 X on the top of a small hill opposite a gravel pit, John Norris was here bumped aged 12 years, from hence round the foot of the Hill leaving a road on the left, then turned short on left hand to corner of Steven Luff's inclosure and Richard Paro's on the Right. Jn. Young here brought a large stone which was placed in center 16th X, the old X being trenched up by Pharo. Thos. Trigg aged 10 was here bumped. Crossed the Turnpike Road foot of Heath End Hill to the stone marked A.P. (sic), about .. chains a X from the stone, from thence Rowhill Coppes corner a X passed a stream that also parts the Counties, Js. Attfield bd. Here the parties separated to avoid doing any damage, went through the Cops following the stream to Alders Meadow, here occurred a doubt as to the stream, it going thro' the meadow in the center, therefrom Mr. J. Wells, Mr. P. Smith, Mr. Cowdrey and several others went along the hedge of the cops, and Mr. Js. Small, Mr. Eyre, Thos. Yeoman and Thos. Pisley followed the stream into the Cops, when Mr. Clement again entered into a dispute respecting the meadow, and as Mr. John Wells who was the leading person said the track he took was the same he had done twice before it then ended, but with Mr. Clement saying he should bring an action at law for the other ground in dispute. Thence a corner of Cops where the stream cross the lane on our left, still following the stream to a bridge at Badshot Lea under which T. Betts junr. F. Attfield and C. Young went through the arch continuing the stream through various meadows in one of which a scramble took place etc. .. On leaving the moor over the hedge at the corner near a gate, on left X, then over the hedge into a ploughed field, thence short on right at a large Helmen tree near a hill, here pushed Wal Moorton off. X at Mr. Boco's field, short on to the hedge, thro' Mr. West's turnips, turn short to hedge right, turn at the corner and follow up the hedge to the top, when close to a Acton Pollard on Rt. X, then thro' the hedge, leaving the same on the right, leaving the chalk pit on the left, turn short at the end near an oak and ash trees. X, turning to the turnpike road at the bottom of which field a X, turning sharp by the ditch 35 paces from corner of last X, again turn short into the road at Whiteways End, under the bridge and through the middle of the pond to an Helme tree opposite.

Cattle found straying in the highways after notice had been given were to be lodged with the Lord of the Manor. Henry Gray, one of the Surveyors, was granted permission to alter his premises in West Street. Mr. Byfield of Downing Street was summoned for allowing carts and other vehicles to remain in the public highway opposite his house. Mr. Menzies of Culverlands was reported to have stopped up a public path and put tenter-hooks into the gates.

The Surveyors were on tenter-hooks themselves over improvements in Crondall Lane. They had encountered difficulties with Mr. Thomas Falkner of Dippenhall and the project had fallen behind schedule, when a letter arrived from Major G. Birch of Clare Park which galvanised the Surveyors into action. The nudgings of the squires of mansions such as Waverley Abbey, Moor Park and Clare had a salutary effect on the authorities. The Surveyors met Major Birch and Mr. Falkner on the site and stumped out the road to the satisfaction of all parties.

. . . . .

The Water Company, though not an elected body, must be mentioned because of its important role in town affairs.

The Company came into being with an Indenture dated 18 March 1836–

> Whereas the Inhabitants of the Town of Farnham aforesaid are not at present well or conveniently supplied with soft water and whereas there are several springs of soft water on a hill above and on the northern side of the said town called Lawday House Common in the Parish of Farnham aforesaid, forming parcel of the waste or Common Land of the Manor of Farnham of which Manor the Right Revd. Charles Richard, Lord Bishop of Winchester is the Lord, who has kindly consented and agreed to grant twenty acres thereof ... for the purpose of supplying the Inhabitants of the said Town with such water and which they have accordingly agreed to do ...

And so on for 98 pages. For a start they raised £2,000 in one hundred £20 shares. The Trustees were William Birch, builder, Andrew Collyer, Henry Gosden Gray, John Knight, William Newnham, John Andrews, butcher, Daniel Edwards, plumber, James Harding the younger, surveyor, Samuel Lewcock, baker, William Mason, solicitor, Edwin Merriott, music master, Robert Nichols, bookseller, John Manwaring Paine, James Stidston the younger, tailor and John Tily, brushmaker.

. . . . .

In the foregoing synopsis, three samples have been chosen at random to give readers some idea of conditions prevailing in Farnham at the beginning of Victoria's reign. Other authorities will find their places in the story as and when they manifest themselves. Certain of these bodies, however, are not of our concern, e.g. The Justices of the Peace who, being 'County' in all senses of the word, and very much the Senior Service, have always considered themselves aloof from local politics. The Board of Guardians, too, became in course of time a County institution.

Perhaps the one omission from the synopsis, apart from brief references, is that most parochial of all parish bodies–the Overseers, with their Assistant Overseers–the Rate Collectors, the 'money-bags' of the community. Holding the purse strings, these Collectors have a way of poking their noses into the business of the precepting authorities for whom they raise funds. Their records, whilst mainly devoted to their own dry-as-dust occupation, sometimes contain minutes of greater interest. Their work needs no introduction; they will take their place, quietly and unobtrusively, in the tableau.

On 20 June 1837, King William IV died and his brother's daughter, Victoria, ascended the throne. The Inspectors of Lighting and Watching, the Surveyors of Highways, the suppliers of water, the Justices, the Guardians and the Overseers paused in their stride to pay their official respects and to join the townspeople in theirs. Then they returned to their agenda.

PART ONE

II

FIRST QUINQUENNIUM

IF YOU look at a Farnham map of c.1837, your immediate reaction will be one of surprise. The township depicted (without its moons–Hale, Badshot, Bourne and Wrecclesham) is of such puny dimensions that it is hardly recognisable as the built-up, integrated conurbation of today. Conspicuous by its absence is the railway, which did not come until the late 1840s; also South Street, which was constructed to connect the town centre with the station. The configuration of the streets is, however, familiar and can be identified–the east-west slope of the main thoroughfare, the broad sweep of Castle Street leading to the bishop's castle with its gracious park, and the narrow side-street which owes its origin to the feet of pilgrims who once left the Winchester-Canterbury road at this point just outside the west gate of the town in order to seek a night's lodging at Waverley Abbey.

That, with the Church lanes and Bridge Square, was all that there was of it in the 1830s. Farnham had not grown much since the days of the pilgrims–some ribbon development along the road through Dogflood, and along the road on the other side as far as the cluster of buildings at the junction of the Crondall road, called Weststreete. The continuous street that now stretched the full length of Dogflood Street, The Borough and West Street, with its bustling central section, the open market of Castle Street and the deceptive promise of things to come at Downing Street, would have given the impression, to a stranger passing through, of a town of some size and importance. But had the stranger dismounted and walked up any of the side alleys that went off at right-angles all along the main street, he would soon have lost himself in the hopfields which encroached upon the town from the north or got wet feet in the low-lying meadows encroaching from the south.

The parishioners lived in the 800 buildings in this township, the rich in the grand houses in West Street and Castle Street, the poor in the cottages and the tradesmen above their shops, a clannish community of persons earning a fat living from exporting hops. It was not until the 1870s that the town began to expand and encroach upon the hopfields and meadows, pushing the boundaries back along the road to Hale, through the hopground of St. Cross and up the hill to the south through the estates of Waverley and Firgrove. This was the beginning. That Farnham, once one of several small towns hereabouts–Alton, Alresford (which it resembled in shape), Odiham and Haslemere–should, within a century and a half, top the 30,000 population mark, whilst the others have remained put, is a matter for conjecture.

. . . . .

The Inspectors of Lighting and Watching were not in evidence on paper to welcome the new Queen to the throne, though doubtless their influence was felt by the loose characters of the town during the nights of celebration that followed. There is no recorded meeting until 2 October 1837, after the annual hop-picking recess. The Watchmen's report showed that nothing of importance had happened since the last meeting on 5 June.

In November, Superintendent John Newell resigned. The strength of the Watchmen now stood at two–James Clear and Henry Downes. It was decided not to increase the number but, in the anticipation of sickness, to keep on hand one or other of the persons–James Spreadborough, William Stannard, Richard Andrews and Thomas Wooderson–who had applied for the job of third Watchman.

The lighting contract with the Directors of the Farnham Gas Company dated 6 November 1837 ran as follows:–

> Whereas the said Directors have at the request of the said Inspectors erected and set up in the said Town 39 Public Lamps with Columns, Heads and Burners complete and have agreed to light such Lamps with Gas for the Term and at the price hereinafter mentioned. Now therefore the said Directors do hereby contract and undertake to light with Gas the several Lamps aforesaid from this time

henceforth every night (Seven days at each full Moon excepted, and the interval of non-lighting between the last day of April and the first day of September also excepted) until the fifth day of November next inclusive, commencing at dusk and continuing until the approach of daylight at and for the price or sum of Three pounds and four shillings per Lamp to be paid and payable by the said Inspectors or their Treasurer for the time being to the Treasurer or Treasurers for the time being of the said Gas Company by three several instalments or payments as follows, viz. the sum of £50 on or before the 1st February next, the like sum of £50 on or before the 1st May following and the remaining sum or instalment of £24 16 0 on or before the said 5th day of November next.

And it is hereby declared that the said Company shall keep the said Lamps in repair and that as such Lamps and the Columns Heads or Burners aforesaid are the Property of the said Company, none of them shall be changed or removed from their present or future situations without the consent of the Directors for the time being of the said Company.

As Witness the Hands of three of the said Inspectors and five of the said Directors the day and year first above written.

George Miller		W. Newnham	
John Knight	Inspectors	Thos. Baker	
Robert Clark		Hy. G. Gray	Directors
		J.M. Paine	
		Rbt. Nichols	

Lethargy set in again and the meetings of the Inspectors were few and far between and were mostly concerned with uninteresting routine matters. The church had been broken into one Saturday night, without Watchman Downes having seen any loose or disorderly characters about the town that night. In August 1838, several knockers had been broken off doors in East Street by Alfred Hyslop and John Lawrence. Downes was reprimanded for not having taken steps to prevent this crime after having heard one of the accused boasting 'of an intention to have a spree'. It is interesting here to note the use of the name 'East Street'–five years earlier they were calling it Dogflood Street.

In the 1838 election, George Smith, innkeeper, lost his place to James Knight, banker. Knight was also one of the Overseers, on whom the Inspectors were leaning for funds. The Rate Collector was having the usual problems in performing the hardest task of all–that of bleeding stones, and was unable to meet the precept deadlines. In one list of rate defaulters, published in detail in the minutes, appeared the names of George Smith, John Newell and Richard Mason.

Next year, James Stevens was replaced by Doctor George Bury. Watchman Clear was sacked for impertinence; John Newell, described as 'the Active High Constable of Farnham' came back as

Serjeant of the Watch at a salary of £30 a year. He was expected to be out in the duties of his office for parts of four nights every week to superintend the Watchmen. In 1841, the Inspectors held only two ordinary meetings and, in 1842, none at all. Maybe, with John Newell around, the Watch was self-winding.

. . . . .

Meanwhile the Board of Surveyors of Highways were taking things more seriously, with well attended and regular meetings. By 1838, six of the original team, Crump, Edwards, Harris, Lidbetter, Small and Stidston had been replaced by William Birch (builder), Francis Stewart, Charles Waterman (tailor of 84 West Street), William Alexander, John Andrews (butcher) and William Barnes. They were progressing nicely, when, on 16 August 1838, Major G. Birch of Clare wrote a letter.

He gave the Surveyors praise for the work already done on the Crondall road but criticised a section about half way, pointing out an obvious remedy which would also shorten the distance by cutting through some land belonging to Mr. John F. Mills and rented by William Pinke Paine (a member of the Board) and John Manwaring Paine. Mr. Mills was approached through his agent, Charles W. Niblett, solicitor of 46 Downing Street, for permission to take the road through his land, but no reply was received. So nothing happened. Four months later, the Board heard again from Birch. The matter was urgently considered at a special meeting and the opinion arrived at that, although Mr. Mills' permission had not been obtained, it was hardly likely that he would have any objection to the road being made across his land. And across the land it went.

On 25 May 1840, the Surveyors were digesting the following letter.

> Gentlemen,
>
> I hereby give you notice that the road or way lately made through and over my land between Farnham and Crondall, and now in the occupation of Messrs William Pinke Paine and John Manwaring Paine, has been made without my consent or approbation and that I shall consider all persons using the said road as Trespassers and shall proceed against them accordingly. And I shall not hold myself bound by any consent which may have been given to you or any other parties for making such road or way for the use of the public by my tenants of

the said land.

Yours etc.,
Charles W. Niblett,
Agent for John F. Mills.

In the end, Mr. William Pinke Paine signed his name to the following memorandum:–

> I, the undersigned, William Pinke Paine, do hereby undertake and agree to indemnify the Board of Surveyors and bear them harmless against all Law Expenses or other proceedings which may arise in consequence of the alterations made in Crondall Lane alluded to in the above mentioned notice.

It is not recorded whether the real villain of the piece, Major G. Birch, was ever sued for trespass as he went to and from Clare Park. As one of Farnham's richest hop barons, Paine could well afford any expense that might have arisen. What is more to the point is the personal risk one takes in giving voluntary service in the public interest.

On 13 December 1838, the Surveyors had increased the wages of the labourers from 10s. to 11s. per week and 12s. to men with large families, in consequence of the high price of bread. Full of seasonal goodwill, the minutes of the Board's meeting at the *Bush Hotel* on Christmas Eve read, succinctly, 'No business was transacted'.

In March 1839, William West, hop-planter of 71 Castle Street, and George Beldham, John Barrett's partner at the Upper Church Lane brewery, joined the Surveyors. And so in 1840 did John Stilwell, John Bartholomew and George Simmonds of Weydon Mill (the Assistant Surveyor was instructed to repair the bridge of Weydon Mill). The labourers' wages were restored to 10s. a week.

In October 1840, the Assistant Surveyor was reported to be ill and Frederick Trimmer, the Rate Collector, stood in for him. The Surveyor died. His Debtor and Creditor Account could not be found. His outstanding salary of £15 was impounded against a sum of £20 14s. 6d. owing from him to the Board. There was worse to come. The Overseers had asked the Board's permission to take over collection of Highway Rates. These eagle-eyed accountants perused the late Surveyor's ratebooks and urgently requested a special meeting of the Highway Board 'for the purpose relative to the apparent embezzlement of a very large amount of the funds of the Board which they have discovered in their investigation of the accounts'.

Over a period of some three years, the late Surveyor had got away with £188 16s. 7¼d.—in those days, money worth getting away with.

Rate Collector Frederick Trimmer's appointment as Assistant Surveyor was confirmed. The local men of sufficient calibre to staff the various *ad hoc* bodies must have been pretty versatile. Like their employers, they drifted around from one job to another, often, like Pooh-Bah, holding down two or three at the same time. The upkeep of Farnham roads in the 1840s entailed little more than digging gravel at Hungry Hill or Shortheath, its cartage by contractors to conveniently placed roadside dumps throughout the area, waiting for the complaints to come in (as they did) and then filling in the potholes. One did not have to be an Associate Member of the Institution of Civil Engineers or a Member of the Institution of Municipal Engineers to superintend this; neither did one have to be a Fellow of the Rating and Valuation Association in order to collect rates. All one needed was to be tough enough to bully the labourers or ratepayers and to withstand the bullying of one's own employers.

In any case, Surveyor Trimmer was provided with a strong-arm man, one Burningham, who was appointed foreman at 14s. a week with authority to discharge any man neglecting his work or who failed to attend from seven in the morning until six at night. All the same, Mr. Trimmer resigned his post of Assistant Surveyor two years later and his successor was William Harding, of the prolific family of Hardings in West Street; like his predecessor, he was also the Assistant Overseer for rates.

. . . . .

The Overseers, although references have been made to them from time to time, have not until now been given an exclusive feature in their own right in this narrative. Rate Collectors have—curiously—always been the poor relations of local government. Perhaps it is that because of shouldering the hardest task of all—that of prising large sums of money from (a) those who have not got it, or (b) those who do not want to part with it, they have developed a sensitive respect for the value of money that makes them stingy themselves and averse to seeing it squandered by the recklessness of other parochial departments. To offset this niggardly complex, there is a side to rating that throughout the years has resulted in the Treasurer of a Council ranking second in status to its Clerk. Indeed, as regards seniority, the Collector probably has the edge on the Clerk for, whilst he did not appear on the statute books until 43 Eliz. 1 c.2, he would almost certainly have gone round with the hat collecting pennies to build Edward the First's bridges.

And then there is another side. A Rate Collector, because his ratebooks are legal documents which must never be destroyed, may study at will the books of his predecessors in office and, if he is sensitive, there will be born in him a respect for the past equal to the hope that, in generations of Collectors to come, his own account books will likewise be regarded with awe. For the bi-annual ratebooks, containing as they do separate entries for each and every building in the area, with the names of its occupier and owner, are authentic street gazetteers as well as providing useful information on newly built houses, land areas, values and the suchlike. It is only a short step to becoming a local historian.

On 2 December 1840, a meeting of the Parishioners chaired by the Rev. Richard Sankey, was held in the Vestry. The object was to receive the report of the Farnham Parochial Assessment Committee upon Mr. Keen's new Valuation List for the Parish; also to decide upon a new formula for the future making and collection of the Rates.

John Manwaring Paine addressed the meeting. The List was approved as being in conformity with the Parochial Assessments Act, 1836, and in accord with the Law Commissioners, and then they got down to the main business on the agenda.

> that the best means of obviating inadvertent errors and of preventing unauthorised and irresponsible alterations in the Rate Books will be the appointment of a permanent Rate Committee to assist the Churchwardens and Overseers, whose business shall be to superintend the making out of every rate and to make such alterations in the rating from time to time as changes of circumstances may require ...
>
> That this Committee should consist of Five Ratepayers who should represent as far as possible the different interests in the Parish. Their duties to include the keeping of regular minutes of all their proceedings, explicitly stating their reasons for every alteration made, and they be especially enjoined to keep a Register of every addition to or alteration in the rating; and also a Register of the annual

variations of land cultivated as hopgrounds. And as regards the fluctuations occasioned by the latter changes, the Committee recommend that the machinery provided by the division of the Parish into Hop Districts for the purpose of determining the Extraordinary Tithe Rentcharge be taken as the standard for adjusting the rating of Hopgrounds, and for determining the amount of alteration consequent upon the grubbing up or fresh planting of hops.

That the Committee would also strongly recommend that the Rate Committee should appoint a proper person (under security) to collect all Parochial rates, who would of course be required carefully to note all changes in occupation etc. occurring between each rate.

The five persons–we have met them all before–elected to form the Rate Committee were:

THOMAS BAKER
HENRY GOSDEN GRAY
CHARLES KNIGHT
JOHN MANWARING PAINE
SAMUEL STEVENS

The first meeting of the Committee of Five was held the following day in Mr. Paine's house. Samuel Stevens was missing but his place was taken by William Birch, Andrew Collyer, James Darville, James Knight, William Pinke Paine and a Mr. Williams. There was no lack of enthusiasm. The Vestry Meeting, though officially called to bless a new Valuation List (a revaluation is always a milestone in the rating world), had been more concerned with an urgent need of a review of the local system of rate collection itself. Whilst referring politely to 'inadvertent errors', they hinted darkly at 'unauthorised and irresponsible' alterations in the ratebooks. The Committee, and their guests, formed themselves into a 19th century O. & M. team to sort things out.

The Highways Board was invited to join the other precepting authorities in allowing rates to be collected by the Overseers. The office of Collector was offered to William Harding; he was required to produce two approved securities of £250 each, for the faithful performance of his duties, together with his own personal security for £500. They were taking no chances. On 9 December 1840, Harding tendered Mr. J. Knight and Mr. W. Wilkins as his two guarantors and his appointment as Assistant Overseer was confirmed. He was instructed to make out a Poor Rate of 1s. in the pound; this ratebook, in Harding's neat, meticulous handwriting is a treasured item in the writer's temporary custody.

The Committee's wide range of duties covered not only the collection for all departments, but also an audit of expenditure.

The minutes of their meetings, whilst primarily occupied with routine matters of little interest unless one has a head for figures, contain many side references to other people's business. Having their fingers on the purse strings, the Collectors liked to see where the money went. Their own world, too, is not entirely devoid of interest—there is always the human element.

It was discovered, for instance, that, in addition to borrowing £188 16s. 7¼d. from the Board of Surveyors, the late Assistant Surveyor had fiddled £126 from Mr. W. Emment, the Governor of the Workhouse.

The occasional references to rating appeals are also of interest in that they tell of people and buildings. In February 1841, Robert Sampson objected to the assessment on his malthouse and brewery in Red Lion Lane, and Joseph Kimber in respect of his public house, the *Jolly Farmer,* Bridge Square. Mr. Keen of Godalming, the Valuer, turned up the files and reported that he had inadvertently overvalued Sampson's premises but had undervalued the *Jolly Farmer.* Moral—to appeal or not to appeal!

Mr. Keen's fees for preparing the 1840 Valuation List for the Farnham Parish was as follows—

7,081 acres of rateable land @ 3d per acre	£ 88	10	3d.
One per cent on £15,527, the Gross Annual Value of other rateable property	155	5	0
Paid for one running reference	4	0	0
	£247	15	3d.

which was quite a large bite out of the rates; the Poor Rate for that year rose to 2s. in the pound, on the new total rateable value of £21,235. This was estimated to produce a nett collection of £1,831.

The Bishop of Winchester offered to renew the lease, at a rent of 2s. 4d. per annum, of the Pest House on Hoghatch Common. Doctor William Newnham reported on his inspection of two lunatic paupers, Frederick Earl and William Spencer, kept on charge to the Parish at Sir Jonathan Miles' Establishment at Hoxton. Doctors Clark and Bury were appointed Parochial Medical Attendants for the year at £130; this appointment was shared by the local doctors in rotation.

In May 1841, it was resolved to sell certain unproductive Parish properties and with the proceeds pay off some of the Workhouse Bonds, which dated from 1790. Mr. John Hollest, solicitor to the

Parish, was instructed to write for the approval of the Law Commissioners, who duly issued their Order for Sale dated 23 April 1841, in respect of:

> (1) All that Tenement or Cottage with the Fuel house, Garden and premises thereunto belonging containing 3 roods and 9 perches, situate in the Bourne in the Tithing of Wrecklesham in the Parish of Farnham, formerly in the occupation of Daniel Clark but now untenanted.
> (2) All those two closes, pieces or parcels of land adjoining each other (the one thereof containing 5 acres, 1 rood and 28 perches and the other thereof containing 6 acres, 2 roods and 19 perches) situate at or near Hoghatch in the Tithing of Badshot in the Parish of Farnham.

Thomas Baker & Sons, Auctioneers, sold the cottage for £40 to James Darville of Snailslynch and the Bishop of Winchester bought the land at Hoghatch for £514.

The Governor of the Workhouse complained of the disorderly and licentious conduct of one of the paupers and was directed to have her removed. Mr. Emment's wife had died and he solicited the appointment of his daughter, Julia Emment as Matron of the Workhouse. Together they got £50 per annum.

The Law Commissioners drew the Committee's attention to the Act of 3 & 4 Vict. c.29 'for the Extension of the Practice of Vaccination'. It was resolved that 'taking into consideration the extraordinary burdens by which this Parish was oppressed during the past year and the liability of which it is not yet extricated, no action be taken at this juncture'. Mr. Mason was paid £2 for preparing a schedule of Deeds, Writings, Books etc. belonging to the Parish of Farnham, which schedule was deposited in the Parish Chest in the Church. Mr. Hollest, Superintendent Registrar, was advanced the sum of £25 11s. 11d. to pay the enumerators for taking the Census on 7 June 1841.

In July 1842, the Committee found that the accounts of the Guardian (not Mr. Emment) were in a very unsatisfactory state and a considerable deficiency was apparent. Investigations were carried out at a special meeting two days later and a full report sent to the Vestry:–

> The Parochial Committee of Management beg to represent to the Parishioners of Farnham that having recently suspected that the Guardian Mr. – –, had obtained various sums of money owing to the Parish of Farnham which, instead of paying over to the Collector agreeably to his instructions, he had appropriated them to his own use, notwithstanding his repeated assurance to the Committee week after week that he could not obtain these several sums from the parties by

Plate 1 *Parish church before restoration*

Plate 2 *Parish church after mid-century restoration*

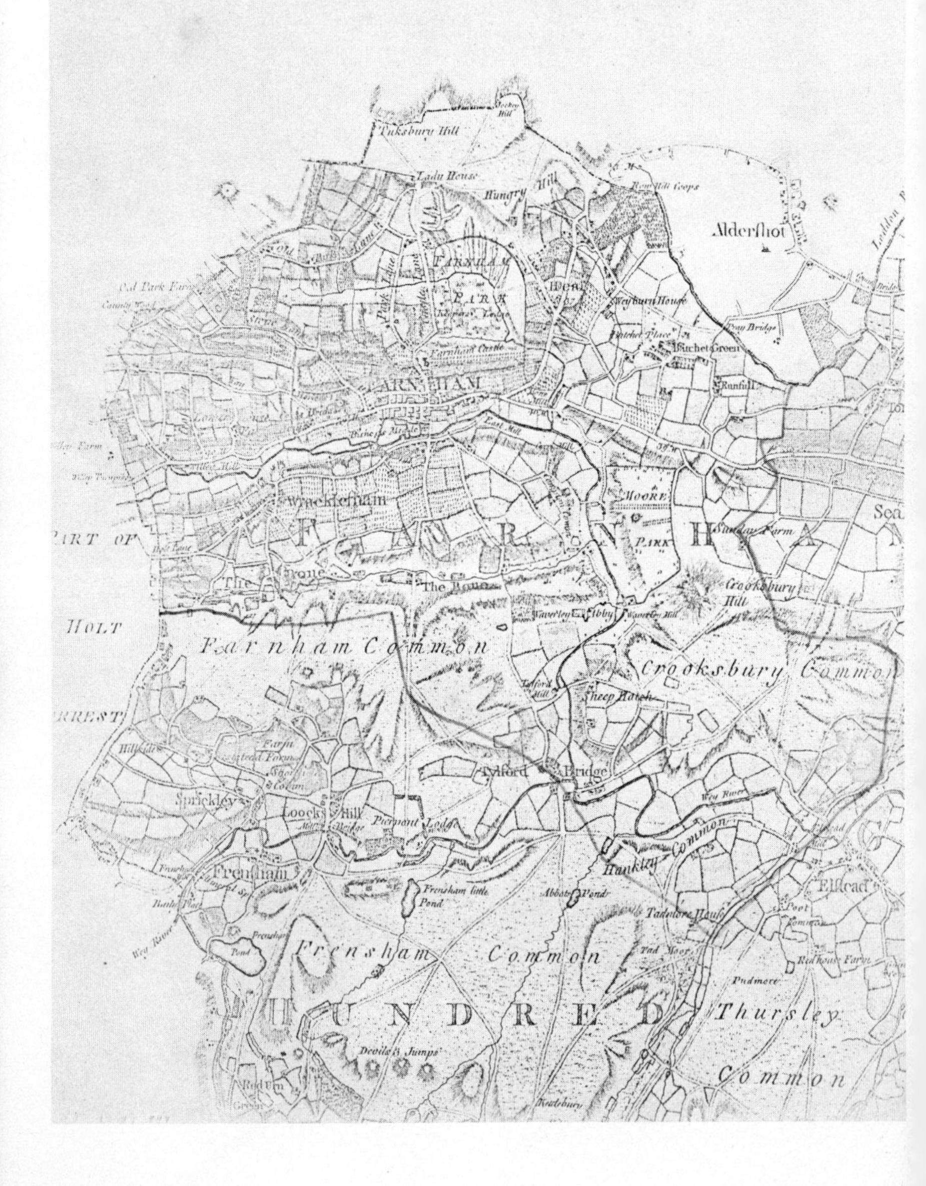

Plate 3 *Parish of Farnham, c.1762 (approx. boundary)*

Plate 4 *Waverley Abbey*

Plate 5 *Moor Park*

Plate 6 *Hopground, Castle Hill, early 19th century*

Plate 7 *Farnham castle, 1830*

whom they were due; and also that he had retained and appropriated to himself other sums of money given to him by the Committee in order to defray various bills owing by the Parish, although he had entered the same in his accounts as duly discharged. The Committee, immediately upon their suspicion being aroused, instituted a strict investigation, the result is as follows–

Money received and not accounted for; Bills not discharged but entered in the Guardians Accounts as paid ... Total, £124 5s. 1d.

This sort of thing was growing so popular that the Rate Committee considered–though there is no minute to this effect–sending to Shaw & Sons for a supply of forms.

The Guardian admitted the correctness of the statement and assigned a Bill of Sale of his effects to his bondsmen, Mr. Baker and Mr. Stewart, which was placed in the hands of the Chairman. As the result of the sale, the sum embezzled was repaid, but the unfortunate Guardian was duly punished. On 20 July 1842 the Vestry found him unworthy of retaining the office of Guardian and also relieved him of his other offices in the town. A year or so later, his name–somewhat pathetically–appears in a list of rate defaulters.

On 5 August 1842, the following candidates for the Guardian's job were interviewed–James Turner, William Hayes, W. Rogers, Henry Hoare, William Edwards and John Newell. Our old friend, the last-named, was appointed at a salary of £60 a year. They went from pillar to post, these men–but some fell by the wayside.

III

SECOND QUINQUENNIUM

EVERY TIME—or so it seems—you walk up Station Hill, on coming to the level-crossing gates the man in the signal-box, who has been watching you in his wing mirror, will, with exquisite timing born of long practice, slam the gates in your face. You should be tolerant, and try to enter into his little game by mouthing obscenities at him. For the signalman's life is a humdrum one and, with a few warmhearted, sympathetic gestures of impotent fury, you can do a lot towards restoring his ego.

This signalman – road-user relationship was established in 1848, with the Affair of the Level-crossing. It all started with the London & South-western, Farnham and Alton Branch Act, 1846, which gave the London & South-western Railway Company powers to construct a branch railway from Guildford, via 'Compton, Worplesden, Perryhill, Burgham otherwise Burpham, Wanborough otherwise Wanborrow, Puttenham, Seale otherwise Seal, Tongham otherwise Twangham, Ash otherwise Ashe ...', to Farnham and on to Alton. Ominously, section 7 of the Act provided:

> And be it so enacted that it shall be lawful for the said Company to carry the said Railway across and on the level of the several public Roads numbered respectively on the Plan deposited as aforesaid, 60 and 123 in the Parish of Farnham in the said County of Surrey ...

Copies of the plan and specifications showing the line and levels had been deposited with the Clerks of the Peace concerned and, one imagines, studied by the townspeople with the eagerness of a schoolboy at a model railway exhibition. Yet there was no campaign for the deletion of section 7—not even of the letter 'L' in the word 'lawful'. The first howl of anguish did not split the heavens until some 17 months after the passing of the Act (16 July 1846), by which time the branch line, having advanced through Twangham and Ashe, was steadily approaching Farnham. It was then that somebody made the interesting discovery, as if for the first time, that the way things were going the line, on coming to the road numbered 60 in the plan, would cross it at ground level.

The natives' name for where X marked the spot on road 60 was The Platt. For the inhabitants it immediately assumed the significance of another Hill 60 in a later war. Allied Command, which the Board of Surveyors became for the brief duration of the conflict, was inundated with petitions, led by George Thomas Nicholson, of Waverley Abbey, Esquire.

The Squire of Waverley, whose routine proddings of the Highways Board were little more than a hobby—albeit designed to keep them on their feet—suddenly found himself in the front line. On this occasion he was personally involved, for Hill 60, which climbed out of the town towards Waverley and Tilford, was his very own road to Farnham. The obstruction threatened by a level-crossing at the threshold of the town he squired would mar the panache of his exits and entrances in the eyes of the local bumpkins.

On 3 February 1848, Mr. James Harris, the Acting Assistant Surveyor, and Mr. Nicholson met Mr. Vance, the Railway Engineer. Though no early photographs of Mr. Vance are to hand, one immediately recognises him as a bearded giant of intimidating character. He had spent the last 17 months travelling down by railway from Guildford, coping on the way with imperious squires and petulant assistant surveyors. By the time he reached Farnham, he was more than a match for anything the town could put up by way of resistance. In Harris' own words, recorded at a Special Meeting held the following day:—

> he had in accordance with the instructions of the Board met Mr. Nicholson and Mr. Vance, the Engineer at the Line. That the latter Gentleman had stated that it was quite impossible under existing circumstances to give the Public a Bridge either under or over on the Waverley Road, but that the Bridge might be formed under the Road leading from Farnham to Tilford which would give a 12 foot headway but that he, the Engineer, did not consider that it would be of any

> service to the Public as the Hill must of course be made much steeper than it was now. But that if Mr. Nicholson and the Board could point out anything else which would be of any advantage to the Public, the Company would be happy to take the same into consideration and oblige them if possible. After much discussion on the propriety of recommending the Company to form a Bridge on the Road to Waverley, a showing of hands was taken when there appeared for the Bridge 2 and against it 6.

Later in the month, the Clerk was instructed to write to Mr. Vance, stating that the Board acquiesced in the proposition of the Company to cross the road at The Platt on a level, provided they would make the road as good as possible. The Thing had come to stay.

. . . . .

The Rate Committee of the Overseers held their meetings at the house of the Assistant Overseer, Mr. William Harding. For the use of the room, they paid him £4 a year rent but provided their own fire and candles. In this cosy setting, the fate of ratepayers was deliberated–which ones to excuse and which ones to summon before the Bench. Things had got so bad that Mr. Harding was told to send out a letter with his next rate demands:–

> ... I am also directed by the Committee to inform all the ratepayers generally that as the business of the Parish cannot be satisfactorily conducted unless the rates be promptly collected, they have ordered me to issue Summonses against every individual who does not pay his or her amount of rates on demand. Your immediate attention therefore is requested to this letter.
>
> W. HARDING.

And, what is more, in May 1844, Harding carried out his threat.

The Income Tax Commissioners paid £3 5s. 0d. for a copy of the ratebook for Schedule A purposes. On 13 June 1844 (was it also a Friday ?), it was resolved that the Workhouse be divided into separate wards for males and females. The tender of William Goddard of £102 10s. 0d. was the lowest for alterations to the Workhouse, which about this time underwent considerable improvements.

A Special Meeting of the Committee sat on 18 February 1845 for the purpose of taking over and reforming on a proper footing an old local charity. The benefactor with the simple name of Henry Smith made a Deed of Settlement on 26 January 1626 of various sums of money to be used for charitable purposes in

Farnham and other parishes. He directed his Trustees to purchase lands and properties, the rents therefrom to be administered by the Churchwardens and Overseers according to conditions imposed in the Deed. In the event of fiddling, the guilty parish had to forfeit the equivalent of a year's income to the Governors of Christ's Hospital in London. The properties purchased by the Trustees in 1650, with rents paid in 1845, were

Hall Farm, Farringdon, Hants—let to Mr. Eames	£114	7	9½d.
Land at Ash, Surrey—let to Mr. J. Pannell	13	0	0
Interest of £233 10 0 lent to Farnham Parish in 1725 by the then Vicar, Churchwardens and Overseers—arising from the sale of timber cut upon Hall Farm ...	9	0	0
The interest of one Farnham Workhouse Bond for £50 ...	2	3	9
	£138	11	6½

Henry Smith had stipulated that gifts were not to be distributed in cash but in goods such as food, fuel or clothing (which had to be of one colour). With the passing years, the administration of the charity had become a little rusty and Henry Smith was turning over in his grave.

The requirements of the Deed are worth reciting in detail:—

(1) to keep minutes of their (the Administrators') proceedings and enter all cases where assistance is rendered from the funds of the Charity.

(2) To meet at least three times in every year, viz. at or about midsummer for electing apprentices, servants, pensioners etc., about Christmas for the general distribution and after Easter before going out of office for the purpose of drawing up the statement of the year's accounts prior to publication.

(3) all cases of relief to be decided in the Meeting by the whole body and no relief given without the sanction of the majority.

(4) not to expend more than £120 a year during the first ten years next ensuing.

(5) to make the following distributions of the funds as nearly as may be—

£20 towards apprenticing young men or women

£10 towards providing young women on going into service with clothes and rewarding them for good conduct

£25 towards relieving a certain number of aged and infirm persons by paying their rent etc.

£65 and whatever sum may not be expended on the above objects in relieving persons having large families in articles of food, fuel or clothing to the amount of 10s. each or thereabouts

(6) to invest the surplus fund in the Farnham Savings Bank in the names of the Vicar, Churchwardens and Overseers until a sufficient sum be accumulated to purchase or build houses for the aged pensioners.

As a means of effecting improvement in the duties of their office, the Rate Committee decided to reorganise their staff (Mr. Harding). He was made Assistant and Clerk to the Rate

Committee, with a salary of £40. A separately created post of Collector was introduced and a Mr. Maurice Goodman was appointed at £26 a year. 10s. a week, even by 1845 standards, was not a lot for what Goodman was faced with. On 9 July 1845, the Committee had a showdown with the rate defaulters—72 in all—by getting them along to the Workhouse to state their grievances. Some were excused but others ordered to pay up within a month.

In November 1845, William Harding resigned and Mr. James Harris was appointed in his place. Four months later it is recorded that Harding was threatened with measures by the Committee if he did not immediately hand over certain Parish Registers that had been in his keeping. At a Special Meeting on 2 April 1846, Harris reported that he had seen Harding, who had 'positively refused' to give up the books. They included the Hop Ground and Alterations Registers ordered to be kept at the Vestry Meeting in 1840. Mr. Hollest, the Parish Solicitor, was instructed to take such steps as required. On the 6 May it was revealed that Harding had handed the records to a Mr. H. Thumwood, who agreed to give them to the Committee provided they would indemnify him against any proceedings that Harding might take against him if he did so. Whereupon the Committee challenged Mr. Thumwood 'in the name of the Committee to surrender the Parochial Books and other Documents belonging to the Parish of Farnham left in his hands by Mr. Harding'. Mr. Thumwood demurred, but finally handed them over.

The Registers were found to be in an 'incomplete state'. It was decided that Harding was not entitled to his last quarter's salary. The most difficult problem for anyone engaged in a tightly scheduled job—in this instance, the collection of a rate within a half-year, each one following upon the last and each with its set of procedures to be observed in meticulous detail—is to keep up-to-date, often under pressure, with the timetable. It is sometimes difficult to keep abreast and, when one falls behind, more difficult to catch up.

Harding fell by the wayside mainly over the Overseers' instructions that the hopgrounds in the district should be reassessed each year according to acreage, which meant riding or perhaps walking round some 1,000 acres of hopfields, measuring up areas newly grubbed and planted or left fallow. With his many other commitments, Harding just did not get around to this. There were, inevitably, consequences; they have a way of building up.

On 11 August 1846, the Clerk of the Peace wrote regarding the yearly returns of rateable value for County Rate purposes. It was explained to him that the hopground assessments, which should have been subject to revision, had been neglected; also that, owing to the negligence of the late Assistant Overseer, rates had been charged twice on a certain piece of land—though only once collected. Then on 29 October 1846, the Poor Law Commissioners of Somerset House wrote and the matter took a more serious turn. In an attempt to water it down, the Committee replied that everything had been alright:

> until Michaelmas 1843, when the Assistant Overseer neglected his duty and on his going out of office last Christmas, it was discovered that he had not made any entry of Hops planted or grubbed for the last three years and consequently those persons who have planted are now paying only the ordinary charge per acre towards the Relief of the Poor as we have no means of ascertaining the amount of ground planted without having the same measured and, great complaints being daily made respecting the unfairness of the proceeding as a large portion of the land has been planted within these three years and as the same would add considerably to the Poor Rate and would be but a trifling expense, the Overseers would feel greatly obliged for your advice in the difficulty, before laying the same before a Vestry Meeting.

But the Commissioners were not satisfied and ordered a revaluation of the Parish. It is not given to any Tom, Dick or Harry to leave his mark upon history by causing a revaluation. In answer to an advertisement in the *County Chronicle* of 15 December 1846, for tenders for 'the admeasurement of the Hoplands in the Parish amounting to 1,000–1,200 acres', a Mr. Edward Ryde of 2 New Inn, Strand, was appointed for the purpose. Edward Ryde would almost certainly have been related to Walter C. Ryde, the man who first published 'Ryde on Rating' in 1900.

The Ratepayers Association submitted a petition dated 30 December 1846, which ran:

> We, the undersigned, ratepayers of the Parish of Farnham, request you to call a Vestry Meeting of the Parishioners for the purpose of taking into consideration the propriety of recommending the Churchwardens and Overseers not to enforce the payment of Rates against persons who are exclusively and entirely dependent upon their own labour for the support of their families, unless their weekly earnings amount to more than a sum as shall be there determined.
>
> J.M. Paine — Charles Andrews — Charles Knight
> Charles Attfield — J. Ward — John Knight
> Thos. Simmonds, Senior — Jas. Shotter

The Committee considered it advisable to obtain the views of the Auditor of the Poor Law Commission, due to arrive shortly, before agreeing to a Vestry Meeting and nothing more was heard of the matter.

In March 1847, to bring the reader up-to-date, the following gentlemen were elected, or re-elected as members of the Rate Committee–

HENRY CAESAR	SAMPSON SAMPSON
GEORGE PEACOCK	WILLIAM BETTS
WILLIAM PULLINGER	MINTY MAJOR
F. STOVOLD	ROBERT BARRETT

. . . . .

24 March 1843–'An adjourned Meeting was called but no Members attended'. There seems to have been a falling off of enthusiasm in the affairs of the Board of Surveyors of Highways, if the short, hurried minutes of their monthly meetings are anything to go by–merely dull recitals of bills and their payment by Mr. William Harding, the Assistant Surveyor.

The Annual General Meeting at the Vestry brought back all the old faces. Their staff of two was reinstated; the wages of Foreman Burningham were reduced to 12s. a week and the labourers' to 8s. From the number of accounts passed for payment, one must assume that, behind the scenes, the real work of the Board was proceeding normally, though little of it was placed on record. Except, of course, on the occasions when Mr. Nicholson of Waverley prodded them about roads in his own part of the Parish and anywhere else for that matter.

Harding's fall from grace, as Assistant Overseer, had its repercussions. On the 3 November 1845, the Board considered that a sufficient supervision had not been exercised over the men employed on the highways and resolved to endeavour to procure a person to act as Assistant Surveyor who should devote his whole time to the office, upon which Mr. Harding tendered his resignation. James Harris was appointed in his place, but they had to share him with the Rate Committee.

The wooden bridge over the stream 'near the Dog Kennels' at Weybourne was replaced in collaboration with the Aldershot Parish Surveyors. On 29 June 1846, it was resolved that all the able-bodied men, including Burningham, should be discharged with the exception of William Clark. Mr. Nicholson complained about an alteration in the road outside Weybourne House, where Mr. Knight lived, but the 'Nicholson Special' Meeting was too poorly attended to be effective.

Then the Squire turned to another matter. He wrote to the Clerk:

> The County having determined to build a 'Lock-up' in Farnham, a site has been fixed up in Bear Lane. It will be extremely important that the drainage from this spot should be as perfect as possible and it has been suggested that, as a mode of making the necessary drain, the various parties interested in the locality might contribute the means. The Trustees of the Road would give something; the parties whose properties would be greatly benefited by such drainage would in all probability subscribe: so that the money required from the funds of the Highways would not be considerable. I have requested Mr. Mason to prepare a plan and estimate of the drain required and shall thank you to lay it together with this note before your Board at their next meeting.
>
> I am, Sir,
> Your Obedient Servant,
> G.T. NICHOLSON.
>
> Waverley Abbey,
> 24th August 1846

The Nicholson Special on this occasion was well attended. Mr. Knight of Weybourne House came to heel; a contract for £9 5s. 0d. was signed by William Goddard to lay the drain from the lock-up in Bear Lane. It only needed Mr. Nicholson to take over the Collector's job and there would have been no silly nonsense over rate arrears.

Robert Sampson, the brewer, had died and his son, Sampson Sampson, took his place on the Board. This fortuitous name for a brand of beer must have been good publicity; to double it up as christian name as well suggests beer of double strength. The family perpetuated its name in the town with a gift of almshouses. They sold their premises in Red Lion Lane to John Barrett, who was brewing in the adjoining Tanyard property. The Barretts extended their brewery to massive proportions.

Farnham, as were most towns about this time, was badly hit by the countrywide glut of labour. The work on the highways required not more than some 15 to 20 men. Seeing a chance for the local unemployed, the Surveyors told Mr. Harris to contact the

Engineer in charge of the railway now approaching the Parish and find out whether it was possible for the Parish to take over the work of a section of the line. Harris saw a Mr. McKensey, who passed him on to a Mr. Ogleby, who was foreman to a Mr. Brassy– and so on up and down the line.

The coming of the railway to Farnham in 1848, whether or not it provided work for the townspeople, brought them something that, as a complete metamorphosis in living standards, could never be equalled. It is doubtful whether more than five per cent of the inhabitants had ever been to London, 35 miles away, or seen the sea. For one penny per mile, by third class (1¾d., second class and 2½d., first class), anyone could now suddenly do just that; it was like a magic carpet.

Robert Tyler Barrett took over from his father in superintending the fire engines. He was born in 1824, one of John's six children, and was later to assume control of the Red Lion Brewery and carry it to great heights. John Leigh Williams of Guildford House, Castle Hill, reported that the gate at the top of Knowles Lane by the Castle had been removed, and a stile substituted by the Bishop's bailiff, one Thomas Ainsley, which prevented persons passing on horseback–the Bishop was duly served with a Notice to abate the nuisance.

A joint meeting of the Guardians, Clergymen and Surveyors was held to consider the provisions of the Nuisance Removal Act. The biggest nuisance of all was the lack of any adequate system of drainage, and consequent diseases. It is difficult to imagine a society that possessed no means of removing unwanted matters except by burying them in the back garden. The Board considered ways and means of surface water drainage through the main street and the Winchester Turnpike Road Trustees came forward with a promise of £50 towards the estimated cost of draining the north side of the street. The Board accepted tenders for the work as follows:–

> that of G. & D.T. Pearcy, for a drain in East Street from Mrs. Falkners to the Mile Stone, and from the Mile Stone to the Bush Ditch ... £85
>
> that of William Snelling in West Street, from Fox Yard to Factory Yard and Potters Gate to the lamp-post opposite Mr. Hayes' garden ... £73

Although strictly for rain water, a lot of the town's sewage found its way into these drains and thence to the river, and to the nudists who bathed in it of a Sunday afternoon.

IV

THIRD QUINQUENNIUM

IN THE matter of streetlighting, Farnham did not conform with modern standards until the 20th century was 60 years old, which was rather late in the day for a town of any size to switch to electricity. In doing so, it sacrificed an essential part of its nocturnal character. The venerable buildings of Farnham do not gain from the harsh glare of electric light; the softer radiance of gaslight emphasised their beauty. It was as if, when positioning the gaslamps in the 1830s, the Inspectors of Lighting and Watching had, consciously or otherwise, set them at the best vantage points to pick out, here, some architectural feature, there, the quiet promise of a side-alley, like artists working on a canvas, sensitive of the beauty caught by their brushes.

In point of fact, it was not at all like that–the only brushes were those the Inspectors had with the Directors of the Gas Company. Doubtless, off duty, they were the best of friends, standing each other drinks after the meetings–those serving on both Boards possibly buying their own, for in the tight little community of 19th century Farnham one could not afford to make enemies. But, once on the job, no punches were pulled.

What almost certainly must have preyed on the minds of the Inspectors was their somewhat hasty venture into gas standards before the 19th century was 35 years old, which cost the ratepayers a lot more money. By the 1850s they had had time to assess the results, to regard the whole exercise as impetuous and to form a nostalgia for the softer radiance of the old oil-lamps–and the less expensive contracts with William Moorton. The yearly lighting accounts, within a pound or so, were on the lines of this one for 1853.

	£	s	d		£	s	d
Balance in the hand of the Treasurer ...	3	6	6	Lighting 40 Lamps one year	120	0	0
From Trustees of Winchester Turnpike Road	20	0	0	Contribution to Lock-up light	2	0	0
From the Collector on account of Rates	164	2	1	Lighting 40 Lamps extra in May, 141 hours @ ½d	11	15	0
				Lighting 40 Lamps extra in August, 188¾ hours @ ½d	15	13	4
				Lighting 4 Abbey Street Lamps, 629 hours @ 2d.	5	4	10
				Salary of Secretary	3	3	0
				Balance in hands of Treasurer	29	12	5
	£187	8	7		£187	8	7

Most irksome of all was the fact that the Inspectors were no longer masters in their own house. The Gas Company not only had a monopoly of gas supply, but owned the lamps as well. To succeed, any form of government, local or otherwise, must hold the whip hand. Being entirely dependent on the good offices of the Directors, the Inspectors found themselves in an inferior bargaining position. The situation was intolerable.

Made to look silly over repeated refusals on the part of the Gas Company to reduce charges, the Inspectors fell back on spiteful complaints about the bad state of the gas supplied to the lamps, the irregular hours of lighting them and the generally dirty condition of the lamps themselves, and followed this up with a demand that the Company should give a definite quotation per lamp. The Directors replied that they 'were anxious to light the public lamps as low as they think they can afford to light them, and in fact as cheap or cheaper than the neighbouring towns, and they therefore offer to do it at the price of £4 per lamp'. After further bickering, and perhaps sessions behind the scenes, the quotation was reduced by 5s. per lamp; the Inspectors—at a price—had won a partial victory.

But the bickering continued. Later in the Queen's reign, the advent of electricity enabled the Inspectors to twist the arm of the Gas Company. The boot then being on the other foot, both sides settled down to some sort of compromise. With mutual advantage and, who knows, an appreciation of what gaslight can do to a town at night, the truce was destined to outlast the Queen by five reigns.

. . . . .

The Inspectors held one of their rare meetings on 13 July 1846 for the purpose of appointing a Day Patrol and Streetkeeper under the superintendence of Serjeant of the Watch, John Newell. John Stevens was chosen for this new post at 6s. a week. They next broke silence on 12 April 1847, when Newell reported on 'various depredations and nuisances committed at different periods of the night, which it was believed must have caused a considerable noise but, as nothing appeared to have been seen or heard at any time by Henry Downes, the Watchman, it was resolved that such Watchman be dismissed from his office on and from Saturday next, when it was directed that James Peacock, one of the Town's Constables, should be employed in his place and stead at the weekly wages of fifteen shillings'. One imagines that Downes, at the first hint of trouble, had decided that discretion was the better part of valour and dived swiftly up a side-street. His replacement quickly brought results, for the following month a Thomas Chambers was arrested for disorderly conduct in the street and fined 15s.

George Cottee, bootmaker in The Borough, complained about an offensive privy, right under his sittingroom window, at the nextdoor *Goats Head Inn.* He requested 'the interference of the Inspectors as Officers acting under the Act of Parliament for directing the Police of the Town under the statute of 9 & 10 Vict. c.96, for the more speedy removal of certain nuisances'. In an age of grievous nuisances, it was as yet nobody's specific duty to authorise their abatement, hence Cottee's cap-in-hand approach to the Inspectors. Two of the Inspectors, Mr. Clark and Mr. Gray, were deputed to call on Henry Wareham, landlord of the *Goats Head Inn* and if this failed John Newell was to lay a complaint before the Justices of the Peace.

In April 1848, Newell displayed his coat and hat, worn out through wear and tear in the course of duty, and was authorised to replace the coat at Stovolds and the hat at Baileys. 'It appearing that Watchman Peacock invariably showed himself to the Serjeant every morning on going off duty at 4 o'clock, it was ordered that he do also exhibit himself at the same time to Mr. Nichols at the Post Office on his way home'. 'It being thought desirable that the Inspectors should hold monthly meetings in accordance with the Act of Parliament with a view to regularity on the part of their Officers, it was resolved to meet accordingly and that the same be notified to the several Inspectors.' And so they held their next ordinary meeting on 12 November 1849–19 months later.

It was reported at the meeting that a violent assault had been made on James Peacock between one and two o'clock on the night of the 6th, when in the execution of his duty. A reward of five pounds was offered for information leading to the arrest of the offenders. Peacock was voted full pay for the four nights he was off duty because of his injuries–now that really was nice of the Inspectors. A Special Meeting was held on 6 December 1849 'for the purpose of considering the subject of an improvement in the Watch by amalgamation with the adjoining district Police patrols.'

> A Deputation from the Committee of the Police Establishment in the country department of the Parish, consisting of Messrs. C. Andrews, C. Knight, J. Nash, S. Sampson and G. Trimmer, attended the Meeting, when a conference being held on the desirability of the Watch and Police Authorities and their Officers acting in aid of and unison with each other, as it being the opinion of the Inspectors present that the watching of the Town will be better provided for and performed by amalgamation with the Police Committee and their Officers, it was resolved to co-operate and unite with them for the purpose.

At an adjourned meeting on 17 December, at which the Police Committee were represented, ways and means were discussed in detail. Five persons were to be appointed, namely one as Day Policeman to perform the duties hitherto carried out by James Stevens, except that such person would be required to watch the Town every Saturday night 'at a trifling increase of wages'. And 'that four other persons be appointed to watch the Parish districts generally and the Town in particular, so that two watchmen be for the most part engaged in patrolling the Town nightly, and three occasionally, and never less than one continuously'. The Inspectors were to contribute £90 per annum to the joint funds.

James Stevens was appointed Day Patrol and Watchman on Saturday nights, fair nights and other special duty occasions, at 8s. a week, with a new coat and hat every two years. The three Watchmen chosen at 17s. weekly were John Reed, Edward

Coulthrop and Christopher Rooney of Church Lane. James McGregor became Serjeant. At a Special Meeting at McGregor's request, held at the *Lion and Lamb Inn* on 19 February 1850, John Reed was charged with misbehaviour. The facts relative to the subject being thoroughly enquired into and sifted and the party, John Reed, being present 'and deemed more in the nature of a disturber than a preserver of the peace on the occasion alluded to', his services were ordered to be dispensed with forthwith. James Peacock, who had been laid off at the time of the reorganisation, was appointed in his place.

In September 1850, the Report Book was again examined. This time, Police Officers Rooney and Peacock were in trouble and were admonished regarding the future, but an allegation 'as to a brothel visit' was disregarded. Peacock was further admonished for having gone home with his wife instead of going on duty. P.O. Peacock was something of a rebel. The following month there was a charge against him for 'undue personal appearance on duty'—possibly, with a name like his, he was given to strutting about his beat displaying his fine hat and coat. Serjeant McGregor resigned to take up a more lucrative position in Kent and our old friend, John Newell, returned as Superintendent of Police.

On 22 April 1851, it was decided that the Town should additionally be lighted during the months of May and August. The point was also raised that the contract with the Gas Company specified that the lights should be left on 'till the approach of daylight', whereas in practice they were often turned out too early in the mornings. This was communicated to the Directors of the Company. Six months later it is recorded that the Directors had only held one meeting 'and then the Inspectors' request of the 22nd April was altogether forgotten to be introduced'. They repeated bluntly 'that it should be particularly understood that the Town lights, being 41 in number (not including that at the Gas Works), be continued as and from the 6th November to the 31st January ensuing until 6 o'clock in the morning and during the remainder of the year, excepting the months of June and July and excepting also the seven moonlight nights of each moon, from dusk until one hour of sunrise each night ... The Company expressed their anxiety to comply with the Inspectors' wishes if practicable, but suggested two hours before sunrise and that, if any extension of the time were required, it could only be met by an increase in payment per lamp'.

Then the Inspectors worked it out that they had been overcharged £25 by the Company for the previous year. The accounts were thereupon investigated and it was found that this was not so—they owed the Gas Company £40. This put up the next rate to clear it. Whatever they tried, the Inspectors just could not win. With the annual contract coming up for renewal, it was a case of either accepting the Company's terms or returning to the dark ages.

James Harris, that man of many parts, added to them by becoming Secretary to the Inspectors at a salary of three guineas per annum.

. . . . .

Farnham's other railway level-crossing, on the road numbered 123 in the Railway Company's plan, was scheduled to manifest itself at Weydon, in the lane which continued from Red Lion to Wrecclesham. Somewhere along the line—though nothing is recorded in the minutes—the townspeople, this time acting before it was too late, won a great victory in persuading the Railway people to erect a road bridge over the line instead. It was discovered that this bridge, instead of being constructed with an agreed slope of one foot in 20, was going up at one in ten. This infuriated the Board of Surveyors who informed the Company of their determination to have it rectified and threatened proceedings if the Railway did not comply. The reply was conciliatory but entirely negative. The Surveyors served notice of their intention to apply to the Board of Trade. They applied to the Board of Trade—who ignored the letter. They applied again and the Board of Trade graciously informed the Surveyors that 'the Lords of the Committee of Privy Council for Trade were in communication with the London & South-western Railway Company on the subject'.. After a decent interval, the Surveyors wrote a third time. And so it came about that Farnham acquired that one-in-ten, kinky little bridge at Weydon, which, no-one will deny, was better than getting another level-crossing.

The bridge over the River Wey in Longbridge was so much a

local landmark that it was referred to simply as 'The Bridge'. It was long in span, in name and in history. Built beside the ford that remains to this day, it saved people, entering or leaving the town by the then only road to the south, from getting their feet wet. It was built of wood and over the years the timbers had worn so that people were again in danger of getting wet feet. Moreover, since the arrival of the railway, the road over the bridge was the only road to the station. The Surveyors decided to replace it with an iron bridge, to the design of a Mr. Craig.

The tender of George Pearcy, builder of East Street, was the lowest at £334 and the work started. The success of an operation of this kind, which must temporarily interrupt the passage of traffic through a main thoroughfare, depends on having all materials assembled in readiness from the word go. This is where Pearcy went wrong. Having more or less dismantled the old bridge, he was faced with the problem of the non-arrival of the iron girders from London. The Surveyors were faced with a claim from a Mr. Mott for £4 10s. 0d. for damage to his dogcart. They all faced each other at a Special Meeting in January 1853, attended by Craig and Pearcy. The latter was told to go up to London and see the contractor for the girders, a Mr. Knight.

On his return Pearcy reported that the girders had all been cast and that he had seen two of them already loaded on to a barge. He was given two more days and then, if the ironwork had not arrived, he was to commence a wooden bridge. The girders, as we know, arrived. What is remarkable is Pearcy's reference to a barge. Does this mean that the girders were transported by the Basingstoke Canal to the Farnham Wharf at Aldershot and hauled overland to the site? Perhaps the railway could not cope with such awkward freight.

I counted two-and-seventy stenches,
All well defined, and several stinks.

Samuel Taylor Coleridge

V

FOURTH QUINQUENNIUM

(I)

SOME IDEA of the confusion which existed as to whose responsibility it was to do something about the appalling sanitary conditions in the town is revealed in a letter dated 5 December 1853 from William Hollest, Clerk of the Churchwardens and Overseers, to the Rate Committee.

> Gentlemen,
>
> You are of course aware that the Guardians have been called upon to carry out the provisions of the Nuisance Acts of 1848 and 1849 and in doing so their attention has been particularly called to the Town Sewers which empty themselves into the meadows, and to prevent further nuisances arising from which, it appeared to the Guardians necessary that these sewers should in the meadows be laid into one drain and to discharge themselves into the River below Mr. Darvill's Mill.
>
> But as doubt arose whether the Nuisance Acts gave the Guardians the power to execute such a work as this, they addressed letters to the Board of Health and the Poor Law Board on the subject, and directed also their Clerk to have an interview with these Boards and their opinion is that the Guardians have no power to execute such a work as that proposed. The Guardians therefore, considering the importance of this matter to the general health of the Town, think it their duty to make known this to the Parish Officers and they would suggest to them the propriety of calling a Public Meeting as to adopting the provisions of the Health of Towns Act in order to remove this great nuisance which is both detrimental to the health and prejudicial to the interests of the Town.
>
> William Hollest.

After consideration of this letter, the Rate Committee issued the reply 'that the Parish Officers did not consider themselves justified in taking upon themselves the responsibility of calling a public meeting of the Inhabitants of the Town unless specially called upon to do so by a requisition by the said Inhabitants and they do not consider themselves the Proper Parties to make the first movement in this case'.

The open ditches that carried the waste products of the town towards the river were sluggish and not always successful in delivering the goods. Of the several channels that crossed no-man's-land between the houses and the river, that known as the Bush Ditch was perhaps the most infamous.

In May 1854 a deputation from the Board of Guardians attended a meeting of the Highways Board to complain about this ditch and another belonging to James Knight. Thomas Thumwood of the *Bush Hotel* and Knight, as members of the Board of Surveyors, were conspicuously absent from this meeting. Closing their ranks, the members present 'unanimously decided that the Board of Surveyors had no jurisdiction in the case, the nuisance complained of being on private property and not under their control whatever'.

Later in the year, someone–possibly the Guardians–brought about a public meeting of the parishioners at the *Bush Hotel* respecting the sanitary conditions in the town and the Surveyors met on 8 December to consider the report and the ways and means within their financial structure of making improvements. The Assistant Surveyor was instructed to take levels of the Bush and Gostrey Ditches and also through Mr. Stevens' Gostrey Meadow, and to prepare rough estimates of expenses of installing drains or culverts. The immediate objective was to roof in the *Bush* and Gostrey Ditches and, in order to ensure their unchecked access to the river, connect them to a new ditch to be cut through Gostrey Meadow, which at that time was no pleasure garden.

To raise means, the Surveyors decided to solicit subscriptions; Mr. Trimmer and Mr. Brown undertook to canvas West Street and Downing Street, and Mr. Thumwood and Mr. Attfield took on East Street and Castle Street. Subscription lists were printed and distributed in the areas that stood to benefit from the project. As there is no account of the work being carried out, one has to assume that the townspeople preferred the smells to parting with their money.

Mr. John M. Paine went to London and saw Mr. Taylor, Secretary of the Board of Health, and put the problem to him that, as sanitary improvements in Farnham would benefit only a small section of the population, the Surveyors did not feel it was right to levy an increased rate throughout the Parish. Mr. Taylor's advice was that the Nuisance Act could not be adopted with any fairness to the ratepayers and that the Act would shortly be amended. And so the Board were returned to square one.

But their abortive efforts were enough to cause the Surveyors to become the town's whipping-boys and complaints from all quarters were showered upon them. The Church Lanes were in a very bad state and needed draining into the river; Abbey Street, too, but this street being handy to the river, they laid in a drain which discharged into the Wey by the Bridge. On 12 April 1856, William Hollest of the Guardians wrote

> I am desired by the Guardians to ask you to draw the attention of the Surveyors to the filthy and unhealthy state of the Fox and Factory Yards and the Guardians think they should not be doing their duty were they not to inform you that Fever is now raging there, and they do this in the hope that a timely abatement of the nuisance existing in those Yards will prevent a spread of Fever which otherwise must assuredly follow.

In reply Mr. Paine told Mr. Hollest something of his own frustrations.

> I shall be in London tomorrow but I will send your letter relative to the removal of nuisances etc. to the Board of Surveyors who meet tomorrow evening. I beg however to inform you that I called the attention of the late Board of Surveyors to the Nuisances Removal Act and after due consideration they declined to act upon it as there was no power in the Act given to any Local Power to impose a Rate on a *limited district,* like the Town of Farnham, instead of imposing the burden on the whole Parish. I may state moreover that I had two or three interviews before Christmas with the Secretary of the Board of Health (Mr. T. Taylor, who framed the Act) and I was distinctly informed that the Act was permissive and not compulsory and therefore with this information the Board of Surveyors came to the resolution that they would not place themselves under the Act, and consequently they have not relieved the Board of Guardians from the responsibility which they have heretofore incurred.
>
> I trust therefore that the Board of Guardians will take immediate steps to remove those intolerable nuisances alluded to in your letter which no one more strongly deprecates than myself.
>
> J.M. PAINE, 14th April 1856.

But the Guardians did not rest there. On the 29 April, the Surveyors met to consider a letter from Mr. Taylor of the Board of Health:–

> I am directed by the General Board of Health to forward to the Highways Board of the Parish of Farnham the accompanying copy of a letter which the Board of Guardians of the Farnham Union have caused to be addressed to this Department, and to request to be furnished with information of the circumstances which have prevented the Highways Board from exercising their power under the Nuisances Removal Act on the representation of the Guardians.

This voice of Whitehall, although it offered no solution to the main problem–lack of money–galvanised the Board into action. It was resolved that 'the Board do place itself under the Nuisances Removal Act and that the same be adopted forthwith'. A Mr. Everett was appointed Inspector of Nuisances with immediate effect, at a salary of £1 per month, and this was such a good investment that, as we shall see, the Highways Board, in their determined assault upon the many inhabitants in the town causing nuisances in some form or other, take more than their share of the credit.

. . . . .

The gentlemen elected, or re-elected, at the Vestry on 25 March 1854 to serve as members of the Board of Surveyors were–to bring the reader up-to-date:–

JOHN MANWARING PAINE	JOHN NASH
GEORGE TRIMMER	F. ANDREWS
GEORGE SIMMONDS	CHARLES ATTFIELD
HENRY G. GRAY	JOHN BAKER
THOMAS THUMWOOD	JAMES KNIGHT
WILLIAM BROWN	CHARLES FALKNER

They proved to be an inspired team. At their first meeting on 3 April they dispensed with the office of Clerk to the Board on the grounds that it was unnecessary and presented his duties to that already overworked man–the Assistant Surveyor, James Harris. As Assistant Overseer, Clerk of Lighting and Watching, Assistant Surveyor and now Clerk–all rolled into one, Harris was indeed 'The Gentleman at the Town Hall'. From the Surveyors he drew £50 per annum. He had to work for it–in general terms his duties were set down as follows; 'that he shall perform the duties of the Clerk, make out the requisite Rates, send in a written monthly report of the state of the roads from his own observations to be entered in a book kept for that purpose, that he be allowed to employ a foreman under the direction of the Board, and that he is expected to look strictly after the men employed on the roads so that the money of the Highways shall be faithfully expended.' There were, as will be seen, countless other matters in which he acted as dogsbody, for much lies beneath the surface of a local government officer's declared terms of reference.

Most of the nuisances in the town could be classified into certain categories, each a routine job of some magnitude. There were, for instance, the nuisances caused by the shopkeepers, who persisted in cluttering up the Board's footways by displaying their goods for sale outside their shops. This practice sprang from ancient origins, for the shop started as a market stall; later it was built into the front downstairs room of the trader's house, so that, instead of going out to push his wares upon the passing public, he was obliged to wait impatiently for customers to come to him. It only needed the shopkeeper next-door to take a chance and revert to the good old days, for the whole street to follow suit. Harris was told to warn, and summon if required, all parties who obstructed the pavements, or whose shop blinds were less than seven feet high. It proved to be a long, hard fight.

Then there were the tradesmen who wanted cellar gratings on the footway. There was nothing wrong about this, except they were in the habit of leaving them open, to the danger of passers-by. William Kingham, who had taken over H.G. Gray's grocery at 18 West Street, was a constant offender in this way and was repeatedly warned by the Board. In the end, the Surveyors decreed that, in order to avoid trapdoors or cellar windows becoming part of the freehold of the properties concerned, the owners should be made to pay one shilling a year to the Board.

The footways were in constant need of repair. It was decided to repitch the whole of the main street pavements and to employ two of the men for this purpose, 'one to begin at each end and continue to work till they meet'. Harris, probably seeing complications ahead, reported that no men were available so it was put out to tender and that of William Snelling accepted. He was ordered to get on with it at once 'and not wait till after the hop-picking as proposed by him'.

To lessen the sewer smells in the main streets, the Surveyors tried out stink traps over the gratings as an experiment, the Austin Trap being favoured. A year later they still had it on approval, and even wrote to Mr. Austin for further samples, though another brand was tested outside Mr. Figg's shop in Downing Street. Later the traps were in use generally throughout the town, though there is nothing to prove that they were ever paid for.

At the end of January and the beginning of February 1855, there were bad falls of snow and a special meeting was held to organise the removal of the snow from the town and the main roads, giving employment to the number of men out of work because of the weather–but only men of the right class, of course, being taken on. Some idea of the severity of the weather may be judged from the fact that Harris' snow-clearance team numbered no less than 175 labourers. They were not all of the 'right class', however, for a letter of protest was received from a Mr. Edwards, who complained that snow had been shovelled from the Frensham road into his hopground and, unless it was removed, he would sue for damages. Mr. Harris was instructed to reply acknowledging the error in not having first obtained permission and hoping that 'no further notice would be taken of it, as it was impossible to open the road to the public without first throwing the snow over his hedge'.

Another Mr. Edwards is given a brief mention in the minutes. He was the Gatekeeper at the level-crossing–by way of being the L. & S-W.R.'s 'our man in Farnham'. Mr. Brown reported that the gates were now being kept closed across the highway instead of the railway. It is not recorded that the Board threw snowballs at Mr. Edwards, though they did serve him with a Notice; they also wrote about it to the Board of Trade, who refused to interfere as it had lately been made a general rule by Act of Parliament for level-crossing gates to be closed across the highways. One's sympathies are more with the Gatekeeper over this. It meant that, instead of the regular half-hourly–or whatever it was in those days–opening of the gates to permit the passage of a train, he was called upon to keep a constant watch for the irregular, unscheduled and much more frequent arrivals of road-users clamouring to be let over the drawbridge. The scene at the Platt must, on occasions, have resembled the Storming of the Bastille.

Meanwhile Mr. Snelling was going about the town, prodded from time to time by the Surveyor, pitching the footpaths with black iron stone. Here and there, parts of these cobbled sidewalks remain today–a picturesque relic of the past. To the feet, however, the cobbles were as hard as iron, which gave rise to the popular belief at one time that the Farnham man was easily recognisable by his fondness for walking on the road in preference to the footway. The Board was very attracted by the prospect of paving with York flagstones, but this proved to be a luxury; the cost, quoted by Mr. Patrick's tender, being 9s. per square yard for York stone as against 2s. for black iron stone. Then a requisition was sent in by Mr. Hazell, who had recently moved to Ivy House and opened a stay factory in the outbuildings, stating that the frontagers on the south side of The Borough preferred York paving and would pay the difference. The Board welcomed this and Mr. Patrick was given an order, but this was later cancelled because the frontagers had second thoughts.

Another category of nuisances took the form of encroachments upon the highways or footpaths. A lot of this was due to the various Inclosure Acts of the first half of the 19th century, particularly the general Act of 1845. Like prospectors at Klondyke, the local wide-boys had staked out their claims, advertised them in the *County Chronicle* and finally been granted absolute possession. They were now fencing in their newly acquired territorial gains in order to keep out the peasants who had formerly wandered freely over the commons and, in doing so, fenced off public rights of way. If there is one way of holding out a red flag to a bull, it is to threaten a footpath under the noses of the local authority. There were several cases—such as the stopping up of the path that led from Gravel Hill, through Mavins, across the waste land and through Henry Kimber's field into Tilford Lane. The Board considered this of advantage to the public and took up arms.

The Bishop, too, was warned for stopping up the London Gate in the Park, and another at Old Park. And then when he did replacc the stile at the former gate, he was criticised because there was no handrail and 'it would be impossible for ladies to go over it'.

Messrs. Lindsay and Edwards, the Fire Chiefs, indented for repairs to the engines and new buckets and hose. Assurance agents in the town were approached for gifts of buckets. Because of repeated calls made on the Fire Brigade by adjoining parishes, the Board felt it would be reasonable to write for yearly subscriptions at the following rates:—

Aldershot, £2; Seale, £2; Tongham, £2; Frensham, £3; Bentley, £4; Crondall, £4; Binstead, £5, Froyle, £4 and Elstead, £3.

Everett resigned his post as Inspector of Nuisances because he was leaving Farnham. A Mr. Hollington was appointed in his place.

In contrast with his ebullient neighbour at Waverley Abbey (who was currently bullying the Board about roads out at Waverley), C.B. Bacon of Moor Park, Esquire, quietly content in the lovely surroundings of his mansion, bothered the Surveyors not at all. It is with some surprise therefore that one reads that he had encroached on the road by erecting a fence at the lodge at Compton Common. He was, of course, requested to remove this within ten days, failing which the Board would do so for him. When they did, that seemingly mild man, Mr. Bacon, was so incensed that he wrote complaining that 'the Assistant Surveyor had pulled down a Fence at Moor Park and had acted illegally in so doing'. Whereupon the Board held an inquest on the fence, at which evidence, in strikingly similar terms, was heard from three persons–James King, John Baker and George Baker, who had lived all their lives at Compton and knew the spot well. Each maintained that the fence had been an encroachment.

The Surveyors were represented by Messrs. Nichols & Potter. This firm of solicitors had been founded in 1834 by Ben Nichols, whose grandfather, Benjamin, had acquired the *Bush Hotel* in 1790; his father, Henry, was at one time a member of the Highways Board. In years to come, Henry Potter, surviving partner, was joined by Mr. E. Crundwell and, later, Mr. Timothy Bridge and the firm practised in these three names.

In the end, the case of Bacon *v.* Board of Surveyors took a more unlitigious course. Mr. Bacon suggested a compromise, which meant that Mr. Harris visited Moor Park to arrange the fence in accordance with the requirements of the Board.

Meanwhile there were troubles over another form of bacon–and a category of nuisances in its own right. A Mr. A. Williams complained that Mr. Aylwin kept pigs on his premises which were a nuisance to the neighbours and a danger to health. Mr. Josiah Bentall, the draper (and now on the Board) raised the matter of the pigs at Ellis' yard, just behind his premises in Bear Lane. George Simmonds kept pigs in Longbridge in a most filthy condition. Mr. Hollington investigated these complaints. At Ellis' yard he found that the blood hole was in a bad state; Aylwin's ten pigs were clean in their sty, but the blood was in a tub and not in a blood hole. Simmonds felt so ashamed that he killed his pigs off.

There was filth running from Mr. Patrick's cottages in Park Lane into the gutter. Mr. W.K. Stevens, who had lodged a complaint, was directed to instal a stink trap at the grating near his own house 'as he was himself the cause of the nuisance there by turning his water-closet into the main sewer'. Mr. Hazell reported that there were eight new houses in Park Lane and these with others formed a nuisance as 'it all ran above ground into the water courses of the highway'. Mr. Nash complained that there was an offensive smell at the Marine Store in Downing Street. Also in Downing Street, a Mr. Dale and a Mr. Rhodes had 'a heap of bones accumulated and they were at times no doubt a great nuisance......'.

One by one, the Board tackled these nuisances; little by little the smells were receding–it was a long, tortuous and often contested process.

VI

FOURTH QUINQUENNIUM

(II)

AND NOW another body comes to life in this narrative; it rendered a more sombre yet nonetheless essential service to the public—that of burying them. Before the mid-1800s, the small populations of parishes were accommodated after life in the area of land around the Parish Church. The churchyard with its ancient tombs is so much a cherished feature that a church without its encircling graves lacks an essential quality. Over the years the churchyards had become overcrowded and one's chance of getting a grave space was about as remote as getting a Council house in the 1960s.

The Farnham Burial Board was formed under 16 & 17 Vict. c.134—the Burial Act, 1853—for the purpose of acquiring and maintaining land in the Parish for use as burial grounds. With funereal pomp, a poll was held in the Farnham Parish Church on 29 March 1855 and the following nine gentlemen elected out of a field of eighteen:—

JOSIAH BENTALL
WILLIAM HAZELL
WILLIAM HOLLEST
JOHN KNIGHT
JOHN M. PAINE
THOMAS THUMWOOD
GEORGE TRIMMER
JOHN NASH
REV. J.S. UTTERTON

All old friends; it must have been difficult sometimes for them to remember exactly which Board meeting they were at. Their first meeting was at the *Bush Hotel* two days later, with the Rector in the chair. Charles William Niblett, the Downing Street solicitor who some 15 years previously had got the better of John M. Paine,

was appointed Clerk and Registrar of Burials. They wasted no time on domestic issues but got straight down to business–indeed their pace over the next few months, measured by Local Government standards, was staggering; the more so because they encountered more than the usual quota of obstacles. Briefly, the events of the first 12 or 13 months may be summarised thus:–
The Farnham Burial Board had in mind three lots of land to choose from; namely a field at Willey Mill belonging to Charles Knight; land belonging to Frances Pennystone near the Railway Station and a piece owned by Thomas Pearce at the end of West Street. One has to be discreet about where one puts a cemetery, not everyone is like the Brontës. Institutions such as the Workhouse, sewage farm and the cemetery were originally sited well outside the town. The Board, for instance, wrote to Stovold of Broomleaf Farm, Nicholson of Waverley Abbey and the Railway Company to get their views about Miss Pennystone's site. But the Board were really more interested in the piece at Willey Mill, which was a nice long way from the land of the living–except for George Simmonds, the Miller, who at once protested. They settled his complaint and then opened negotiations with Charles Knight, with a figure of something like £150 an acre in mind.

Knight quoted the Board £200 an acre, if they would take the whole of his field; plus a lump-sum of £50 if only part was taken; plus £90 for fixing it with George Simmonds (and moving his pig sties out of the way); plus compensation settled at £90 to W. Betts, another tenant. Being in a hurry, the Board accepted without haggling. They chartered William Birch to prepare plans and estimates for two chapels–episcopal and dissenters–and a cemetery lodge; to be built of stone 'of the Upper Green Sand, which is dug in the Parish', and costing from £500 to £900. They even wrote to the Bishop to book him for the consecration service. All this in the space of less than two months.

And then they added it all up and approached the Vestry for sanction to borrow £3,500. On 24 May 1855, rather subdued, the Board considered the Vestry's decision to limit sanction to £3,000, all-in, with a recommendation that they drop the Willey project and try again with James Knight, who owned a likely bit of land at Coxbridge.

So Mr. Niblett set off again, to treat with Mr. James, who asked the sum of £975 for 3 acres 1 rod 30 perches. The Board haggled, but finally gave way. Mr. Birch was instructed to produce a fresh set of plans and tenders were invited. Two tenants on the land, Groves and Carter, claimed £25 and £40 compensation. The tender of Mr. Mason, builder, was accepted and his contract specified that work should commence on 1 October 1855, the two chapels to be completed by 29 December and the lodge by 29 January 1856.

Then the Board decided that the geography of the site would be improved if ¾ acre was taken off the bottom and added to the top. James Knight did not go along with this, so–in short–the Board washed their hands of the whole exercise and went and saw Thomas Pearce, who owned the adjoining field. Pearce wanted £1,200. On 18 October 1855, one month later, both parties had exchanged contracts and Mr. Birch got busy again. Mr. Matthews, sitting tenant, was voted £125 to get up and go; Goddards, builders of East Street, were given the signal to commence building the chapels and lodge. The chapels turned out to be too small and were lengthened by three feet. The walls of the lodge were, in Birch's words, 'considerably out of an upright', and the Royal Exchange Assurance Office, who were putting up the money, had second thoughts–just as the bills were starting to arrive.

Lesser men, opening up a cemetery, might at this point have given up the ghost and become their first customers. Not so our Board; Mr. Niblett was sent to look for another source of funds–and found it; a Mr. Duke was engaged as Clerk of Works, to Goddards' annoyance; Thomas Trusler was taken on the strength to landscape with tree-planting; the confines of the cemetery area were walled in, with a dwarf wall and railing on the West Street frontage; arrangements were set in hand for selling off land surplus to requirements; the paths were laid; grave-spaces planned out; interment fees decided upon. Richard Wooderson was appointed Sexton at £10 a year, his duties being 'to take charge of the Chapels and attend the Gates, to keep the paths swept and edge the grass and generally keep the Ground in order, with the exception of mowing the large plots–for which he had to live in the Lodge'. Wooderson moved in on the 1 May 1856. In the space of 13 months, the Board had gotten themselves a Cemetery. They were now in business and—two days later, on 3 May 1856—the first customer arrived. Over the ensuing ten years, an annual average of 80 to 90 people came to be buried.

In May 1857, the Board ordered 'that all papers, books, documents and writings, Seal and Chest and other things belonging to the Burial Board, now in the custody of Mrs. Niblett, be at once demanded of her and that the same (if given up) be deposited with the Rev. J.S. Utterton'. Then the thunders of the Vatican roared in the form of a summons from London solicitors acting for Sophia Barling and Alfred Barling of Farnham, Judgement Creditors, for Charles William Niblett, Judgement Debtor, and the Farnham Burial Board—to be heard in the Court of Common Pleas on 11 May 1857, in respect of a debt of £82 15s. 8d. The unfortunate Clerk's balance of salary was paid into the Court on account. On 26 May 1857, it was resolved that 'Mr. Niblett, not having appeared to discharge his duties as Clerk and Registrar, that he be discharged and is hereby discharged from this day forward from these Offices'. Mr. Henry Potter was appointed in his place.

Membership of the Board had already changed out of all recognition—perhaps they did not care for the role of the town's grave-diggers. The dominant personality was now Dr. Robert Oke Clark of 10 Castle Street. Also on the Board were George Cooke, James Tily, William Rudge and Sampson Sampson. Their recorded business almost exclusively concerns routine administration matters; of the customers, hardly anything. The Victorians who died and were buried at Farnham Cemetery are of equal importance in this book to those who lived.

There was an application by the family of John Randall, late chemist, to erect railings at his grave; an iron border was allowed around Ann Herridge's grave; Mr. Clark was granted permission to plant a cypress tree over the grave of his late children.

The Burial Board, too, had to press the Overseers for money. In March 1860, the accounts stood as follows:—

The 4th instalment of the Principal Sum of £1000 advanced by Miss Ann Nash	£50 0 0
Half a year's Interest on £850, the Balance of the Principal now remaining to Miss Nash	21 5 0
The 4th instalment of the Principal Sum of £1000 advanced by Miss Jane Nash	50 0 0

Half a year's Interest on the Balance of the Principal now remaining	£21	5	0
The 4th instalment of the Principal of the Sum advanced by Miss Rowlandson	50	0	0
Half a year's Interest on the Balance of the Principal remaining due to her	21	5	0
Amount of Mr. Snelling's Bill for repairs	13	6	4
The like–Mr. Hughe's Bill	8	10	0
	£235	11	4

. . . . .

In contrast with the unseen business of the grave-diggers, the objectives of the Inspector of Nuisances were palpably obvious to anyone with a nose. Although now the proclaimed authority on sanitary matters, there was nothing that the Board of Surveyors could do apart from bullying the offenders. What the town needed was a few hundred pounds spent on providing an effective drainage system, if only into the River Wey. Getting no help from Whitehall, the Surveyors asked the opinion of the Magistrates and Mr. Thresher, the Chairman, advised them that, should any ratepayer object to an item of expenditure for drains, the Magistrates would have no alternative than to disallow it. The Board's genuine but frustrated desire to meet the demands made on them was pathetic. East Street was especially bad–Birch's new houses near the White Post, Gatcum's house, Goddard's premises and others. Passing travellers running the gauntlet from the White Post to the Cemetery at the other end held their noses and whipped up their horses.

That elder statesman, John Manwaring Paine, offered to sell the Board a strip of land at his factory at Dippenhall for road widening. He was told that there was no precedent for buying land for such purposes–so would he give it? Paine's factory made bricks of a whitish colour; they were used in the first Town Hall soon to be built on the site of the old *Goats Head Inn.* Paine was perhaps the best known figure of early 19th century Farnham. When he died in May 1858, the mark he left on the town proved to be indelible. Certain names–Paine, Knight, Trimmer, Mason, Stevens and others–spring immediately to mind, whilst lesser men who played their parts died and were forgotten.

The Surveyor was instructed to write to the Police respecting boys playing at Marbles and Pitch & Toss on the pitching (where better?), thus causing holes and damage on the footways. Also to draw their attention to damage done to the bridge by some parties maliciously knocking off the tops of the iron standards.

At a Special Meeting on 5 May 1858, the Board discussed James Harris' resignation from the Office of Assistant Surveyor. A change of Surveyor was a local event of some magnitude. Harris remained as Clerk. Circulars were distributed throughout the Parish and also in Guildford, Godalming, Alton and Odiham, which proclaimed:–

> SURVEYOR WANTED
>
> The Board of Surveyors of the Parish of Farnham require the services of a Competent Person as Road Surveyor for the Highways of the Parish. The Salary is fixed at £52 per annum. He will be required to devote his whole time to the duties of his Office, and to find Securities to the extent of £100. Testimonies as to competence and character to be sent to Mr. John Nash, Farnham, the Chairman to the said Board, on or before Monday, May 17th next.

There were seven applications, including that of George Vanner of the Wrecclesham family of farmers, but the Surveyors were not satisfied and re-advertised in the *County Chronicle, Sussex Express* and the *West Surrey Times,* at an increased salary of £60. There were five replies, including one from George Vanner. Three attended a meeting on 8 June 1858–Joseph Humphreys of Artington, Surveyor of Mickleham and father of five children; William Grant of Tunbridge, farmer and father of four and George Vanner, who offered to take the job at the original £52 per annum, and got it.

Mr. Aylwin was in trouble again with his pigs, which he had not cleaned out for some time. Gatcum of East Street was still making a smell. A Mr. Cullum wrote complaining about Robert Attfield's yard in Downing Street whilst Mr. Attfield complained about Cullum. Messrs. Daniels & Chitty had carted and tipped some glass bottles at the side of the Upper Way to Wrecclesham, and Messrs. Speakman & Haynes had also thrown some rubbish down near the Bridge. And so it went on.

The Rev. E.J. Ward, Vicar of East Clandon and owner of Firgrove, wrote:–

Plate 8 *East Street in the 1830's*

Plate 9 *Farnham station pre 1860, when disc signals were discontinued, showing level-crossing gates and, beyond, farm bridge in Broomleaf*

Plate 10 *Farnham, from the Meadows*

Plate 11 *Town centre before demolition in the 1860's*

Plate 12 *The Bourne's former church, and cemetery*

Plate 13 *Farnham in the 1860's, showing influence of the nearby Aldershot Camp*

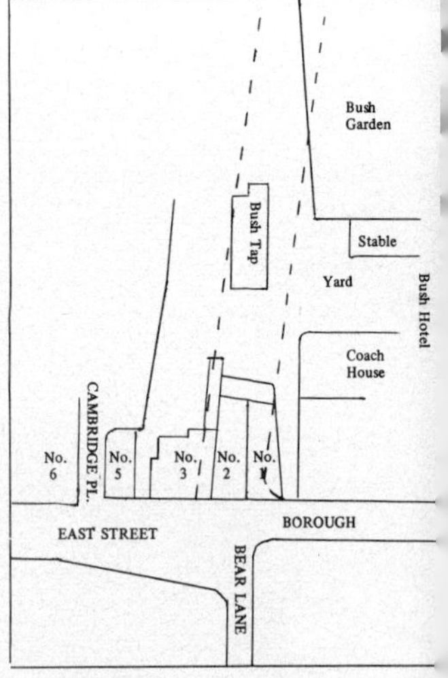

Plate 14 *Farnham Town Hall, 1866*

Plate 15 *Plan of South Street*

> I am induced to address these few to you, as Surveyors of Highways, for the purpose of laying before your Board a proposition for improving a part of the road leading to Tilford, near to the Farnham Station.
>
> At the spot to which I would draw your attention, the road is not more than 12 feet wide and consequently will not admit of two carriages passing which is not only inconvenient but here, from its proximity to the Station, is also dangerous. The South-western Railway Company have very liberally consented to give about 8 feet or such a portion of their field adjoining the Station and abutting on the west side of the road leading to Tilford, as is requisite to make the said road 20 feet wide.

The Board pleaded poverty. The greatest damage caused by the railway to any one property in the town was perhaps the splitting in two of the Firgrove Estate, which stretched from the river up the hill and over the Ridgway, and, in width, from Tilford Road to where Weydon Hill Road came. In an endeavour to save the house itself, the Rev. Ward forced the Railway Company to include in their 1846 Act a section to the effect 'that no part of the said railway .. shall .. be nearer than Fifty yards to the south-east Walls of the Garden'. Nevertheless, the splendour of the House diminished and the severed land on the hillside was sold off later in the reign in building plots.

Labourers were two-a-penny. The Board studied their list of workmen—and sacked 17 of them, but 'if found to be out of work at the expiration of the week, the Surveyor was directed to set on again some of those who were worst off'. Mr. Edwards' proposal that the men be paid by cheque was not intended to be funny. The Board were concerned about the unemployment problem in the town. Their own requirements were about 38 men according to the extent of road work. They were pleased therefore when Henry Jowning, farmer at Shortheath, offered to employ a certain number of roadmen to pick up stones in his fields if the Board would buy them at 9d. a load.

On 28 December 1858, Mr. Vanner reported that a boy named Frederick Clark of Red Lion Lane had been seen by a son of Frederick Stovold to throw a stone at the ironwork at the Bridge and knock off one of the arrow heads. The boy appeared in Court and tell-tale Stovold was awarded £2. A man named Jefferies encroached on the highway by digging a well thereon. The Rector applied for a stink-trap at the grating opposite his house. On inspection it was discovered that 'the nuisance complained of arose from water closets having been laid into the common sewers and that Mr. Utterton had himself turned his own Church into the sewer'. Cleanliness, they say, is next to Godliness.

He hath a tear for pity, and a hand
Open as day for melting Charity.

William Shakespeare

VII

FIFTH QUINQUENNIUM

THE CHURCHWARDENS and Overseers of the Parish found space on occasions to record the grants made to deserving individuals from the funds of Smith's Charity. The following cases, taken at random from the long lists of beneficiaries, shed interesting sidelights on the way the other half lived in the 1860s. 'Going out to service' was the lot of the daughters, the cottagers' savings going on apprenticing their sons with local trades. In this world of the poor, apprentice and servant met and married, begat their like, grew old and finished in the workhouse. Their struggle so preyed on the mind of the man named Henry Smith that by his Deed in 1626, he cushioned the harshness of their lives, not so much by the temporary material help he gave them as by the more enduring sweetness that once there had lived someone who cared.

Louisa Scarlett, 13, dau of Elizabeth Scarlett. Been with Mr. Romsey, Shepherds Walk, City Road, 12 months; board and lodging only .. granted 10s.
Caroline Downs, 14, dau of John and Ann Downs. Been with Mrs. Mott as nurse 1 month; wages received 1s. per week .. granted 10s.
Elizabeth Chuter, 16, dau of George and E. Chuter. Been with Miss Stratford 3 months and receiving 9d. per week .. granted 10s.
Elizabeth Eades, 17, dau of William and E. Eades. Been with Mrs. R. Ellis 3 years and receiving 1s. 6d. per week .. this application was refused.
Alice Wells, 14, an orphan. Been with Mrs. T. Edwards 9 months and receiving 50s. per annum .. granted 10s.
Caroline Fry, 16, dau of W. and H. Fry. Proposed Master, Mr. Croft, baker over Bridge. Been there 11 months at 1s. per week .. granted 10s.
Elizabeth Blackman, 12, dau of C. Blackman, Bourne. Proposed Master, Mr. W. Dare, publican, Wrecclesham 16 months; no wages .. refused.
Eliza Stock, 13, dau of Richard Stock. With Mr. Hale, bootmaker; been there 12 months at 3d. per week .. granted 10s.

Elizabeth Lovell, 15, illegitimate dau of - Lovell, mother in asylum. With Mr. Blackie 4 months at 1s. per week .. granted 10s.
Mary Quennell, 12 years, dau of Jno. H. Quennell. With Mrs. Goucher, Ovington, 3 months, 1s. per week .. granted 10s.
Emma Cranham, 20, dau of man in Union, no mother. Mrs. G. Baker 3 months service at 1s. 6d. .. granted 10s.
Emily Jones, 16, dau of W.G. Jones. With Mr. Stokes, *Fox and Hounds;* been there 9 months at 1s. 0d. per week .. refused as being at a public house.

Apprentices seeking help towards their premiums included:—

Henry Cole, 13, son of Henry and Jane Cole, Factory Yard. Proposed Master, Mr. Smither, Hale road, baker. Premium asked £4, the boy to receive board and lodging and clothes .. granted £4.
Charles Worthington, 16, son of Michael Worthington. Proposed Master, Mr. W. Whiting, coach builder, Hale; been there 12 months, to be apprenticed 7 years. Premium asked £20, to receive, 1st year nil; 2nd year 4s. per week .. refused.
Jane Wright, 17, dau of Widow Wright, Crondall Lane. Proposed Mistress, Miss Murray, milliner; been with her 10 months, to be apprenticed 2 years. Premium asked £2 .. granted 10s. for clothes only.
Frank Grover, son of George and Jane Grover. Aged 15 years. Proposed Master, Mr. Sturt; been with him 2 years and 3 months. Premium asked £10. Decided that the sum of £3 be offered only.
Archdeacon Utterton reported that he had in hand the sum of £3, which was originally granted to a boy named Steer, who was to be apprenticed to Mr. Henry Patrick but who now said the Boy was of no use in the trade.
Stephen Loveland, 13 years, son of Widow Loveland. Proposed Master, John Figg, shoemaker, Downing Street. Premium asked £5, to receive 2s. per week up to 15 years of age and 1s. per week increase for every year afterwards .. recommended that the sum of £3 be granted to the Boy if a satisfactory Master can be found, but not to Mr. Figg.
An application was made by a widow, Mrs. Swayne, for help to get her son and daughter out to California. She had collected a considerable sum, but short about £10. The case was recommended by the Archdeacon and she was granted the sum of 20s. for clothing.
Henry Hole, 15, son of Widow Hole. Proposed Master, Mr. F. Sturt. Premium asked £10; wages to increase till 21. Granted conditionally £3 10s. 0d. Mr. Sturt agreed to take Henry Hole at £3 10s. 0d. premium.
An application from Mrs. Brooker, widow, for clothes for her son; subject to fits .. granted 12s.

There were 15 pensioners on the charity's Books in 1860. As they died, others took their place—there was no shortage.

. . . . .

From the early 1860s, the Rate Collector was John Thorp. He was a chemist who had arrived from Thame to a pharmacy at 16 The Borough. By some chance he had become involved in public service and, seeing in it a better future than retailing Holloways Pills and other medicaments, he ended up by becoming a full-time Officer of the Parish and other plums such as Secretary to the Farnham Market House & Town Hall Company.

The affairs of the Rating Department had grown a little sluggish. A canon of rating law was to get the ratebooks signed by the Magistrates, the Churchwardens and anyone else who could write, otherwise the rate was invalid and, in the eyes of the Law, no-one was obliged to pay it. On 7 May 1863, George Henry Elwin of the Railway Company's Rates and Taxes Office, Waterloo Bridge Station, wrote:

> I beg to call your particular attention to the fact that the Farnham Poor Rate made 2nd January 1863 has not yet been allowed by the Magistrates.

and, on 12 May,

> Will you please let me have a reply to my note of the 7th instant as to the non-allowance by the Magistrates of the Poor Rate made 2nd January last.

Mr. Harris, whose job it was to make out the ratebooks, reported to his Committee that he had already replied to Mr. Elwin to the effect that 'being laid up with Rheumatic Gout at the time the Rate should have been signed by the Magistrates, it had afterwards escaped his memory, but that it was now signed and allowed by two Magistrates'.

In June, the arrears list was studied and the Committee gave instructions for summonses to be issued. The names included Henry Patrick, Andrew Crosby, Frederick Attfield, Henry Smither and George Trimmer!

An oak chest was ordered from Mr. F. Birch in which to deposit the Parish documents. It was to be 6ft. 3ins. long, 2ft. 6ins. wide and 2ft. 6ins. deep, of well seasoned oak 1½ins. in thickness, lined with zinc, with two superior well made locks and with a partition to part the maps etc. from the books and other documents. It cost seven guineas and was duly placed in the Church in December 1863 and the contents laid to rest.

In no time at all, the maps were exhumed because the Assessment Committee wanted to borrow them. This Committee was a newcomer under the Union Assessment Committee Act 1862 and was elected annually by the Guardians for the purpose of valuing properties for rating purposes, hitherto a somewhat hit-and-miss affair performed by the Overseers themselves–

sometimes with the assistance of the ratepayer concerned. On 2 November 1864, the Rate Committee studied a new Valuation List produced by the Assessment Committee. Oddly, this list, which is in the writer's temporary custody, is neither signed nor dated, a point which would have been of interest to Mr. Elwin.

The Overseers distributed bread to the value of £22 from the funds of Smith's Charity, to the poor and needy. At a subsequent meeting, a member referred to 'the disgraceful scenes which occurred at the Church Doors February 2nd last in giving away the Bread and suggested that an application should be made to the Commissioners to alter the system of giving it away'.

Mr. Lucy wrote requesting a share of the printing of Parish documents as he had done nothing for some four years and it was ordered that he have the printing for the next year. Arthur E. Lucy published and printed the *Surrey & Hants. News* at 1 The Borough and also at Aldershot and Guildford. It had been running since 1859 and circulated in a wide area of Surrey and Hampshire. These early local newspapers make interesting reading nowadays. The front page is devoted to local tradesmen's advertisements:–

> E. Bromley, Wine & Spirit Merchant. Gin 2s. per bottle, Rum 3s. 4d.; brandy 3s. 4d.; Cognac 5s. 6d.; Whisky 3s. 4d.
>
> J. Mallam, 51 The Borough; men's tailor ... C. Borelli, 11 East Street; Watch and Clock Maker, Silversmith, Jeweller etc. ... Charles Keen, East Street, established 1800; Coach & Carriage Builder ... J.W. Barfoot, now opened at 1 New Exchange, The Borough; Decorators ...
>
> Mr. Chitty, Farnham every Thursday at Mr. Harrington's, Jewellers, 47 The Borough; Artificial Teeth constructed upon the principle patented by Mr. Chitty, are adapted to the mouth without extracting or filling any of the remaining teeth or stumps. They are fitted without wires, springs or other mechanical contrivances, in a manner to become immovable only at the will of the wearer. These teeth occupy less space in the mouth; they are very much stronger and far more durable and can be worn with greater comfort than those made on vulcanite, india-rubber, gutta-percha and other so-called self-adhesive bases. From 10s. each.

Pages 2 and 3–Home and Foreign News, culled from the national press. They loved a good murder–'The Mysterious Murder in London', 'The Sad End of a Wretched Life', 'A Revolting Murder', 'Burnt to Death' ... Pages 4 and 5–public notices, editorial and local news of towns and villages in the circulation area–

> (21st April 1866), FARNHAM. Grand Concert in the New Exchange. In celebration of the opening of the New Town Hall which, it will be remembered, was inaugerated a few weeks since by a grand banquet ...

Page 6–Parliamentary reports. Page 7–more magazine. Page 8–more advertisements; Holloways Pills; Mrs. Arnshaw's Soothing Syrup; Brown's Bronchial Troches; Blunden's Gout & Rheumatic Pills ...

. . . . .

Those who didn't respond to pills made heavy demands on the Burial Board. The Rev. J.S. Utterton wrote to the Board on 31 August 1861:

> The Inhabitants of the Bourne have expressed a strong desire that a burial ground should be attached to the Chapel which is being erected there. The Bishop approves of this arrangement and the Government also, who have sent an Inspector to examine the Ground. It will not only be a boon to the people in the Bourne, but also to the Parish at large as the Cemetery is filling up very fast. I shall be glad if you will call a meeting of the Board and ascertain whether they have any objection to the arrangement. Mr. Ward of Fir Grove has given the ground. The Bishop will defray all the expenses of consecration and I intend to raise the money by private subscription towards inclosing and laying out the Ground.

As far as the Farnham Burial Board were concerned it was almost a *fait accompli* but, from an administration angle, there was a snag. They wrote to the Burial Board, Whitehall 'respecting their power to consent to other burial places in the Parish independent of the Board'. In reply there was a letter from a Sir George Grey saying that he would consider the case upon receiving an application for *his* consent. To which the Board wrote back asking again whether *they* had the power to consent. Without waiting for the next salvo from Sir George, the Board gave their consent to the proposed new cemetery and presented him with a copy of the resolution.

On 25 March 1862, the Vestry agreed amended regulations and scale of fees submitted by the Board and a copy was sent to Whitehall for approval. Sir George Grey replied '... with respect to the 13th proposed regulation, by which it is required that in every grave purchased for the use of a family a layer of earth 18 inches in thickness be left between each coffin, it would seem that this involved a contradiction as, by the 10th proposed–when more than one body is intended to be interred in a purchased common private grave–the layer of interposed earth between the coffins is to be only one foot thick'. The Board admitted the clerical error and settled for 18 inches. With regard to the scale of fees, Sir George struck out the fees proposed for the Minister, Clerk and Sexton, and for searches in the Register, as these were already provided for by statute. But never mind—the Bourne got its cemetery.

The two chapels at Farnham Cemetery were insured for £100 each with the Sun Fire Office, and the Lodge for £200. The Lodge had proved a problem child since the time it was built. The roof leaked, the chinmey smoked and the pump didn't work; the back and sides were affected by damp, the washhouse got flooded and the stonework wanted repointing. In 1859, these defects and all other necessary repairs to the cemetery buildings, listed by Stapley, the Board's surveyor, were put in order.

On 7 May 1866, the Grave-diggers met for the first time in the Board Room at the new Town Hall, paying £5 per annum, including gas, firing and attendance. With so many *ad hoc* bodies requiring a meeting place, the Farnham Market House & Town Hall Company Ltd. did quite well out of this room at £5 each. It was the room on the right as you went in. The tenants had no great love for it; for one thing they had to share it; also it did not belong to the town and, to representatives of local government, this was irksome.

A conspicuous feature of Farnham cemetery is the number of child burials. Infant mortality was high; people had big families, but not all of them survived. Mrs. Bellenger sought permission to include in the inscription on her husband's grave references to her son, buried at Farnborough, and daughter, buried at Slough. Mr. Annesley applied to plant a tree on the grave of his child, buried on 26 July 1865. Miss Mary Nash had left word that she wished to be buried in section E of the cemetery, this being the first interment in that section. Mr. Chapman asked to place a headstone between the graves of his two children, recently buried in adjoining graves. Permission was given for the following inscription on the grave of James Corps, buried 19 December 1865:

We cannot tell who next may fall
Beneath the chast'ning rod.
One must be first, so let us all
Prepare to meet our God.

And, on the stone of Ellen Mary Stovold Mallam, buried 9 January 1866

> Farewell thou little blooming bud,
> Just bursting into flower.
> We give thee up, but Oh! the pain
> Of that last parting hour.

. . . . .

In the end the smells forced the inhabitants of the town into taking an epochal and irreparable step—that of abandoning the satellite villages, the rich hopgrounds and the country mansions, in order to cut the area of authority down to the Trouble Spot, namely the town part of the Parish. It was a momentous decision to make and the parishioners fought over it for at least a year. Suddenly to reduce one's realm in size from some 10,000 acres to a mere 234 called for some nerve; but the Smells won—there was really no alternative. That the authority which took over the town would by a series of boundary extensions in the course of time regain, with the exception of Tilford, the territory jettisoned in 1866, would have lulled many a conscience at the time.

The formalities began in the usual way with a requisition to the Summoning Officer, Mr. Richard Mason, to call a meeting of Owners and Ratepayers for the purpose of taking into consideration a resolution for the adoption of the Local Government Act 1858.

> I do hereby give Notice that a Meeting will be holden at the *Bush Hotel* in Farnham on Wednesday the Twenty-fifth day of April 1866 at Two o'clock in the afternoon, in pursuance of a Requisition duly signed, for the purpose of considering a Resolution for the adoption of the Local Government Act 1858 in the District of Farnham within the Parish of Farnham.
>
> Dated the 19th day of April 1866,
>
> RICHARD MASON, Summoning Officer.

Robert Oke Clark chaired the meeting and put the resolution. By a show of hands it was defeated. Whereupon Samuel George Sloman demanded a poll.

At No. 8 Richmond Terrace, Whitehall, there was a department called the Local Government Act Office. In this office there was a Mr. Arnold Taylor and a Mr. T. Taylor (nepotism?) who, during the long period which Farnham took to make up its mind, exercised care and patience (at times sorely tried) in guiding the locals in their hour of torment. In Richard Mason, they had an opponent who played his pawns with cunning.

Mr. T. reassured Mr. Mason that a Local Board formed under the Act would be entirely independent of any central authority, except for the borrowing of money, which as usual would require the sanction of the Secretary of State. Mr. Arnold came down to Farnham on more than one occasion to talk to the inhabitants, having first been genned up on local colour ('some good positive evidence to show the necessity for sanitary improvements in Farnham, such as prevalent diseases or the evils of nuisances arising from want of drainage or the absence of proper sanitary appliances, will all serve to strengthen my hands and support your case').

To cut a whole file of it short, the voters of Farnham adopted the Act by 300 for, 249 against and 102 don't knows. A major point was the settlement of boundaries for the new Local Board's area. These were skin-tight to the town, and the River Wey which was earmarked as the main sewer. The boundary made a special diversion to take in the Workhouse in Hale Road, cut across to the south bank of the river, included the railway station and Firgrove House, crossed the Meadows to Coxbridge, over the Turnpike road to include the West End Grove estate, along the backs of the houses in West Street and Long Garden Walk, up round the Castle (but not the Park), along the rear of East Street properties back to the White Post.

It was like moving out of Moor Park into a Council flat. Yet the Local Board which came into being on 2 June 1866 became the nucleus of local government in Farnham. At once it assumed the duties of the Board of Surveyors and the Inspectors of Lighting and Watching. Other bodies, with a purely local interest, joined at some later stage–Burials, Rating (in 1929). For some 30 years, until the County Councils were formed, the Board enjoyed absolute sovereignty. The Guardians, who had always acted in a union of parishes, stayed in the clouds until the County adopted them; the Magistrates, of course, owed allegiance only to their Maker.

Such was the prescience of Westminster that the future of local government was conceived in 1858 which, during the next 100 years, became the envy of, and often the pattern for other countries in the world. And it all came from defective drains.

PART TWO

THE LOCAL BOARD, 1866–1895

I see you stand like greyhounds in the slips,
Straining upon the start.

William Shakespeare

VIII

NEW BROOM

At the First Meeting of the Local Board held at the *Bush Hotel,* Farnham on the 31st August 1866.

THE WORD 'At' is arabesqued in pomp, pride and circumstance. Robert Tyler Barrett was unanimously chosen as Chairman of the Board for the ensuing year. The certificate of Richard Mason, the Summoning Officer appointed by the Secretary of State, of the result of the Election of the Local Board was produced and delivered to the Board; the following persons were thereby certified to be duly elected, viz.–

GEORGE TRIMMER	WILLIAM JACOB HOLLEST
JOHN NASH	GEORGE CROOK
WILLIAM MASON	HENRY POTTER
SAMUEL ANDREWS	JOSIAH BENTALL
WILLIAM BROWN	ROBERT TYLER BARRETT
WILLIAM HAZELL	SAMUEL GEORGE SLOMAN

These gentlemen made and signed the Declaration of Qualification required by the Public Health Act 1848 and the Local Government Act 1858.

Richard Mason was appointed Clerk to the Board, at a salary of £25 a year–with (added in his own handwriting) a bonus at the end of the first year as the Board should think necessary. The Offices of Surveyor, Inspector and Collector to be combined in one person at £75 per annum, the same to be advertised for in *The Times,* the *Surrey & Hants. News,* the *Hampshire Chronicle* and *Sheldrake's Aldershot Gazette.* Mr. Luffrin was employed as Inspector *pro tem.* The Knights of Farnham Bank were appointed Treasurers.

After this heady experience, the next meeting on 11 September was more like old times, except for an exciting reference by the Clerk to the choice of a design for the Seal. Business was back to normal–an overflowing privy in Downing Street belonging to John Clark; an accumulation of filth in Factory Yard belonging to Warner and Mahoney; an overflowing privy in West Street on the premises of Benjamin Fry and another in Bear Lane at William Harris'.

It was resolved to hold ordinary meetings of the Board on the first Tuesday in every month but such was the nature of their programme that they met much more frequently. There were 24 applications from all parts of the south-east for the job of Surveyor-Inspector-Collector, mainly from surveyors or clerks of work–though there was a porter, a warehouseman, a railway clerk, a grocer and a schoolmaster. A Mr. Hector Harding of Aldershot was appointed, his duties to commence on the 12 November 1866. Luffrin was discharged as from that date and given 50s. for his services as privy counsellor.

The Board notified the Inspectors of Lighting and Watching:–

> That the powers conferred upon them by the Acts of Parliament under which they were constituted were, as from the 20th day of August last, so far as the District of the Local Board was concerned, superseded by the Acts from which the Board obtained its powers.

In October 1866, the Local Board met for the first time in the Board Room of the new Town Hall. It was opportune, though fortuitous, that this large public hall at the corner of Castle Street and The Borough was completed at the same time as the advent of the Local Board. Had the Board, with their new-found strength, been in existence a few years earlier–who knows–they might have said 'no' to the demolition of the Market House in the street outside.

Money troubles were over; they had a built-in authority to levy a General District Rate to cover all expenditure according to law. For a start they wanted some £303, the cost of getting established (£50 for legal fees alone), and, in the months ahead, £50 for lighting and £100 for highways. A rate at 6d. in the pound on the rateable value of £14,097 14s. 6d., would, with the normal irrecoverables, produce £318 13s. 9d. so they imposed this on the ratepayers. The big expenses would come later.

The first stirrings of the giant came in the form of a rumble from Dr. Sloman about obstructions on the footways and it was decided that a public notice be given 'that all obstructions on the pathways within the District shall be removed in accordance with Section 28 of 10 & 11 Vict. c.89 (Towns Police Clauses Act, 1847)'.

The old Board of Surveyors intimated that they had instructed their Surveyor no longer to interfere with that portion of the highways of the Parish within the District of the Local Board and that the Fire Engines were handed over to the Local Board as from the 29 September. And with this act of surrender, the Surveyors yielded up the Citadel and disappeared into the bush. It is like saying goodbye to an old friend. Also to other old friends, the Inspectors of Lighting and Watching, for on 10 October the Gas Company wrote:–

> The Directors of this Company have hitherto been under a contract with the Board of Inspectors of Lighting to supply the Public Lamps of the Town with gas etc. from the 5th November to same date in succeeding year at the rate of £4 per lamp per annum. I am informed that the contract no longer exists ... having only just been made aware of the non-existence of the Lighting Board ...

The Local Board had to start from scratch. The Surveyors had taken all their tools and know-how with them; so, as the Gas Company's letter suggests, had the Inspectors. Harding was told to open up shop–no mean task.

The Doctor again rumbled, this time taking the bull by the horns–'that steps be taken to effectively drain the town'. He could not have picked a more precise way of putting it, even if it did mean splitting an infinitive. All in good time, said the Board who, as an experiment, instructed Harding to prepare a report on the best means of repairing Castle Street 'for the purpose of Traffic on the outer market'–presumably where the Market House had once stood. Then they remembered that some of Castle Street did not belong to the town–it belonged to the Farnham Market House & Town Hall Company, so–galling thought–they had to write to the Company for permission to include the site in their plans for Castle Street. The Town Hall Company (to use a shortened version of their title) wrote back on 14 December 1866, saying:

> In answer to your letter of the 5th instant, I am directed to inform you that the Directors of the Farnham Market House & Town Hall Company consent to

> the request of the Local Board to be allowed to alter the portion of Castle Street belonging to the said Company on condition that the Local Board sink the corner stones marking the site of the old Market House in acknowledgement of the Farnham Market House & Town Hall Company to the freehold therein and the right of the said Company to levy tolls in respect thereof.

Harding reported that he would require some 500 loads of gravel and was ordered to dig this at the Parish Pit at Hungry Hill and arrange cartage. Then they remembered that this pit was not theirs at all but belonged to the old Board of Surveyors who still functioned in the bush area of the Parish, including Hungry Hill at Hale. This really was trying—in the area of the Local Board, there were no sources of gravel at all. So they wrote to the Surveyors to get them to acknowledge the Board's right to take gravel and on what terms; they also wrote to the Local Government Act Office and the ubiquitous Mr. T. Taylor replied:—

> I am directed by Mr. Secretary Walpole to acknowledge receipt of your letter of the 30th ult as to the right of the Local Board to take materials for Road repair outside the District. I have to state in reply that I quite agree with you in your opinion that the Local Board succeed to all the rights, as well as the duties, of the Surveyors of Highways.

The *Surrey & Hants. News* requested leave to attend meetings of the Board to report proceedings and it was resolved to admit the Press. In the papers the reports appeared on the lines of the minutes—a single paragraph of unrelated subjects, many of which, separately treated, would have made interesting news items in themselves.

Advertisements were put in *The Times, The Engineering Journal,* and the *County Chronicle* for submissions by engineers for the best means of draining the District, prizes of £100 and £50 being offered 'for the best and second best schemes for draining the District and disposal of the Sewage thereof'.

The bad state was discussed of the road leading out of Castle Street called 'Blue Gates Road', leading to the *Hop Blossom Inn* in the hopgrounds. This name could be considered in any future redevelopment of Long Garden Walk.

Committees were formed, one to draw up Bye-laws and another to take over the financial business; the form of present-day local government was taking shape. The scope of the Board's activities was increasing. There was, for instance, a voluntary body in the town called The Committee of Subscribers for Watering the Streets of the Town. In the days before the use of tar on the road surfaces, there was a very real nuisance caused in dry weather from the dust stirred up by carts or even by a strong wind, and the need for vehicles to go round sprinkling the roads with water was essential. The Board wrote to Charles Austwick of Castle Street, the Hon. Secretary of the Committe, suggesting that the Board should take over the duties of watering the streets and inviting terms. Mr. Austwick replied:–

> In reply to your favour of the 13th February 1867, I have been requested by the Committee of Subscribers for Watering the Streets of the Town of Farnham to inform you for the information of the Local Board that the liabilities of the Committee amount to the sum of £12 and that the assets comprise two water carts and the pump situated in East Street, which will be at the service of the Local Board for the sum of £12.

The area to be watered was 'West Street, starting from Mr. Stokes' House at the West End; The Borough and East Street to the White Post; Castle Street to Miss Girardo's House and Downing Street and Abbey Street to the lower Gates of the Railway Station'. It was quite an expensive business. A new galvanised iron water cart that the Board bought cost £28. The tender of Mr. Ambrose Pharo was accepted for watering the streets–wet weather excepted–at £3 15s. 0d. per week, 'using three horses' (presumably with carts on the back).

Mr. W.J. Hollest, 'having failed to qualify himself to sit on the Board' had to resign and Mr. Hewitt, who had received the next highest number of votes in 1866, took his place ... The offer of the Town Hall Company to house the Fire Engine in the newly completed Engine House at the Town Hall was accepted, the Company undertaking to furnish the necessary protection to the engine by gates or otherwise ... The Water Company agreed to the Surveyor having a duplicate key of the valve of the water main for use in case of fire ... Mr. Barnes, the District Auditor, in connection with his forthcoming audit of the Board's accounts, requested the Board to name his fee, pointing out that other Local Boards usually paid him five guineas. It was resolved to pay three guineas, including travelling and all other expenses. This praiseworthy display of thriftiness could not have failed to impress the Auditor–one way or the other.

Meanwhile the Board's main commission–the Town's Drainage–had not gone unnoticed by readers of *The Times,* the *Engineering Journal* and the *County Chronicle,* for a rash of plans and schemes had arrived from outer space. These were handed over to Harding to digest and report on, which proved easier said than done for a man who, having scratched about in his own backyard, suddenly finds himself confronted by Civil Engineers from all parts of the country trying to get in on Farnham's proposed drainage scheme. But a man-of-the-world came along in the person of John Frederick Bateman Esquire, the new owner of Moor Park.

Mr. Bateman had a personal interest in the matter. The River Wey wound its sluggish course through his Park within noseshot of his house and on the bosom of the stream was borne that portion of the town's unwanted matter that had made the journey so far. He offered to introduce the Board to a Mr. John W. Leather, Civil Engineer of Leeds, who, for a consideration, would analyse the applicants' entries. A fee of 40 guineas was arranged with Mr. Leather, who asked the Board to forward all the plans to him in Leeds, which the Board reluctantly did.

The Board took a tougher line on approving building applications. In June 1867, they refused Samuel Newman, basket maker, permission to alter his shopfront at 4 The Borough to bring it forward into line with his neighbours, Restall & Bevan, tea dealers at No. 5 ... Complaints were made to the Town Hall Company about the mess left by a recent fair in Castle Street. To the Board, these fairs were an abomination but there was nothing they could do about it because they were held on private ground. Under Section 40 of the 1858 Act, the Board took over maintenance of the Turnpike Road and thus became responsible for all streets in their area.

In July 1867, the Board considered a petition signed by several ratepayers praying that the hours be regulated for bathing in the River Wey. They decided that this was a matter for the Police. Apart from the fact of sewage, the most noteworthy feature of the sport was that, not being able to buy bathing costumes in the town, the bathers dispensed with this formality so that the scene on the river banks on a summer's day must have resembled a painting by Rubens or perhaps Cézanne.

It had been decided that members retiring at the end of the year should be the four with the lowest number of votes in 1866, namely Crook, Andrews, Hewitt and Bentall. The Clerk produced eight nominations for membership, of which four had been withdrawn, and a certificate was signed by the Chairman as required by Section 27 of the Public Health Act 1848, declaring George Crook, Samuel Andrews, James Hewitt and Josiah Bentall to be duly elected. Mr. Barrett remained as Chairman.

The 'new' Board met on 3 September 1867. Mr. Kingham had submitted plans for proposed new buildings in West Street, which were approved ... The Bye-laws had been printed—by Lucy and Nichols for £4 16s. 0d.—and were put in circulation ... The Surveyor reported that some of the stays supporting the palisading of the bridge had been broken and repairs and painting of the bridge were ordered.

The coming of the Army to Aldershot in 1855 had changed Farnham to a remarkable degree. As a garrison town, Farnham was invaded by the soldiers of the Queen in their thousands. Aldershot, then a mere hamlet, had no pubs; furthermore, the railway promoters in the 1840s had passed it without a second glance. Farnham supplied these two essential needs—a dozen or more new pubs sprouted along East Street and a fleet of horse-buses plied between the Station and the Camp, whilst bulkier army stores were floated in on the Basingstoke Canal and unloaded at what used to be the Farnham Wharf.

Whilst this new-found prosperity was excellent for the locals engaged in the beer trade and the cab business, it was not good enough for Her Majesty's Secretary of State for War. To move troops in an emergency—stopping all along East Street on the way to Farnham Station—was not an encouraging start to thin red lines in various theatres of war. What the camp, and the emerging town of Aldershot, needed was it own railhead. This was a long time coming, for it was not until 'Anno Vicesimo Victoriae Reginae Cap ciii' that the South-western (Aldershot) Railway Act, for a proposed railway from Pirbright to Farnham, received Royal Assent—possibly because the project, with two ancillary branches, would cost the Railway Company £160,000. Completion was scheduled for within three years of the passing of the Act on 19 June 1865, with a penalty of £50 to the Crown for every day after the expiration of the period. In 1868, the Company was trying to withdraw from this game of forfeits.

In March of that year, the Local Boards of Farnham and

Aldershot acted jointly, and promptly, in opposing the Bill before Parliament for an extension of completion date. The L. & S-W.R. urged withdrawal of the opposition and met a deputation of the Boards on 19 March 1868, wherefrom Barrett, Trimmer and Potter returned with the news that work on the Pirbright–Farnham railway had already been started and would proceed, though later than originally planned (it was finished in 1870). The link, because it gave a quicker journey to Waterloo than the Farnham–Guildford–Waterloo line, became the main route to London. The original railway, along which trains pulled by funny little engines had carried the sybarites of Farnham on their trips to town since 1849, was eventually scrapped, leaving a scar through the Ticeland of Badshot.

Mr. Leather had to be repeatedly prodded into making his report as umpire of the drainage applications and, on being given an ultimatum expiring on 21 February 1868, had produced his findings. Let the words of the Minutes of 24 March speak for themselves:–

> ... The Chairman having reported on the result of his consideration thereof that, after having devoted several hours to its perusal, he experienced nearly as much difficulty now with the Report in his hands as he had hitherto done without it ... and the Members present having expressed themselves as having met with equal a difficulty in their consideration of the Report, it was resolved and the Clerk was directed to write Mr. Bateman and explain the position in which the Board found themselves and inquire of him if he would favour the Board with his advice and assistance.

On 7 July 1868, the first mention is made of what was to become South Street.

> The Chairman on the Requisition of five Members of the Board having mentioned the subject of the desirability of increased Road accommodation between the Railway Station and the Town, the subject was considered and, after some discussion upon the question whether (a considerable outlay of public money being involved in the scheme) the Board should take any steps in the matter without some evidence of the wishes of the Ratepayers and others interested therein, at length resolved not to do so but to await some manifestation of the wishes of their constituents.

In July, Mr. Bateman declared No. 9 and No. 5 the Winner and Runner-up of the drainage competitors. They were Messrs. Hassard & Anstey of Westminster Chambers, Victoria Street, London (codename 'Fortuna') and John Bailey Denton of 22 Whitehall Place, under the motto 'Engineer'. They were awarded the prize-money.

At the Board's second Annual General Meeting on 25 August 1868, S.G. Sloman, William Mason, Thomas Smith and William Burningham were declared Members. It was, also, a reluctant goodbye to the Chairman. Robert Tyler Barrett, then 44 years old and father of nine, was rich enough to move to a country house at Frith End, Kingsley, where he lived until he died in 1883. The polite exchanges at the meeting were sincere. Mr. Barrett in a speech of some length 'offered an opinion upon the drainage of the town and upon other public matters which he thought must soon come before them for consideration'; he expressed his reluctance at resigning from the Board and his thanks to the Members for their courtesy. In a return speech, Dr. Sloman tried in vain to induce Mr. Barrett to continue his valuable services to the town.

IX

THE ROAD BUILDERS

IN MARCH 1869, the Farnham Burial Board waived the customary fees for the interment of Richard Wooderson, the Sexton. His widow was voted a gratuity of £5 in consideration of the additional cost she had been put to during her husband's long illness; she was allowed to remain at the Lodge, and continue the Sexton's duties (did she dig her husband's grave?), until the following 1 May. In her letter of thanks to the Clerk of the Board, Mary Wooderson wrote:

> May I ask you very heartily to thank the Board for their kind letter of condolence and expression of approval of my late husband's services. I shall always esteem this letter as one of special value.

John Hudson, a servant of the Bishop of Winchester, was appointed as the next Sexton. The cemetery was given another spring-clean—the walls repaired; the railings painted brown; the chapels cleaned and painted by Gibbons & Sons; the shrubs trimmed by Trusler, the nurseryman, and the Lodge fitted with a new kitchen range from Mr. C. Hart's costing £4 12s. 4d.

The Rev. G.E. Fox of Hale wrote in December 1869:

> When Hale Church was erected in 1844, a certain portion of ground was set apart in connexion with it as a burial place for the people of Hale. The Ground is now so fully occupied that urgent need exists for an enlarged churchyard or other burial place in Hale.
>
> Within the last few weeks two Vestry meetings have been held in Hale Church to consider the matter. At these meetings it has transpired unexpectedly to us that we have a claim to inter our parishioners in the Farnham Cemetery in consequence of the Farnham Cemetery having been constructed out of Funds for which the whole of the original Parish of Farnham, including Hale, is rated.

The Board found that this was indeed so, but having an ample number of clients of their own, suggested that Hale should apply to the War Office for a grant of land and constitute their own Burial Board. But the Hale Vicar protested that they had no such intention.

Hudson reported that he had trouble in preventing visitors from trampling on the grass, and even picking flowers from the graves. The usual notices were posted at strategic points but people still walked on the grass. So Hudson was told to keep children out of the cemetery. Only the dead ones were allowed in. Mrs. Bartholomew, wife of the Downing Street chimney-sweep, was in trouble for planting flowers on the graves of her two children; the grave of Mr. Hewett's child was inscribed:

> It was not meet that she should longer tarry from that bliss which God reserveth for the pure in heart.

Sometimes grown-ups were buried too. One was John Cann–'For 27 years he laboured as a Wesleyan Lay Preacher in the Neighbourhood.'

. . . . .

The way the Ratepayers of Farnham belaboured their Local Board into making a new approach road from the centre of the town to the Railway Station is a good example of the *vox populi* when stirred by mass emotion. It is an old game that is still played, though the attitude of a Council today has toughened. It is all a matter of money. The germ of an idea leads to the lobbying of Members who, fearing the reaction of ratepayers to the cost of the project, play safe by having nothing to do with it, thus rousing the ratepayers to greater efforts, so that no-one can complain when the bills come in. We have already seen how in July 1868, five Members of the Board raised the desirability of having a street to the Station and how the Board stated their reluctance to spend public money on it (which the *Surrey and Hants. News* was pleased to copy) and then waited for the next move from the townsfolk. They even refused the first requisition because it had too few signatures. Then came:

> We the undersigned Ratepayers within the District of your Board, being convinced of the desirability of direct and more commodious Roads between the

> Town and the Railway Station, respectfully request that you will take the earliest opportunity of considering the subject and of carrying out such scheme or project as shall to you appear most advantageous to the Ratepayers of the District and the public service.

Signed by the Bishop of Winchester, followed by 84 prominent citizens of the town, enough to hold down any dissenting ratepayers at a later stage. The Board were now free to do what they probably wanted to do in the first place.

The introduction of an entirely new street in the shopping centre of a town is not a matter to be undertaken lightly. A manifesto issued in December 1868 showed that the Board did not consider it a frivolous matter.

> In 1849 the South-western Railway Company opened their Station at Farnham in such a position as necessitated the whole of the traffic passing along a narrow, tortuous and in one part dangerous route, called Abbey Street, and so on up Downing Street into the town. Besides being occasionally productive of collisions, and always dangerous, it necessitates a long detour to all persons and vehicles bound for the Station from the Eastern end of the town and neighbourhood.
>
> This state of things has from time to time given rise to what may be called a 'new street' fever or ferment, but from the want of some Local Body invested with power to carry forward any such scheme, it has invariably fallen to the ground, and would not, probably, now have assumed any tangible shape but for the Board recently formed under the Local Government Act.

The Board approved a draft plan and conjectured the likely cost, and the initial response of the owners of properties and land affected was heartening. On nearing the town, the proposed road would slice off about eight feet of the *Bush* garden, go straight through the *Bush Tap,* No. 1 East Street, occupied by William Williams the Baker, No. 2 East Street occupied by William Lindsay, Plumber and Glazier, and shave off the flank of No. 3.

The Committee formed to look into details reported favourably:—

> That they had seen the principal proprietors concerned in the matter who expressed no disapproval in the main of the Plan adopted by the Board. They are willing to give all the ground as set out in the Plan and will remove all the buildings in which they are interested, this making a clear line of 35 feet to the river, with such extra feet at the opening in East Street as marked on the plan. The two properties affected by the Road on either side of the river having already been offered for the sums of £200 and £45 respectively, there remain but Williams' house and Linday's house to be provided for ...

The biggest landowners involved, the Knight brothers and

George Trimmer (the boundary between their fields passed down the centre of the road as far as the river) offered the Board the required strips for nothing (could this have been with an eye to future value of building plots fronting the road?). The Committee estimated, optimistically, that the overall cost of the whole scheme would be in the region of £2,312; they were about £700 short. They also estimated, pessimistically, that voluntary subscriptions would produce £500; they were £511 short. George Trimmer, in addition to his gift of land, donated £200. The Board worked it out that they would need a loan of £1,600 and applied for sanction to borrow, which was granted by Mr. T. Taylor. They then set the ball rolling by advertising for tenders.

The ordinary business of the Board was pushed into the corners. In one sat Mr. Leather of Leeds, asking for an increase in his agreed fees of 40 guineas as drainage consultant—so they sent him a cheque for £42. As an interim measure they had paid Goddards £196 to put in a new drain across Gostrey to the river; this helped only to add to the pollution of the river. In another corner, the Board took out the age-old squabble with the Gas Company over the price of gas, dusted it and put it back. The Knight brothers sought permission to lay York paving outside their new Bank premises in Castle Street. This was Norman Shaw's extravaganza—that towering, pseudo-Elizabethan, timbered, overlapped flight of fancy that was replaced by a pink-faced Lloyds Bank in 1931.

In the fourth corner was fermenting a row over the Post Office run by Robert Nichols at 25 The Borough. It was right in the narrowest part of the bottleneck and the Board desired its removal to a less congested position.

> Mr. Trimmer called the Board's attention to the inconvenience caused to the public from the position of the Post Office in the Borough and the danger from the increase of business which would shortly accrue to the Post Office by its being made the Public Telegraph Station. It was resolved that a Memorial for the removal of the Post Office from its present position to a more central and convenient site in the Town, together with a petition signed by the Ratepayers be handed to one of the Members of the County for presentation to His Lordship the Post Master General.

In March 1869, a Surveyor of the G.P.O. came down, looked around and was not impressed. In May, Robert Nichols was formally approached and his reply was conveyed to the P.M.G. with a covering note of the Board's 'displeasure at the tenor and discourtesy thereof'.

The tenders for the construction of the new roads and bridge ranged from £1,089 to £1,588, with one at £883 that was highly suspect until it was found that it was for the bridge only. The next lowest brought the original estimate of £2,312 up by £400 and this rather took the wind out of their sails. It was Henry Potter, who had regained his seat on the Board in Robert Barrett's place, who grasped the nettle:–

> That nothing be done with reference to a further loan until it had been positively ascertained what the total cost of carrying out the proposed scheme will be and if on enquiry it should be found that such total cost would necessitate a charge on the Rates of more than £400 in addition to the sum already authorised, then that such proposed scheme in its entirety be abandoned and in lieu thereof efforts be at once made to carry out that portion only of the present scheme which comprises the Road from Mr. Birch's corner to the Railway.

This meant discarding the stretch of road from East Street to where the link with Longbridge came about halfway down–a galling prospect. It had a sobering effect on the Board and checked their headlong flight towards a financial crisis.

For a space they indulged in trivia–such as smells, and some stuff that had arrived from Whitehall on petroleum regulations and the Workshops Regulations Act 1867. They returned to it on 13 April 1869 with a concise and more realistic statement of debits and credits prepared by William Hazell. This showed a total estimated cost of £2,755; assets were put at £3,005, which included a maximum loan of £2,000 and expected subscriptions of £955, and left a surplus of £250. It was encouraging. Fresh tenders were invited, this time for the roads and the bridge separately. Some people called Yates & Ridgers won the roads at £472 and Goddards got the bridge at £332. The way ahead was clear now; Mr. Taylor was asked to sanction a further £400 and the Committee were pressed to 'continue their labours and take such steps as they may deem necessary to collect and get in the promised contributions'.

The gentlemen who financed the making of the new streets, acting in the livery of the Atlas Assurance Company, were Thomas Chapman of Bryanston Square, Benjamin Buck Greene of Kensington Palace Gardens, John George McLean of Lime Street, Joseph Gote of Threadneedle Street and Sir William John Walter Baynes of Austin Friars, Bt. The loans were repayable over 30 years, in half-yearly instalments of £66 13s. 4d., with interest. That was the only interest those gentlemen took–they probably never so much as walked along the streets in their lives.

Mrs. Caroline Paine, widow of John Manwaring Paine, complained of a nuisance from an open ditch at George Trimmer's brewery and Mr. Smither about overflowing closets in Lower Church Lane. Mr. Potter raised the question of altering the date for holding 'the so called Holy Thursday Fair'. Mr. Crook tendered his resignation from the Board membership because of ill health. In July 1869, James Knight died and his son, James Knight junior, took his place in the Bank and as co-Treasurer of the Board.

In the 1869 Election, the electorate participated for the first time and the Clerk was paid a gratuity of 15 guineas for acting as Returning Officer. The result was as follows:–

POTTER Henry	Castle Street	Solicitor	322	elected
NASH John	Downing Street	Auctioneer	354	elected
TRIMMER George	West Street	Brewer	307	elected
HAZELL William	Ivy House	Manufacturer	313	elected
WONNACOTT Thomas	West Street	Architect	105	
TILY James	Castle Street	Ironmonger	54	
BIRCH F.C.	Downing Street	Builder	180	elected
WILLIAMS Anthony	West Street	Wine Merchant	49	
ELSLEY E.E.	East Street	Brewer	97	

In the following October the Post Master General applied for consent to erect four poles in the road being constructed to bring the electric telegraph wires from the station to the Post Office. The Board being peeved that the P.M.G. had done nothing at all in the matter of having the Post Office moved, the Clerk was:

> directed to inform him that although the Board were fully impressed with the importance of the work upon which the Post Master General was engaged and the great convenience to accrue to the public from its accomplishment, they yet feel compelled to withhold their consent to the erection of the poles in question for the reason that, did they assent thereto, they would be assisting the Post Master General to increase the business of an Office which from its position they considered unsuited to its purpose and thereby add to a nuisance and inconvenience of which they and the public had already complained.

This brought a Mr. Yates down from London to attend a Special Meeting of the Board to see what was going on and report back. On 12 November, the Post Master General wrote that he 'had abandoned the attempt for the present to give Telegraphic Accommodation to the Town of Farnham'.

In September, Harding had reported progress on the new roads.

Demolition of Williams' bakery at 1 East Street had begun and his new premises started behind the old *Bush Tap* for future frontage on the new street. Lindsay the plumber at 2 East Street hung on to the bitter end–he had been troublesome throughout. In the end, John Thorp, the rate collector, came to the rescue by offering to let Lindsay have his shop at 16 The Borough, he himself moving to 9 Downing Street–for a compensation of £30.

The Local Board held a Special Meeting on the New Bridge at 10 o'clock on the morning of Monday, 24 January 1870. Having viewed the roads, they adjourned to the *Bush Hotel* where the Surveyor 'in reply to enquiry made of him, having stated that the Roads had been completely finished according to the terms of the Contract and that he had certified to that effect, it was moved by Mr. Potter, seconded by Mr. Nash and resolved that the Surveyor having so certified the Roads be now taken from the Contractor'.

The final balance sheet was as follows:–

Loans	£2000	Purchases:	Lindsay	£700
			Williams	700
Contributions	£1011 17 0		Rev. Ward	45
			Darvill	225
Materials from			Balchin	45
Lindsay's house	£ 29		Burningham	10
		Construction:	Roads	£472 10 0
			Bridge	332
			Fences	35
		Compensation:	Bromley	£ 40
			Thorp	30
		Law Costs		£180 14 10
		Incidental Expenses		£ 72 17 6
		Balance in Hand		£152 14 8
	£3040 17 0			£3040 17 0

They called it South Street; Station Street would have been even worse. On the not unimportant subject of street-names the preference for applying the points of the compass signifies a lack of imagination; it also implies an invitation to get out of the town. It is fortunate that Castle Street was not called North Street–if only after Bishop Brownlow North. In Farnham, the names 'The Borough' and 'Downing Street' have individuality. The fast disappearing side-alleys, too, have names of character. The name, 'Bridge Street', was proposed for the road through Gostrey Meadow linking South Street with Longbridge. An amendment changed this to 'Union Road'–what was wrong with 'Gostrey'?

A similar lack of concern is abundantly evident in the way in which South Street was allowed to be developed in the years which followed. The street had been conceived with the sole purpose of providing a direct route to the station–there the Board's mission ended. George Trimmer got a fine corner site for the *Royal Deer* public house. The Knights were so delighted with the improved access to the *Bush Hotel* that they donated £50. Little was done by the Board to control the hodge-podge of unrelated architecture that prevented South Street from acquiring a charm, though–as if in compensation–the street came to be honoured with a Lutyens building.

The time has come, the walrus said,
To talk of many things.

Lewis Carrol

X

POT-POURRI

THE FUNNY thing was—no sooner had the Local Board brought to a triumphant conclusion the formation of the new road from the station, because of the 'narrow, tortuous and in one part dangerous route called Abbey Street', than they embarked upon a costly scheme to widen and improve Abbey Street. The idea originated from the Surveyor's report of the threatened collapse of a boundary wall to some land belonging to George Trimmer. When its replacement was being discussed, Mr. Trimmer offered a strip of frontage—a temptation which no Board could resist. It was thereupon resolved to accept his offer and widen this stretch of the street to 24 feet. This had the effect of causing a pair of cottages belonging to James Harris, which stuck out into the roadway, to look more like a sore thumb than ever; their purchase and demolition were inevitable. Having already paid Patricks £61 for the new wall, the Board at first demurred at the further expense of £50 for the cottages but, being more or less committed, finally gave in and applied the full treatment.

This was largely a period of routine everyday matters though, below the surface, surged the strong undercurrent of the dire need of sewage disposal; the spectre of this enormous undertaking loomed ever nearer.

There was a bit of everything. Charles Austwick grumbled about the nuisance arising from 'the presence in Castle Street and the long stay of the so called Cheap Jack or travelling auction van' ... Henry Potter called attention to 'the abuse of his Office by the Town Crier in having recently repeatedly published offensive and

Plate 16 *Robert Nichols' post-office*

Plate 17 *The* Jolly Farmer, *Bridge Square, birthplace of William Cobbett*

Plate 18 *Lower Church Lane; entrance to waggon yard on left*

Plate 19 *Group of cyclists:* left to right *(back row) Frank Mason, Robert Sampson, W.J. Wells, – Mesher, T. Turner; (front row) –, – Garrood, R.W. Mason*

Plate 20 *Samuel Bide, nurseryman*

Plate 21 *George Trimmer, brewer*

Plate 22 *George Robins, builder*

Plate 23 *Ernest Crundwell, solicitor and public servant*

Plate 24 *Hopping scene; Farnham's greatest industry*

Plate 25 *Mr. Hart's ironmongery at 117 West Street*

scandalous matter affecting individuals in the Town'; the Clerk enquired of the Steward of the Manor as to whether the appointment–and dismissal–of Town Criers might be vested in the Local Board ... the Surveyor was directed to obtain a 50-rung ladder for use as a fire-escape and place it so as to be readily accessible against the wall of the churchyard in Church Lane ... the railway being built from Pirbright to Farnham was single-line only and the Board sponsored a memorial from the residents to 'compel or induce' the Railway Company to lay a double track.

The Clerk announced that it was imperative upon any person on erecting a dwellinghouse to submit plans to the Board before proceeding. Presumably this edict also applied to other types of property, for in May 1870 plans were approved for 'Hoppers Barracks' in Red Lion Lane (perhaps aptly described), and the Farnham Co-operative Society Limited's new slaughterhouse in East Street.

Doctor Sloman proposed that the Board should surrender to the Post Master General's application to erect the telegraph poles in South Street, but it was resolved that 'the Board having informed the Public are to have the accommodation of the Postal Telegraph at the Railway Station, are of the opinion that it would be more desirable for the present to use the office there than to consent to its connection with such an inconvenient office as the Post Office'. A memorial signed by the Ratepayers urged the Board to consent. Then in July Postmaster Nichols volunteered a statement that he was now willing to consent to the Board's wish to remove the Post Office to a more central position at the corner of Castle Street, provided he could secure the lease of the premises from the existing tenant, a Mr. King. Mr. Nichols also demanded £200 from the Board by way of compensation for the annual loss he would sustain. So the Clerk waited upon the Rev. J.M. Sumner, asking him to ascertain from the Bishop whether he would favour the proposal and assist in raising so large a sum. Mr. Sumner replied that the Bishop would give £10. They even touched the Post Master General for a subscription. Then Nichols reported that he had failed to dislodge Mr. King from 10 The Borough, so the Board had a go.

At the meeting on 6 September 1870, it was reported that King asked terms far in excess of the value of the lease. They were in the middle of discussing this, and the latest letter from the P.M.G., when Mr. Jewell from the P.M.G's. Office turned up, joined in the discussion and then withdrew. This so impressed the Board that a motion was put to the meeting 'that the Post Master General's request to connect the Post Office with the Telegraph System of the Country be granted'. It was defeated by five votes to four by an amendment 'that it would be in the interests of the Town to put up with a slight inconvenience rather than offer facilities for perpetuating the present objectionable situation'. The P.M.G. was informed of this decision and also a Mr. Preed of the Post Office Engineering Department, Southampton, who was conceivably standing by with his Poles.

Then there was a letter dated 27 August 1870 from the Surrey Coroner, conveying the request of the Jury summoned to determine the cause of death of one William Annels, drowned whilst bathing at a hole in the river called the Penstock, to the effect that the Local Board should have the Penstock filled in or prohibit bathing at this point ... And a communication from The Native Guano Company extolling their 'A.B.C. Process for the Utilization of Sewage and conveying a protest against what they called the "partyzanship of the Government Officials" in favour of irrigation system, and urging the Board to join a deputation to the Home Secretary to ask for a searching enquiry into their system with a view to decide whether it does or does not offer as claimed a solution of the great Sewage question'.

At the Annual General Meeting on 30 August 1870, Mr. Hazell, Returning Officer, announced the result of the Election held on the 25th. James Hewitt, china-warehouseman of The Borough, headed the poll with 221 votes; then came Frank Birch, builder, (218); Josiah Bentall (217) and E.E. Elsley, brewer of the *Unicorn Inn,* East Street, (208). Henry Poppleton, the East Street schoolmaster, lost with 99 votes. The half-year's rate rose to 1s. in the pound; £115 went on the South Street loan and Abbey Street improvements.

In September, Mr. Hazell, referring to a recent fire at Attfield's hopkiln in West Street, raised the question generally of the existing inadequacy of the prevention of loss of property by fire. The hazard of fire was great in the 19th century, probably because of the inflammable means of house lighting; fire-fighting services, on the other hand, were unsophisticated. The engine was kept locked up in the Engine Room at the Town Hall, the fire-escape was on the wall of the churchyard and the Surveyor had the key to the water main. By the time the component parts had been assembled and it was decided who pumped and who held the hose, there remained little more to do apart from damping down the ashes.

It was Mr. E.E. Elsley, brewer of the *Unicorn Inn* opposite Cambridge Place in East Street, who made history on 6 September 1870 by suggesting to the Board that a Volunteer Fire Brigade be formed, and offering to organise such a body if the Board would provide the uniforms and sponsor it generally. He was asked to submit a detailed proposal at a later meeting and produced a list of names of persons willing to form a brigade, together with samples of uniforms. On 1 November, the Board resolved to form a Brigade and advertisements were put in the local press inviting the co-operation and assistance of all persons taking an interest in the subject. The response, in spite of Mr. Elsley's list, was negative. Thereupon it was decided to appoint two men, at 3 guineas each per annum, to keep the engines and equipment in good working order. George Elliott, of the prolific family of local blacksmiths, and Frederick Edwards were chosen and designated as Superintendents of the Fire Engines. With the Edwards family, it became a tradition, passing from father to son, that continued well into the 1930s. Then the home-spun began to disappear from the livery, and the proud boast of the volunteer firemen of a flat few minutes from alarm to turn-out–and they came running from their places of work in the town–ceased to have any significance.

Plans were approved for George Trimmer's new *Royal Deer* public house in its outstanding corner position at the top of South Street. Williams, the baker, was already installed, also the new *Bush Tap.* The Wesleyan Church came two years later. Slow to start, South Street never quite made it; a hundred years later, it is still only partially developed. It was constructed as a means of getting to the town from the station–it still is this. People do not tarry in the street, as they do in West Street and The Borough and–cautiously–The Woolmead.

They passed out of 1870 into the thirty-fourth year of the Queen's reign. There was no difference, except that the Queen and the Board were a year older and a year more tired.

In January, the Post Master General announced the decision to remove the Post Office from its present site and asked the Board to recommend an alternative site. This could be regarded as a victory over Whitehall but, for some reason, the Board took no action in the matter ... The Guardians wrote about the outbreak of smallpox and urged the Board to enforce the regulations of the Lodging Houses Act and the Surveyor was appointed Inspector of Common Lodging Houses ... Doctor Andrews wrote about illnesses in Red Lion Lane caused by the total absence of drainage facilities there ... smells too numerous and tedious to mention ... Mr. Smith, draper of The Borough, and Mr. Price, grocer of Downing Street, asked permission to erect poles on the pavement to carry sunblinds ... Charles Keen, then building his premises in East Street, was paid £30 for frontage to widen the pavement ... On 6 June 1871, only one member turned up at the meeting ... 4 July 1871: present—Mr. Bentall and two others.

On 18 July more members attended a Special Meeting to consider a plan submitted by Mr. Nichols for new Post Office buildings but as these were considered unsuitable, they were turned down. In August, Nichols attended a meeting and was told either to move or enlarge the Post Office accommodation at 25 The Borough. He chose the latter course, provided the Board agreed to the P.M.G's. application, and in due course a compromise was negotiated and Mr. Preed brought his poles and connected 25 The Borough with the telegraph system of the country.

At the A.G.M., adjourned to 5 September because of poor attendance, William Mason, coal merchant of East Street, Doctor Robert Oke Clark of Downing Street, and the architect, Thomas Wonnacott of Kenmure Villa, Abbey Street, joined the Board.

The growing criticism directed against the Board because of their failure to cope with the drainage problem seemed to be approaching a climax. As usual, the Board parried the numerous complaints with ineffectual orders to the Surveyor to attend to them. The *Surrey Advertiser* of 31 July 1871 published a report of a meeting of the Board of Guardians at which the Rev. Jones, Vice-Chairman, had stated that one of the Medical Officers in the town had informed the Local Board of twenty-five nuisances, but no steps had been taken to abate any one of them. In August, the Board turned down one appeal for action on the grounds that 'in all probability the Board will shortly be obliged to proceed with a General System for their District'. It is easy enough to criticise the whipping-boy, yet the Board's efforts to control nuisances were, on their own minuted admissions, futile in the extreme. Over the bad state of the river—that receptacle for what did manage to get away from the town—the Surveyor was instructed to interview the owners on either bank and, optimistically, ask them to remove 'the trees, mud, etc.' in the bed thereof. The prospect of removing the et cetera must have been daunting.

Mr. Wonnacott put an end to the road-sweepers working on Sundays ... Disgraceful scenes were enacted at the 1871 commemoration of the Gunpowder Plot ... There was a bad fire at the *Jolly Farmer* ... Police Superintendent Newland was appointed Petroleum Inspector ... Mr. Elsley proposed moving the pump and milestone, which protruded into the roadway at the bottom of Bear Lane, to a more convenient site (can one move a milestone without moving the towns named on it?). Dr. Clark proposed that the milestone be moved and the pump taken away altogether. Mr. Nash proposed that the pump remained where it was and that the milestone only be moved. And the Clerk pointed out that Mr. Nash's amendment as to the pump was a negative to Mr. Elsley's motion and the proper course was for Mr. Nash and his followers to vote in the negative on such motion. When it came to parish pump politics, these men were unbeatable. In clean white paint, with its medieval lettering picked out in black, the milestone today forms a welcome feature of The Woolmead; it is a pity that the removal of the pump robbed the area of another mitigating influence.

Mr. Eyre of The Borough was told to abate the nuisance arising from his candle factory ... William Williams in South Street complained about the dungpit at the *Bush Hotel*. He also made the useful suggestion that the name 'South Street' should be painted in some conspicuous position. It could be that the idea of labelling streets had not occurred to anyone, for the Surveyor, as the outcome of Mr. Williams' suggestion, was told to obtain and fix enamelled plates bearing the names of the town's streets.

The Election in August 1872 introduced William Kingham, then busy expanding his grocery business in West Street. Henry Potter had retired from the Board. In the tangle of small-town politics, there was no doubt a reason—could it have been that, as Solicitor to the Squire of Moor Park, he saw trouble brewing over the continued and increasing pollution of the river, and didn't fancy shadow-boxing on this issue?

At the September meeting Mr. Wonnacott drew the Board's attention to the accommodation provided by hop-planters for their pickers and asked what powers the Board had of 'preventing the herding together of old and young, married and single, and male and female, the which he had himself witnessed on a visit made by him to a Barrack near to West Street'. There was no authority to intervene, unless overcrowding was discovered, so Mr. Wonnacott, who felt rather strongly about all things of a sleazy nature, 'remarked severely upon the conduct of Hop-planters in the matter and expressed the hope that having called the Board's and by that means, through the Press, public attention to the question, to see an effort made to remedy the indecency and immortality which in his opinion must be and was the result of the practice'.

In October the same Member entertained the Board at length on the subject of Earth Closets, explaining 'the principles upon which they were conducted'. He suggested that 'as an experiment they might be tried out in a part of the District'. He then introduced a Mr. Caffen of Alton, who had been waiting outside, which gentleman explained to the Board 'the modus operandi of an Earth Closet brought out, and proposed to be patented, by him'. But the Board, with their usual shyness of innovations, postponed the subject.

They were given to bursts of enthusiasm, followed by withdrawals. When Doctor Sloman moved, for instances, that the area of the Board be extended, under the recently passed Public Health Act, 1872, to include the whole of the original Farnham Parish, Mr. Nash put an amendment, carried, that, whilst an extension was desirable, the time was not yet ripe.

. . . . .

Those back-room—slightly anachronous—parochial officers, the

Churchwardens and Overseers, were still functioning in the town, though now completely overshadowed by the mighty local Board. At their meeting on 13 October 1870, as if pioneering something, it was proposed by Churchwarden John Bevan 'that henceforth all minutes of their meetings be entered in a Book to be kept for that purpose'. This explains the absence of the previous two year's minutes (which the writer wasted hours looking for). The lethargy, however, was understandable, for their Clerk, James Harris–that man of many parts–had died some six months earlier. They died in harness, these employees; there was no period of retirement on pension. At the approach of death, their work deteriorated. Then they died and their widows received an abrupt demand to deliver up all parish deeds and documents found in the house to their successors. Before the emergence in the 20th century of a professional body of local government officers, trained and qualified in their respective fields to advise and recommend on technical aspects–a nicely balanced Councillor-Officer relationship, the elected Members bore the whole brunt whilst their staff stood mutely by awaiting orders.

Alfred James Nash of 35 The Borough was appointed as the new Clerk at £50 a year and, with due ceremony, the key of the Parish Chest was placed in his custody. They also at this time took their place in the Board Room at the Town Hall–though Mr. Barnes, the District Auditor, later queried their authority to spend money in renting a room, thus taking a further step away from the Mother Church, whence all forms of local government sprang.

The Churchwardens and Overseers in their unpretentious role performed little apart from the collection of the Poor Rate and the administration of the Charities, though their records contain snippets of information not to be found elsewhere, and are a useful guide to new assessments for rating purposes–George Ransom's newly-built shop in 1871 on the opposite corner from the *Royal Deer,* also big additions to the Workhouse.

The section of railway on the new route from Pirbright, within the Parish area, measured 1 mile 10 chains 25 links. This was assessed at £125 rateable value, against which George Harvey Elwin of the Railway Company lodged an appeal. This astute man, who had once caught James Harris out over the ratebooks not having been signed, again discovered a technical anomaly in that, although the new line had been opened in May 1870 and rates paid from that date, the assessment itself had not been formally passed by the Assessment Committee. He therefore claimed a refund of a year's rates.

Mr. J.F. Bateman's offer of the renewal of the lease, at £2 per annum, of the recreation ground at Compton was passed to the new owner of Waverley Abbey. Mr. Thomas D. Anderson replied on 28 February 1872 to the effect that he would be pleased to rent the ground under the same terms and conditions which Mr. Nicholson did. This chronicle has now entered within a hundred years of the present time. More and more, names will be mentioned of persons whose descendants–grandchildren, perhaps children–live in Farnham today. Thus family links will be established relating the events of Queen Victoria's reign more tangibly with those of the 1970s and, in consequence, this history will become a more personal matter.

A Father kind, a Father dear,
A loving friend lieth here.

Inscription on a headstone in Farnham Cemetery

XI

MATTERS OF GRAVE CONCERN

THAT ENERGETIC body, the Farnham Burial Board, had opened a branch at Hale, an operation which had passed off with no more than the usual number of stumbling-blocks. Having ascertained from the Burial Acts Office that the provision and supervision of a burial ground in this outlying area of the Parish could be undertaken as a charge against Parish Funds, subject to Vestry sanction, the Board seized the reins from the Rev. George Fox and his parishioners, who had themselves got as far as acquiring a piece of land, and were probably wondering what to do with it. At a meeting at Hale Church on 4 April 1871 it was announced:

> that the offer of the Farnham Burial Board to provide a new Burial Ground and Chapels for Hale out of the Poor Rates of the whole Parish be accepted and that the two acres of land on the Common granted by the War Office to the Parishioners of Hale for the purpose of a Burial Ground be made over to the Burial Board of Farnham for this object.

Within one hundred yards' distance of the boundaries of this piece of land there were thirty-one houses and it was a legal requirement to obtain the consent of each and every one of the owners to the establishment of a cemetery in their midst. All save two raised no objection. Of these, one was a few yards within the 100-yard limit so his objection was disposed of by the simple expedient of a slight alteration in the boundary line. The other, a Mr. William Crate, owned a pair of cottages right opposite and was deaf to the persuasion of both the Burial Board and the people of Hale. Then a Mr. T.B. Jefferies, owner of a neighbouring pair of houses, was also attracted by the unique opportunity of easy money and joined Mr. Crate. A Mr. Wickham also claimed £150 compensation but as he too was only just within the limit, they again shifted the plot. The owners of the other twenty or so properties must have regretted their hasty consents, a lack of forethought not as a rule associated with Hale residents of the 19th century, on hearing that Mr. Crate had been promised £50 and Mr. Jefferies £40 in compensation.

The plot of land, which was adjacent to the Bishop's school in Hungry Hill, had been donated by the War Office, possibly as a gesture of the good-will that existed between the troops and the people of Hale who, more in keeping with their reputation, were reaping a fat harvest from providing the former with beer, clean laundry and other things that soldiers liked. In a nice letter of confirmation on 19 February 1872, Captain C.E. Luard R.E. wrote:

> In accordance with instructions received from the Secretary of State for War to hand over to you on account of the Farnham Burial Board a piece of ground at Hungry Hill, 2 acres in area, I have to inform you that instructions have been issued for the removal of certain W.D. boundary stones at that site (the limits of which have been pointed out by Lieut. Wilson R.E. to you) and that the Board above mentioned may consider itself henceforth the proprietor of the said 2 acres of land.

Sidney Stapley was appointed architect. Tenders were invited for the construction of the two Chapels, Lodge, the gate and walls–that of Goddards being the lowest, and the Rev. Fox, doubtless bewildered by this display of urban know-how, was invited to become a member of the Grave-diggers Club.

The expenditure ceiling had been set by the Vestry at £900; already the estimate exceeded this by £150. The Board referred back to the Vestry and won the day only on a poll. They applied to the Public Works Loan Board but that august body only agreed to £1,000, so they wrote to Hale saying that, as the end product–to use an apt metaphor–was all theirs, could they not raise the balance. To which John Henry Knight of Weybourne House–and a member of the Burial Board–said 'no'. So they took the £1,000 from the P.W.L.B. at 5 per cent over twenty years and hoped for the best. All told, when completed and equipped, the Hale cemetery cost £1,150, but money has a way of coming out in the wash.

Goddard's contract was due for completion by 2 September 1872 and on that day all that remained to be done was the landscaping. The Board attended at 10.45 a.m. on Friday, 1 November 1872, for the consecration ceremony by the Bishop of Winchester. It was a slick, smooth operation of some eight months, during which the land was acquired, two minor churches built, a lodge erected, the plot walled in and the whole site transformed from a piece of rough War Department wasteland into the special beauty of a burial ground.

Samuel Bide was nominated by the Hale Churchwardens as the Sexton. Mr. Bide was the Sexton and Clerk at Hale Church. He proposed to carry out his duties at the new cemetery through his brother, Richard Bide, who would live at the Lodge. Mr. Bide, it seems, was something of a personality in Hale society; he dictated his terms for the appointment so the Board had him in, cut him down to size and got him to agree to £10 per annum all-in, on their terms.

Meanwhile at the Farnham cemetery, things were as normal. The rain now came in through the roof of the lodge and the interior walls were covered with mildew. John Hudson, the Sexton, applied for an increase in wages but 'on account of the unsatisfactory manner in which he performs his duties at the Cemetery', this was refused; indeed the Board reprimanded him on more than one occasion for neglect of duty ... A mechanic named Maberly was let off with a single fee for the burial of his two children 'who had died almost together and were buried in the same grave' ... A tombstone erected to the memory of Arthur Douglas, beloved infant son of John Cornish and Anne Trestrail, who died at sea three days from England on 7 June 1871, aged 1 year 6 months, was inscribed:

In some rude spot where vulgar herbage grows,
If chance a violet rear its purple head,
The careful gardener moves it ere it bloom
To thrive and flourish in a nobler bed.
Such was thy fate, dear child,
Thy opening such
Pre-eminence in early bloom was shown,
For earth too good, perhaps,
And loved too much.
Heaven saw, and early marked thee for its own.

After this they gave up quoting inscriptions in the Minutes.

Since its inception, the Board's Chairman had been Mr. J.S. Utterton, Rector of Farnham; he was made an Archdeacon in about 1860. The minutes of the meeting on 8 June 1874 were signed 'J.S. GUILDFORD'. He lived at Guildford House, Castle Hill–was his title responsible for the change of name from 'Castle Hill House'?–under the shadow of the Bishop of Winchester's Castle. On becoming the Suffragan Biship of Guildford, the Burial Board invited him to resign because of his increased ecclesiastical duties and he accepted in a letter of 21 April 1875 to Mr. Henry Potter:

> Will you be good enough to notify the Farnham Burial Board that I beg leave to resign my seat as Chairman and also as Member of the Board and at the same time to express my grateful sense of the courtesy which I have always received at the hands of the successive Members of that Board since its formation.

His successor, the Rev. James Richard Philip Hoste was inducted as Rector of Farnham on 25 March 1875. He was elected to the Burial Board at a Vestry held on 7 May and assumed the Chairmanship. He was Rector until 1893. The surname occurs in the Nelson genealogy.

. . . . .

In January 1873, the Town Hall Company wrote to the Local Board that 'on the ground that it was a great public convenience, the Board should take over for repair the Clock in the Tower of the Town Hall'. The Board could hardly refuse and agreed to an annual grant for upkeep of the clock ... In February Mr. Nash reported that the Town Crier, one Stevens, had placed in his hands 'the Badge of Office, namely the Bell', and given notice of his intention to resign.

The prevailing lull in the affairs of the Board continued. Mr. Stapley pressed for a depot in which to store the Board's equipment ... It was decided to channel and kerb the footways in South Street (presumably all one with the roadway) ... George Trimmer proposed a new sewer from the Gostrey Ditch eastward through the back gardens of East Street into the river, which provoked a rumble from Mr. Potter on behalf of Mr. Bateman and so was not proceeded with ... Mr. Mason had not attended Meetings for several months and risked expulsion ... The Congregational Church Trustees sought permission to pave with bricks the footway in front of their new Church in South Street–the old

Church at 80 East Street was incorporated into the adjacent British School.

It was almost too uneventful. At the Annual General Meeting on 30 August 1873, only one Member (Robert Oke Clark) attended. At the Election, Mr. W. Vine, grocer of Castle Street, had replaced Frank Birch, the builder. The Surveyor was instructed to inspect public lodging-houses and places set apart for lodging hop-pickers and report on numbers of both sexes and children living in each, with conveniences existing for the separation of the sexes, closet accommodation and so on. His subsequent report was published in the local press with, it was hoped, the desired effect.

Then they considered again the infamous Gostrey Ditch. It was decided to fill it in and substitute an 18-inch pipe to the river. This brought another howl of anguish from Mr. Potter, to which the Clerk was instructed to reply 'for Mr. Bateman's information, that the Board had resolved to proceed with the scheme of filling in the filthy Ditch in question and substituting for it a pipe drain'. George Mesher's tender at £65 was accepted for the work. About this time, other drains were laid to the river from points in East Street. Curiously, when pressed to clear the River Wey of obstructions, the Board denied responsibility on the grounds that the river was private property.

In May 1874, the Board decided to go ahead with the provision of the pavements in South Street and the north side of Union Road. The tender of Mesher was the lowest at £500, for kerbing and paving with plain black Fareham bricks, obtainable of Messrs. Brace & Co. of Fareham. The Local Government Board sanctioned the loan but the Public Works Loan Board were difficult about it and kept the Board waiting. The work had commenced and in July Mesher was due for a first instalment of £195 under the terms of his contract; so they had to borrow it from Knights, the bankers. Then the P.W.L.B. were sticky about loan charges, so the Board went to the Atlas Assurance Company and finally got the money from the same gentlemen who had advanced the £2,000 for making the streets. Then Mesher went into liquidation and Brace & Co. demanded £150 in payment for the bricks supplied to the contractor, which the Board had to refuse because, not only were the works not completed but the Liquidator, Mr. Nash, might claim the £150 as a debt under the contract. In the end the pavements were finished to everybody's satisfaction, except perhaps the unfortunate Mesher, but it just goes to show how 'the best laid schemes o' mice and men gang aft a-gley'.

Were they men or mice? In June, when considering the inconvenience to the public 'from the so frequently, and often for so long a time, closing the gates enclosing the level-crossing over the Railway near the Station and the way to Waverley and Tilford', it was decided that any action should be by means of a 'Memorial from without' ... Also that no action be taken when Mr. Pearcey of West Street complained of a nuisance 'arising from the use as a urinal of the western wall of the *Wheatsheaf Inn* by men frequenting that house'.

£20 of the previous Poor Rate could not be accounted for and Hector Harding pleaded that illness prevented him from attending a Special Meeting on 3 November 1874 to hear his explanation. In the following month it was reported that the money had been paid in but nevertheless Harding offered his resignation as Surveyor and Collector and the Board accepted it. There is a familiar ring about this. He was retained for a temporary period of three months as Surveyor only and John Thorp was taken on as temporary Rate Collector.

At the end of the three months, the Board reviewed the staffing position. Applications for the post of Surveyor had been received from Sidney Stapley, Thomas Wonnacott and (pathetically) Hector Harding, of Farnham, Charles Hall of Frimley, William Jenkins of Aldershot and James Grenham of Ewshot. Stapley, architect and surveyor of 23 West Street, was appointed. Applications for the Collector's job came from John Thorp and James Lee, the Collector of Income Tax, and the former was chosen. In March, Thorp reported to the Board that he was having difficulty in obtaining the account books from Harding, who was given seven days in which to hand them over. In the end it was the District Auditor who worked out exactly how much Harding was down the drain–in his Surveyor's account, £39 1s. 4d., and as Collector, £17 11s. 4d. a total of £56 12s. 8d. His sureties paid up, less £21 due in salary to Harding.

In January 1875, plans were approved for alterations to 24 The Borough, now occupied by John Griffith, pharmacist. In April,

Doctor R.O. Clark, because of increasing calls of his practice, resigned his various public offices and in his place on the Local Board came a Mr. Wyatt, wine merchant of Castle Street, with the curious christian name of Esdaile. Sidney Stapley proved a very able surveyor. He anticipated the Board's intentions and, for the most part, it was he who made the suggestions–and the Board who sat on them. Unhampered by the petty cares of extracting rates from reluctant ratepayers, he went around the town like a new broom, sweeping it clean.

He discovered that the Water Company, who were laying a new main in Castle Street, were taking the easy way out and poking their pipes through the drains. The Board decided that, provided proper care was taken, the water would not be contaminated and the Company were allowed to proceed ... Serjeant Trimmer was appointed as the new Town Crier at £5 a year ... William Simmonds of Bourne Mill complained about the gate on the Turnpike Road, which impeded his access to the town. The Home Secretary's Office on being approached informed the Board that the gate would cease to exist on 1 November 1875.

For some time, the Board had been looking round for a suitable place in which to store their equipment–carts, fire-engines and all the curious trappings of a local authority. They went after several sites. In July 1875, James Knight offered part of the Waggon Yard in Lower Church Lane, which the coming of the railway had robbed of its former busy purpose. But the Knights were as usual meticulously insistent on their pound of flesh and frightened the Board away from what would have made a very good site for a yard and–later on–Council Offices, with a civic centre at the nearby Red Lion Brewery.

About this time, the Board became conscious of an additional source of smell, the nocturnal one which emanated from carts that moved about the town emptying privies. It was George Trimmer who, on 6 July 1875, called the Board's attention 'to the filthy practice of Night Soil Men removing the contents of Privies in Carts unfit for the purpose'. These carts operated on much the same principle as a cat's dirtbox, only larger. Mr. Trimmer reported that he had seen carts in Guildford made especially for the purpose and advocated the purchase of one. It took Stapley five months to jog the Board into getting one, which was hired out to those remarkable persons, the Night Soil Men, at 1s. a load.

On 4 January 1876, Stapley sought permission to continue the South Street pavement across Abbey Street to the pitching at Ashley Terrace, past the *Railway Hotel* to the station fence and, if possible, through the railway yard if the Railway Company agreed–which they didn't ... In February he asked, and was allowed to pipe in the open Conduit in Castle Street–that gift of water from a one-time Bishop at the Castle ... At the prompting of the Local Government Board, a Medical Officer of Health was appointed under the Public Health Act 1875; he was Doctor Samuel George Sloman, whose father of the same name was on the Board ... Mr. Wonnacott brought up the question of damage caused by boys throwing stones in the streets ... A letter of 4 July 1876 from James Knight, Henry Goujon, William Vine and William Gilbert complained of the nuisance caused by street preachers ... Stenches reported from manure stored at the railway station ... A memorial, now that the Post Office had been moved from The Borough to West Street, for a pillar-box in the neighbourhood of the old site–the Post Office people obliged with one at the bottom of Bear Lane.

In the first half of the year 1877, there was a marked falling off of business. Two new Members arrived–Samuel Andrews, the hop-planter, and Thomas Matthews, brewer of the *Lion and Lamb.* Then in July and August, there was another burst of enthusiasm over the drainage problem. A committee was formed to collect statistics and information on the subject. The reason for the renewed interest was a letter dated 12 July from Messrs. Potter & Stevens on behalf of Mr. Bateman threatening proceedings if the Board 'should, after the lapse of a reasonable time, permit the stream to be polluted with the sewage of the Town'.

The letter threw the Board into a dither. Some Members were in favour of asking Mr. Bateman himself for advice. Others suggested that a qualified Civil Engineer be consulted; perhaps they were not unmindful of the £42 wasted on Mr. Leather in 1868–to say nothing of the £150 squandered in prize money for the two best schemes entered. The Clerk referred to a recently published Report, or Blue Book, on the modes of treating town sewage and was told to get copies. The Clerk on the advice of the Board replied petulantly to Messrs. Potter & Stevens stating that the subject of the town's drainage was under consideration and, in fact, had been so before their letter arrived. And then—as always—the burst of enthusiasm was followed by a withdrawal and the whole matter subsided.

In October came a requisition signed by ratepayers in the so-called Fairfield Estate near the railway station, praying for the erection of one or two streetlamps. The Surveyor was instructed to fix two, which, in contrast with the Board's usual parsimony in street-lighting matters, was generous. As it so happened, no less than four Members of the Board lived in The Fairfield. This small residential enclave was a new departure. It established the fashion for the town's wealthier citizens to cease to reside at their places of business in favour of private residences outside the shopping area. And it heralded a general development of the town's perimeter areas which, over the next twenty years, more than doubled the size of Farnham.

As one who long in populous city pent
Where houses thick and sewers annoy the air

John Milton *(Paradise Lost)*

XII

FITS AND STARTS

AT THE Local Board's meeting on 1 January 1878–evidently with good resolutions–Dr. Sloman proposed that a Mr. Baldwin Latham be engaged to advise the Board on sewage disposal; Mr. Trimmer fancied Mr. R.B. Grantham or Mr. J.W. Barry; Mr. Mason, a Mr. Hennett; Mr. Wonnacott, a Mr. Eachen; Mr. Hazell, Messrs. J.B. Denton, Hille, Lemon, Peggs, Pritchard and Rowell; and Dr. Sloman came up with another one, a Mr. Law. There was no shortage of Civil Engineers in the country to advise Sanitary Authorities. Mr. Mason, the Clerk, was instructed to write to them to enquire whether they would be willing to visit Farnham with a view to reporting on the most efficient method of draining the town.

This chapter–as indeed are many others–is rather overflowing with sewage. The limitation imposed on a writer of history is that his plot is geared to the facts, whether they be exciting or dull. The long accepted fact of drainage has blunted public interest in this menial task of a local authority, so that the reader may be excused for becoming impatient with the Farnham Local Board's preoccupation which at times amounted to an obsession. To the Board, and to the reader's grandfather, however, drainage–particularly the lack of it–was of marked importance.

One engineer was much the same as any other, so the Board picked on the one alphabetically at the top, Mr. Barry, and invited him down. Although the date of the meeting, 12 March 1878, was of Barry's choosing, he informed the Board that he had not come prepared with any definite scheme–one would have thought that he would have done his homework. After a desultory discussion, a further visit was arranged for 20 April and the Surveyor was told to put Barry in the picture as regards local conditions. Mr. Barry duly made his report and was questioned by Members. In a subsequent debate it was resolved that the Clerk should write thanking Mr. Barry in the name of the Board and inform him that they were not prepared to carry the matter further. This adventure cost the ratepayers ten guineas.

But having picked Barry's brains, and possibly forming the opinion that putting the town on the sewer did not warrant the fees of a Civil Engineer, the Board voted by four to two to place the whole matter in the hands of their Surveyor, whereupon Mr. Stapley 'addressed the Board and stated that, in consequence of the observations he had heard, he felt he must decline to take upon himself the responsibility of devising a scheme'. And there the matter rested.

They returned to things they understood. Plans were approved for the East Street Schools near St. James Church ... The Railway Company agreed to open a gateway, to meet the new pedestrian footway, in the fence surrounding the station yard, but still refused to continue the pavement across the yard ... At the Election on 6 April, Mr. A.J. Bentall joined his father, Josiah, as a member; unsuccessful candidates included John Henry Knight, who had lost his seat previously, Harry Loveless, dealer, and Daniel Goddard, the East Street builder, of whom we shall hear more.

It wasn't long before they had another try. The Chairman referred to Mr. Lemon, one of the engineers he had favoured in January, and 'having furnished to the Board information in regard to him and to the works which he had executed or which were in course of execution by him, it was on the motion of Mr. Bentall, seconded by Mr. Nash, resolved that Mr. Lemon be invited to visit the District and report upon the matter upon the terms set forth in his letter of the 1st February last'.

Mr. James Lemon—with a partner, the firm is still in existence—of Southampton attended a Special Meeting on 18 June 1878 and at considerable length explained his scheme for the disposal of sewage in Farnham. This interview went further; Mr. Lemon was asked to seek a suitable site for the sewage works and also to arrange to see Mr. Bateman of Moor Park and get his opinion. In July, Mr. Lemon submitted his report. It was considered and published in the local press. And that's as far as it got.

Plans for the rebuilding of Barrett's *Ship Inn* (17 The Borough) which, for compensation of £35, was set back nine inches on the west side and fifteen inches on the east side ... Mr. Stapley was indignant that, at a recent fire outside the District, the engines had been used without his knowledge or consent. The Board agreed that the Surveyor's approval should first be applied for and obtained–it is not recorded that Mr. Stapley was attached to the wall of the churchyard so as to be readily accessible ... Andrew Crosby's tender at £27 was the lowest for installing hydrants in The Borough, West Street, near the pump in East Street, at the bottom of Downing Street and the corner of Upper Church Lane.

It was Mr. Wonnacott who moved the next pawn–'that Mr. Lemon be instructed to prepare plans, specifications and estimates for the Local Government Board with the view to tenders for works in connection with the proposed Drains or Sewers, providing his commission for so doing shall not exceed 2½ per cent on the estimated cost'. The Local Government Board were first approached, their reply was considered and the matter again dropped.

The Railway people agreed to panel in the sides of the footbridge by the station, which was considered dangerous ... A memorial signed by Andrew Marshall and Robert Hewitt asking the Board to allow hawkers to use the Market Square on Saturdays ... Plans for building in The Fairfield by Messrs. Foot & Robins ... More trouble with shopkeepers obstructing the pavements, though 'since the Board has had the subject under consideration' the nuisance had been much abated ... Robert Nichols complained that his shop window had been damaged by a servant of the Board breaking stones–the Surveyor admitted this and was told to see to its repair ... Plans for George Ransom's house in The Fairfield.

In February 1879, the Medical Officer reported a fatal case of diphtheria in Park Place, Bear Lane, blaming the well water. Also that enteric fever had broken out in Beavers Yard. Tests proved that water from the wells contained organic matter. The Water Company were urged to lay additional mains in places in the town not provided with water, particularly in Bear Lane. For various reasons, the Company refused. Formed with so much aplomb in 1836, the Farnham Water Company had since lost interest; the fact that someone had died failed to move them. Many residents in Farnham, especially in the side streets, had no piped supply and had to depend on well water. The wells were in close proximity to inadequate drainage arrangements; the first signs of trouble were serious illnesses and the Board acted rather late in the day in serving the owners of the properties with a notice to make the water fit for drinking.

Mr. Trimmer called attention to the increasing nuisance of barrows and trucks being wheeled on the pavements and of carts remaining stationary on the highways for long periods. Mr. Stapley added that carts supplying gravel used for the cattle market had broken the brick paving in South Street ... A letter was received from the Local Government Board enquiring whether the Local Board had given consideration to the question of sewerage of the District since correspondence of December 1878 and the Clerk was directed to reply thereto in the negative ... The Clerk of the Peace invited the Board to apply to the County Authority that certain roads passing through the town might be declared main roads maintainable out of County funds, which led to a nice little contribution of about £50 a year.

Sidney Longhurst of Willmer House was unlucky in the 1879 Election ... Mr. Sturt, stationer of The Borough, complained about costermongers placing their barrows in front of his shop for the sale of fish and other articles ... Mr. Wonnacott went on and on about the necessity for 'separate sleeping and closet accommodation for the different sexes of hop-pickers visiting the District' ... And then Mr. Henry Potter wrote.

In letters dated 17 and 24 July 1879, Mr. Potter served notices of Mr. Bateman's intention to proceed, under the Rivers Pollution Act, 1876, to restrain the Board from permitting sewage matters to flow into the river.

Jonathan Swift, in his *Imitation of Horace*, wished for:

> A handsome house to lodge a friend
> A river at my garden's end.

It could be that he wrote these words whilst living at Moor Park as Sir William Temple's Secretary; if not, there is little doubt that they were inspired by memories of that gracious house, with the River Wey flowing through the grounds. Had Swift lived a century and a half later, it is likely that these lines would had been lost to English literature.

Mr. Bateman had been patient for many years, during which the river at the bottom of the garden had borne increasing evidence of the presence of other people a mile or so upstream. It was always the same with river folk–the chap downstream was on the receiving end of what happened upstream, and so on down to the sea.

The Board's immediate, and sensible, reaction was to form a Committee consisting of Mr. Hazell, Mr. Nash and Mr. Wonnacott to confer with Mr. Bateman. Their report was considered at a Special Meeting of the Board on the 16 September 1879 and entered verbatim in the minutes:–

> First — That Mr. Bateman would do nothing harsh but that he desired the Board to do something to remedy the present state of things and remarked that hitherto they had done nothing.
>
> Secondly — That the present pollution of the River would not be permitted to continue, and
>
> Thirdly — That he, Mr. Bateman, would be happy to render any help and give any advice in his power to the Board or its Engineer or Surveyor.
>
> The Committee further report that, when they pressed to know whether remedial measures would be accepted as a temporary amelioration of the state of things and whether they would be effectual in staying the threatened proceedings, he, Mr. Bateman, made no direct response but advised the doing of the drainage completely and at once, rather than attempting to remedy piecemeal or patch up a temporary amendment of the evils complained of.

A discussion ensued 'bearing for the most part upon the question of how to avoid the threatened litigation'–like children fearing punishment. A resolution was passed that Mr. Lemon be invited to say if he was at liberty to undertake the drainage of the District and, if so, on what terms. Routine matters went by the Board. Such as Dr. Sloman's proposal to frame bye-laws in relation to new buildings (the Board were unhappy about Robert Nichol's plans for cottages in the Bush Meadow–Victoria Road–on the grounds that they were too small, lacked space and that 'the privy accommodation was objectionable as being much too open to the public' which was discussed half-heartedly and dropped ... Also Mr. Hazell did not proceed with a motion for an extension of the boundary of the District.

The Clerk produced correspondence with Mr. Lemon which was studied at the October meeting. The Chairman also tabled a report by the Sanitary Authority of Taunton, and he and Mr. Kingham and Mr. Wonnacott were deputed to go down to Somerset to inspect the sewage disposal system installed in that town. They went on the 1 November 1879 and a printed copy of their report is pasted in the Minute Book—a rare opportunity for learning something about that lowly service of local government which few people know about but nevertheless is not without interest from a technical point of view. Since 1879, the system of sewage disposal has undergone many improvements, notably with the co-operation of a small insect which, together with its friends and relations, is so fond of the fare provided at the sewage farm that the end liquid (the writer once dipped his finger in it and sucked it) is (the writer hoped) completely free of organic matter. The basic principles, however, are much the same.

REPORT OF THE DEPUTATION APPOINTED BY THE FARNHAM LOCAL BOARD TO VISIT THE SEWAGE WORKS AT TAUNTON.

In accordance with the desire of the Board, we beg to report that we, the undersigned, visited Taunton and carefully examined the Drainage Outfall Works, and the process of dealing with and purifying the sewage of that town and district. We regret to state that owing to domestic affliction, our Surveyor was unable to accompany us. He has since visited the town and will doubtless report the result to the Board at their next meeting. We paid three visits to the Outfall Works and were greatly and most kindly assisted in our investigations by the Chairman of the Sanitary Committee of the Town Council and the Borough Engineer. We also had the privilege of a conversation with the Mayor, who confirmed the information received from the foregoing gentlemen.

The town is situated in a valley, and is similarly circumstanced, with regard to its elevation above the River Tone as Farnham is to the Wey. Its population is about 17,000 and the area drained is—for sewage 1,200 acres, and for surface and storm waters 2,000 acres. The average amount of inflow from this large area is 320,000 gallons a day, but provision is made for dealing with 1,000,000 gallons.

The Sewage Works consist of a large store tank 117 feet long, 25 feet deep and about 30 wide. This is arched over level with the ground, and upon it is reared a substantial building in three compartments. In the first are two tanks in which the chemicals are mixed, and also a centrifugal pump. In the second are three contractors pumps, a 10-horse power engine, and a water tank for supplying the mixing tanks. In the third is the engine boiler. Behind this building are the precipitating tanks in two series, each consisting of one tank 33 feet by 18 feet and 7 feet deep, one of 100 feet long, 33 feet wide and 7 feet deep, a third of 33 feet by 18 feet by 6 feet, then a filter bed 50 feet by 33 feet by 8 feet deep, in which a layer of coarse gravel, brick-bats and shingle, in all about 3 feet. Besides the foregoing there are two sheds for drying the sludge, each about 50 feet by 12 feet. Altogether the works, the approaches and all connected therewith cover about three acres of land.

> The motive power is a 12-horse power turbine, worked with a 4 feet 6 fall, and with a flow of water not more than about half the average volume of the Wey. Ordinarily only the turbine is needed, and it works six days in the week, 12 hours each day. Besides the turbine there is a supplementary 10-horse power engine which is seldom required. The turbine and engine together are quite equal to pumping 1,000,000 gallons a day.
>
> The process of working is extremely simple. We will describe the operation for one day. The one man in charge mixes, as if for mortar, 10 cwt. of lime with three quarts of carbolic acid, and one and a quarter cwt. of common coarse salt. This paste is put into a trough in one corner of the mixing room and from it, as occasion requires, a portion is put into a tank containing 750 gallons and kept gently stirred. From this tank, through an inch pipe, a jet is poured down the side of the pumps and mixing with the sewage as it entered them is brought up with it to the tanks. As the foul fluid enters the first tank the smell is unmistakeably offensive. From the first to the second tank it passes in a thin wide stream; here, although the distance traversed is only 18 feet, a marked difference in the colour and consistence of the sewage water is discernable. In the second tank further precipitation takes place. In the third tank still further precipitation; and it then falls in a thin cascade about 5 feet down into the filtering bed, thence to the shallow tanks and over white tiles, a clear, almost perfectly inodorous stream directly into the River Tone. The precipitation is so rapid that in the first 18 feet of the tanks the average depth of sludge deposited in about eight weeks (the period they are allowed to be in use before being cleared out) is 3 feet. In the next 100 feet, the average depth is 1 foot and in the third tank only 3 inches. At the outfall, the stream, at the time of our visit, was so pure that fish were seen sporting in it. We also saw two fish caught there in less than a quarter of an hour, and Mr. Alderman Taylor informed us that his nephew a few days before had caught a fine trout there ...

In addition, the Board studied a report of the system in use at Chiswick, and also wrote for information from the Local Government Board. The result of their investigations gave them sufficient confidence to proceed further in their negotiations with James Lemon, who attended a meeting on 6 January 1880 to outline his scheme in greater detail. He was asked to leave the room whilst the Members cogitated and it was resolved that, at this stage, Mr. Lemon's terms of reference should be limited to a survey of the District and the preparation of a scheme with draft plans etc. Mr. Trimmer, however, had read of cases where disposal by means of precipitation had not been successful and proposed that the Board should seek the views of towns that had tried the system, also to make enquiries about the alternative process of irrigation and filtration.

Mr. Lemon came back on the 6 April with a printed report, a copy of which was handed to each Member, and detailed plans which were exhibited on the walls of the Board Room. He then left the Board to think it over. Two years and eight months later, this amazing Board were still thinking it over.

It had been a cold winter. Mr. Wells of the Water Company called attention to the hydrants, which were frozen–and what would happen if there was a fire? ... The Medical Officer reported typhoid in Babbs Mead, believed to have been caused by impure water from a well. His father was acting Chairman at the meeting which decided that the Medical Officer shouldn't just mention it but should take positive action to establish and eradicate the cause ... There was little or no water at the end of the Conduit because of a stoppage in Castle Hill ... The residents in The Fairfield wanted a pavement and Mr. Trimmer, who did not happen to live there, was against it ... James Hewitt lost his seat in April and Thomas Matthews did not seek re-election; in their places came John A. Lorimer, doctor of 33 Castle Street, and Donald George, merchant of West Street. William Hazell, who had been Chairman for so long that his re-appointment each year had become a matter of form, acknowledged the gesture on this occasion but declined 'owing to advancing years and diminished hearing and eyesight'. George Trimmer became Chairman. One of Farnham's most prosperous sons, he had built up his brewery from scratch; he died, in 1892, a very rich man. He gave to the town that had made his fortune faithful public service during the greater part of his life and a hospital which bears his name.

The District Auditor queried the Board's authority to pay the wages of a town crier, with the result that the gentleman's services, on a paid basis, were discontinued ... Twenty ratepayers complained of a nuisance arising from Mr. Aylwin's pigs in Lower Church Lane ... Another memorial about Mr. Eyre's candle factory in The Borough. Mr. Eyre contended that the boiling of tallow was permissible by the Metropolitan Board of Works, so the Board wrote there and found that Eyre had been misinformed ... At a Special Meeting on 14 September 1880, the surveyor reported 'that all the fire engines were faulty and that one small new one would be more effective in extinguishing a fire than probably all the old ones put together'. So a new engine was ordered from Merryweathers' at £42 ... In January 1881, a Member called attention to 'the disgraceful scenes savouring of faction fights enacting on Sunday evenings in the Town, but which it was suggested were caused by visits of Aldershot lads'. The police were asked to take action. It was wrong perhaps to lay the blame on the troops, so much as on the lads from Hale. These belligerent characters in the later years of the century gained a reputation for descending their hill at weekends to the night life of the town and, after a few drinks in the pubs in East Street, spoiling for a fight. One could not expect the soldiers of the Queen to run away.

The Board understood and were adept at handling these trivial problems. The files are full of such matters–memorials for additional street-lamps, the abatement of smells, the removal of petty nuisances, this, that and the other, signed by as many residents as could write their names, the more the better, some even signed by Members of the Board. Perhaps local government had not, after all, progressed far along the road to confidence. The Farnham Board, after a promising start, had proved a weak reed in the face of important issues.

The charge is prepar'd, the lawyers are met,
The judges all ranged; a terrible show!

John Gay

XIII

THE SHOT IS FIRED

WILLIAM MASON had again been playing truant, this time for more than the statutory six months' absence. When asked his intentions, he stated that he wished to resign his seat on the Local Board ... A Member reported that close to the station he had observed an opened drain 'from which a very bad effluvia proceeded' ... The Registrar General sought the Board's co-operation in the forthcoming Census, and asked if they would number houses in the roads–which they wouldn't ... First signs of a take-over by Aldershot? The Local Board of that town proposed a communal County Court, the sittings for the two towns being separate and distinct. But the Chairman referred darkly 'to what had been done in the past' and explained that he had reason 'to fear that the movement now made might result not in separation but in wholly superseding Farnham, if Farnham were not active to avoid it'. A memorial was addressed to the Lord Lieutenant of the County and a deputation of the townspeople waited upon him ... Ambrose Pharo, who had watered the streets ever since the Board took it over, and probably before, lost the job to a rival, George Riches.

Edward Bromley of the *Bush* had been nagging the Board about the worse-than-ever state of the *Bush* Ditch. When a petition arrived signed by visitors to the Hotel, the Board were so surprised that they had the ditch replaced by a piped drain. Like the Market House, another feature of the town was swept away.

The 1881 Election was fought on the issue of the sewage disposal. Thomas Wonnacott and A.J. Bentall lost their seats;

William Mason had retired. In their places came Daniel Goddard, the East Street builder, Thomas Smith, draper in The Borough and Edward Barrett, described as hop-planter of The Fairfield. Barrett–later Colonel Edward Barrett–was then 27 years old; he had married in 1879, which accounts for his having left the home of his father, Robert Tyler Barrett, for a house of his own in the new Fairfield Estate. It was he who sold the Red Lion Brewery to George Trimmer in 1890, to form the Farnham United Brewery, of which he later became Chairman.

Mr. Lorimer, who at the last meeting had given notice of his intention to propose a move on drainage, made a long speech in which 'he saw in the result of the election that it had been fought on the issue of drainage or no drainage, and that it was obvious that a majority verdict was for no drainage', so he withdrew his motion.

George Trimmer, re-elected Chairman, made an impressive speech in relation to the water supply and its effect on the general health of the town and that the position was quite satisfactory. A speech which Mr. Lorimer spoilt rather by denouncing cesspits as being likely to contaminate well water.

The result of the Census had proved that the population of Farnham, 5,080, had increased whereas that of Aldershot had decreased. The Board saw something sinister in this, in that 'it bore upon the County Court question', and hurried to inform the Lord Lieutenant ... On 16 May 1881, Doctor Hayes of The Fairfield wrote a letter to the Board recommending the removal of dust and refuse from houses in the District. The idea of dustmen was new to the Board, who discussed the matter and dismissed it. So Doctor Hayes wrote to the Local Government Board in London, who passed on a copy with a covering letter. It seemed that refuse collection had become a recognised service of a local authority, and the Clerk wrote round to other towns and asked them how they went about it. In September it was decided to initiate the service in Farnham and tenders were invited 'from persons willing to act as Scavengers on Tuesdays and Saturdays'. The tender of Abraham Smith, at 4s. 3d. per day, was accepted. Residents in the town desiring to avail themselves of the service were asked to place a card marked D in their windows. Thus Abraham Smith became Farnham's first dustman, D-day being 11

October 1881. No arrangements were made for a refuse tip; presumably Mr. Smith took it home and used it.

William Hazell was dead. The depressing feature of recording history is that, from time to time, a figure emerges who stays put, so that the time inevitably comes when one has to record his death, having in the meantime formed some sort of affection. Mr. Hazell, that manufacturer of women's corsets in the outbuildings of Ivy house, Downing Street, was another of Farnham's dedicated public men. His long office as Chairman of the Board reflected the opinion of his fellow Members. He seldom missed a meeting and his last attendance was on 1 March 1881, two months before he died. With the approval of the Local Government Board, his replacement was chosen by the Members and Mr. Wonnacott came back in like a homing pigeon to its cote.

It wasn't only the *Bush* Ditch. An Extraordinary Meeting of the Local Board was held on Saturday, 23 July 1881, in the meadows at the rear of Vernon House Garden, convened by the Chairman:–

> The Chairman having explained that his attention had been called to the filthy state of the Backwater, then in view of the Board owing to its having become perfectly dry, the water usually flowing there being diverted into another channel to enable the cleansing of another part of the river bed then proceeding, an inspection of the whole of the Backwater was made and after considering the subject it was on the Motion of Mr. Smith, seconded by Mr. Goddard, resolved that the whole bed of the so called Backwater be forthwith cleaned out and the refuse matter (Mr. Trimmer consenting) deposited on the banks until fit for removal and that the same be then removed at the cost of the Board.

The short approach to the Park from the top of Bear Lane was widened by the purchase of a strip of land from the Rev. M.O. Stevens for £26. The Bishop of Winchester was asked for sanction to replace 'the dangerous step-stile' with a turnstile. For some reason the steps were retained and visitors to the park have since had the choice of either stile ... The Town Hall Company asked the Board to bear the cost of renovating the clock face at the Town Hall but the Clerk pointed out that at the last Audit the annual grant towards winding the clock had been queried. So the Town Hall Company proposed that the Board should lease the clock, at a rent equivalent to the cost of maintenance and to this the Auditor gave his consent ... The Railway people agreed to roof in the footbridge at the station for the convenience of the public ... Plans for alterations in East Street to Mr. Sturt's property and to Mr. Drover's blacksmith's shop in Church Lane;

houses in The Fairfield for Messrs. Foot & Robins and a house for Miss Allden at the West End Estate (Send House–now demolished).

In January 1882 they were much concerned about the state of the footways and, for a start, decided on a major project to repave East Street. Bricks were chosen in preference to pitching, which was most uncomfortable to walk on, with a stretch at the far end 'tar paved as an experiment'. They estimated the cost at between four and five hundred pounds, so halved this by deciding to do the north side of the street only, rather than be drummed out of town by the ratepayers. A Committee consisting of Messrs. Smith, Andrews, Bentall and Goddard was formed, to deal with the matter 'under the advice and assistance of Mr. Wonnacott, should it prove that the Surveyor (who had intimated fears of it) was unequal to the duty'. Mr. Wonnacott certainly assumed full command of the situation. He measured the pavement from the bottom of Bear Lane to St. James Church and found it to be 1,316 feet; this was to be 'paved with bricks six feet wide' (and twelve feet long?); the 800 feet from the Church to the *Albion* was to be tarred and the tender of Thomas Free of High Wycombe was accepted at 2s. 2d. per yard super. 26,000 bricks were purchased at £2 11s. 4d. per 1,000; the whole job came to about £225, which was paid for out of rates, it being anticipated that the Public Works Loan Board would raise objections. Mr. Stapley showed some interest after all and was allowed to engage a Clerk of Works.

The Aldershot Board wrote in reference to a Bill before Parliament for the extension of the Great Western Railway system into Aldershot and inviting Farnham's co-operation in support of the scheme. It was resolved 'that this Board approved the Scheme of the Promoters of the Windsor and Ascot Railway to obtain running powers on the Pirbright, Aldershot and Farnham branch of the London and South-western Railway Company into Farnham, which this Board considers will be highly beneficial to the Town and District'. Mr. Trimmer even attended and gave evidence before the Committee of the House of Commons.

Sidney Stapley handed in his resignation as Surveyor. No reason is given, nor was there any hint of trouble–apart from the rather obvious snub over the East Street paving. Stapley had a busy private practice in the town; if there was feeling, it was no doubt reciprocated. There were no less than eighty-eight applications for his replacement. The Board met on 27 June and, splitting into two, took half each and waded through them, finally whittling them down to a short list of three; the applicants were asked to attend an interview on 11 July.

A complaint had been made of a nuisance at the rear of Nos. 43 and 56 East Street and the Committee formed to view the locus entered their report in the minutes in detail. It is worthy of repetition as an example as the sort of thing that was normal in the 1880s.

> The Committee met on June 19th and inspected the outbuildings and gardens at the back of these houses and found an open ditch running parallel with the street at about 25 yards distant from the dwellings. This ditch receives not only the drainage from sinks but also the overflow from several privies, most of them being without cesspools and others too small. Vegetable and other refuse is also thrown into it, thus making the ditch one large filthy cesspool.

On 11 July, Mr. R.F. Hankins of Pemberton near Wigan was appointed Surveyor at £100 a year, and £12 for the rent of an office. From time to time in the annals of Farnham local government, there has emerged on the staff someone 'from up north', who, by his different mould and strange accents, has breathed a little vitality into southern stillness. Mr. Hankins' offer of security to the Board was the title deeds of his house, 'Hill Top', Newent, estimated to be worth £500. His duties in Farnham began on 15 August 1882. Perhaps, if he could have anticipated immediate events, Mr. Hankins would have chosen to remain at Pemberton near Wigan.

The Meeting in September 1882 opened in much the same manner as any other ordinary monthly meeting, that is to say, the minutes of the last meeting were read and confirmed. Mr. Stapley reported that the nuisance in East Street had been abated; he also reported an encroachment by George Robins on the footway in front of his shop near the railway station. George Elliott, one of the Fire Chiefs, was allowed to order equipment for the use of the Fire Brigade. The Medical Officer reported a case of typhoid at the house of William Foot near the station.

All fairly routine stuff. Then the Clerk,

> having reported that he had been served with a Notice from Mr. Bateman of his intention to proceed against the Board under the Pollution of Rivers Act 1876 for

> polluting the stream, and having read such Notice and the Chairman having in a speech of considerable length reminded the Board of the steps taken from time to time in reference to the drainage of the District, and having explained the difficulties which beset the question and pointed out the evil consequences which had resulted from drainage works in other towns, and the matter having been discussed, it was on the Motion of Mr. Nash, seconded by Mr. Barrett (Mr. Bentall only dissenting), resolved that the Clerk do write Mr. Bateman's Solicitor and express the Board's regret and surprise that Mr. Bateman should have deemed it necessary to take even the initiatory step of such Notice and to add that, should he resolve to follow it up with the threatened process, the Board would take it to be their duty to answer him and defend themselves and their constituents'.

On the last occasion, a special meeting had been summoned and a deputation sent post-haste to Moor Park. The new anti-drainage policy of the Board now resulted in a mixture of obstinacy and injured innocence, almost disinterest in the matter. At the next ordinary meeting in October, beyond reading a letter from Mr. Potter, outlining his client's legal position in the threatened proceedings, they were more interested in two other matters raised by the Leader of the Opposition, namely that the Board spent ratepayers' money in removing private nuisances in the town, and criticism that the Board had not taken steps to seek a provisional order to enlarge the area of the District. Indeed the Special Meeting summoned on 24 October 1882 was not for the purpose of a maudlin contemplation of being dragged through the Courts but to consider these two points raised by Mr. Potter. However Mr. Goddard did ask the Clerk what remedy the Board had against persons sending sewage into the surface water drains and thence to the river. The Board took the view that it was their duty to provide drains for rain and sink water and, if they had been abused by the conveyance of sewage matter, they, the Board, failed to see how they could be answerable for that.

The Clerk reported in December that he had been served with a Summons to appear before a Special Sitting of the Aldershot County Court on 24 January 1883. He informed the Board that, being one of the Registrars of the County Court, he was precluded by law from representing the Board. Mr. Martin of Messrs. Hart, Hart & Martin of Dorking was instructed.

The case of Bateman *v.* Farnham Local Board was a protracted one. It opened on 24 January 1883 at the Aldershot County Court (Mr. Vernon Lushington Q.C.) and was adjourned five times over the next four months. The Plaintiff, represented by Mr. Morgan

Howard Q.C., sought an Order 'to restrain the Defendants from allowing solid or liquid sewage matter to fall or flow, or knowingly permitting it to fall or flow, into the River Wey'. The Local Board (Mr. Douglas Kingsford Q.C.) pleaded numerous endeavours in the past, some fifteen in all, to install drainage. But the issue was the pollution of the river and facts were facts. Judgement was in favour of Mr. Bateman and an injunction was granted against the Board with effect from 1 January 1884, a somewhat optimistic deadline, with leave to appeal to the Court for extra time if the circumstances warranted it.

The six-day action cost the Board £214 4s. 10d. for Mr. Bateman's legal expenses, and their own, £342 11s. 1d. These added to the bill for sewage disposal works to which, as the Board now realised, they were unconditionally committed. Of the Court proceedings there is no mention whatever in the Board's minutes; perhaps they did not wish their ignominy to be placed on permanent official record.

XIV

THE ANSWER'S A LEMON

FOR A breath of fresh air let us turn again to the more inspiring affairs of those men of iron will and grim purpose–the Farnham Burial Board. One cannot suppress a feeling, however, that their verve was prompted more by the impatience of the bodies waiting at the gate than by an ambition to be one up on the other authorities in the town. For their membership at this time included such men as William Hazell (soon to move in), Josiah Bentall, A.J. Bentall, Sam Andrews, Thomas Wonnacott and Thomas Smith who, as members of the Local Board, were content to pollute the River Wey with all manners of smelly unmentionables yet, for some reason or other, drew the line at floating dead bodies downstream in the direction of Moor Park.

In January 1879, the Burial Board took stock: of the 2,655 grave spaces in Farnham cemetery, 594 remained untenanted. With lettings averaging about two a week, this gave some six years in which to expand–plenty of time, one would have said, for a Board which had taken twelve months to establish the cemetery, eight at Hale and practically overnight at The Bourne. The reason for their decision to act without delay is apparent. There was only one way to extend–that was to the west, in a 13-acre field belonging to Mr. John Knight, and Mr. Knight was planning to develop on the lines of the West End Estate on the other side of the road. He already had a name for it, 'Hollow Oak Estate', and an estate road constructed. On this land, right under the cemetery wall Knight had a row of five cottages, fronting the main road, with gardens stretching the full depth of the cemetery. Cottages were no great obstacle but a full scale housing estate was another matter and unless the Board moved quickly any extension of the cemetery could only take the form of a separate burial ground elsewhere in the District, with the additional expense of its own chapels, lodge and other necessary equipment.

The negotiations between the Board and Mr. Knight, as it happened, occupied no less than two of the six years. John Knight came of a family renowned for their dauntless and imperturbable character; moreover he had other–well advanced–plans in mind. The Board, by the demands of their calling, were equally determined men. Their Clerk, Henry Potter, and John Knight were well matched and the events of these two years read like one of those periodical attempts of mankind to get to the bottom of what happens when an irresistible force meets an immovable body.

Briefly, the duel can be summarised as follows. Potter led off with a letter dated 14 January 1879, seeking Knight's views on selling the Board a piece of land for extending the cemetery. Knight parried this by not replying until 3 March, when he declined the invitation because a house was about to be built on the land. In July, Potter waylaid Knight–a quicker means of communication than writing him a letter–and was told that the position remained unchanged. In October, Potter wrote again and, one month later, Knight replied that he was now in a position to sell part of the Hollow Oak Estate and would follow up 'in a few days' time' with details. In January 1880, these details had not arrived, so a liaison committee of the Board was set up and Potter wrote to Knight to arrange a meeting. By March no reply had been received but Potter managed to buttonhole Knight and, with some close in-fighting, to arrange a meeting with the committee for 11 March. They met on the site and agreement was reached on the piece of land the Board wished to buy and Knight promised to submit terms. In May, he had not yet done so, although Potter had written twice to remind him, but a letter was handed in at the meeting in which Knight apologised for the delay, named a price of £850 and promised particulars 'in a few days' time'. To which the Board wrote back asking him to be good enough to make a definite offer in time for a special meeting on 12 May. At that meeting, Potter reported that he had written–twice–but nothing had arrived; he was directed to write again, giving Knight a week.

It could be said at this stage that honours were pretty even and, whilst some slight advantage accrued to Knight, it was still difficult to forecast the outcome. The next move came from Knight—possibly rattled by a two-months' dead silence from the Board—on 23 July, offering a piece of land coloured pink on the plan for £850, or a larger area coloured pink and blue for £1,600, and specifying a 7-foot high boundary wall with a 9-foot wide plantation inside, also that the Board should pay the Vendor's legal expenses—a true Knight touch. What is more, he met the committee again on 7 August and agreed to submit an amended plan more suitable to the Board's requirements. On 13 September, he was given until the 27th to produce it.

This sort of thing can only go on so long before one side snaps. It was Potter who showed the first signs of cracking. He approached the owner of some hopground opposite, who offered the Board about 2 acres for £1,200. Knight may have interpreted this as throwing in the glove and felt that he could now afford to be more generous, for he came up with a further offer, and a third meeting with the committee, and final terms to suit both parties. These arrived in January 1881, the second anniversary of Potter's initial letter. The number of vacant grave spaces, meanwhile, had fallen to 409.

Mr. Knight offered 7a. 1r. 14p., including the five cottages, for £4,900, or 3 acres for £1,950 and the cottages at £700. The second proposal was adopted at a poll of the townspeople by 146 votes to 97. The Board borrowed £3,300 from some of the same gentlemen who had financed South Street—and who must by now have developed a sense of proprietorship—and set to work; there was no particular hurry with this one. An interesting feature was that the boundary wall was built of stones taken from the old footway in East Street—which the Local Board were replacing with bricks—and bought for 2s. 6d. a yard. The Bishop of Winchester consecrated the new extension, which doubled the size of the cemetery, on 20 June 1883.

John Hudson, the Sexton, died in April 1881 and his successor was Mr. W.H. Wheeler ... Mr. J.S. Hickley replaced Mr. Chessell as a member of the Board; he resigned two years later and Alfred Henry Stevens of Castle Street took his place ... To provide access to the extension, two grave stones were placed flat on their graves, with the consent of the relatives of the deceased persons ... The Board, as landlords of five cottages, were having tenant trouble; rents were 3s. a week.

The names mentioned in the minutes in connection with headstones of those who came to be buried read like a directory of the town. In the end, one after another, they all came.

. . . . .

If the Members of the Farnham Local Board were licking their wounds after their defeat in the County Court, they showed no signs of it at the Special Meeting on 9 May 1883. Instead, they thanked Mr. Martin and Mr. Douglas Kingsford for their conduct of the defence 'which had been highly satisfactory to the Board'. The use of this adjective can only be interpreted as the victorious cry of the seweragists on the Board who, hitherto thwarted by the opposition, suddenly saw the green light. Indeed, as the whole town now knew, there was no option left in the matter. On the advice of Mr. Martin, the Board voted eight to four against an appeal and having accepted the verdict turned their minds towards the major project ahead—an awesome prospect that was cushioned to some extent by the comforting presence in Southampton of Mr. James Lemon, C.E.

Concerning Mr. Lemon, the Board had a strong sense of guilt. They had, a few years back, put him to a great deal of trouble and expense in preparing a detailed drainage scheme and their lack of interest ever since was churlish in the extreme. What is more, they had not paid Mr. Lemon one penny towards his fees and expenses. Neither had the patient Mr. Lemon sent in a bill; the occasion for this was if the Board, when the time came, took their custom elsewhere—a fact of which the Board was well aware. The Board's position was (a) they had to instal drainage, with a Civil Engineer to see to it, (b) they owed Mr. Lemon for preliminary work done in the past and (c) why pay twice for the same spade-work to be done by someone else? So the Board grasped the nettle and asked Mr. Lemon for a statement of his claim for services rendered up-to-date and, when this arrived, it was rather frightening. Whatever other qualities they lacked, the Board were astute with the ratepayers' money—their constituents being vigilant over such matters, and they squeezed the lemon by suggesting that, if he were appointed as engineer to carry out a full-scale drainage system, would he be prepared to waive his fees for work done in the past? They also asked Mr. Lemon whether he would have any objection to their seeking the advice of a Consultant as to the efficiency of his proposed methods. Mr. Lemon wrote from Lansdowne House, Southampton, on 14 July 1883:–

> Referring to my interview with the Local Board on the 10th instant, I beg to say I am willing to accept the proposition made by the Chairman, viz.–that I should forego my charges against the Board except travelling expenses on condition that the Board pay me 5 per cent commission and travelling expenses for my services as Engineer on the cost of the works (exclusive of the purchase of the lands), also that the Plans be submitted to an Engineer of eminence named by the Board and approved by me.
>
> I think it desirable that you should prepare a short agreement between the Board and myself as the Board cannot bind their successors except by Deed and difficulties often crop up with the Auditor. I have every confidence in the present Board as I have shown by trusting them four or five years, but I once had a case in which the new Board repudiated everything their predecessors had done and rescinded all the resolutions.

The Clerk considered that Mr. Lemon was rushing things rather, but the Board was hardly in a position to dictate and, on 24 July 1883, the great decision was made 'that Mr. Lemon be appointed Engineer to the Board for the purpose of carrying out a Scheme of Sewerage for the District upon the terms of his letter of the 14th instant and that the Clerk be directed to reduce such appointment into writing and produce the same for sealing at the next Meeting of the Board'. Mr. Lemon, who was present, thanked the Board and said the Scheme should be put in hand forthwith, and mentioned various sites which had occurred to him 'for receipt of the sewage matter'. His air of confidence betrayed his over-estimation of Farnham people; the installation of sewerage, which occupied most of the remaining years of the Local Board's reign, proved to be not as simple as he imagined.

Another matter which claimed the Board's attention in the summer of 1883 was the extension of the District; the question had flickered briefly and gone out from time to time over the past few years but had now become urgent, not only because Mr. Potter said it was, but because the town was spreading eastward in Hale Road and St. James, and up beyond the station, where the Waverley Estate–Tilford, Alfred and St. Georges Roads–was in an advanced stage of development. The people who lived in these new houses were townspeople, sharing in many of the amenities provided by the Board, yet paying rates to the rural parish. The deciding factor was the inability to include these housing estates in the proposed sewerage unless they were brought into the Board's area.

The proposed new boundary line was traced out on the map and Mr. Hankins was told to prepare the papers for the application to the Local Government Board. The new boundary was again drawn almost touching the houses. The Local Board had no wish to be lumbered with the trouble and expense of the upkeep of roads in undeveloped areas of no practical advantage to them. Indeed, where the proposed line passed along a road, the Board were careful to leave the roadway itself in the hands of the Rural Highways Board, whilst making sure of the ratepayers–a point duly noticed and adjusted by the Local Government Board. The application was not due in until the following January, which would give the Board time to include the site of the sewage farm, when that was settled later.

Other boundary extensions were to follow. At first piecemeal, then the wholesale take-overs of Hale, Heath End, Weybourne and Badshot Lea in 1914 and in, 1924, of Waverley, The Bourne, Wrecclesham, Boundstone, Rowledge and Dippenhall, so that the day was to come when the whole of the old Farnham Parish, with the unfortunate exception of Tilford, was again under one roof.

Mr. Lorimer mentioned 'a serious accident from the use of firearms at a stall at the Fair in Castle Street' ... A Member proposed reviving the old Borough of Farnham ... A privy shared by the houses in Factory Yard was investigated and found to be totally inadequate for the needs of the houses there ... Mr. Wonnacott proposed separate accommodation for male and female hop-pickers, but found no seconder ... Richard Mason was away ill for some weeks and Mr. J.R. Nash executed his duties as Acting Clerk ... Mr. Chuter, watchmaker of Downing Street, reported difficulty in keeping the Town Hall clock going ... Slaughterhouse licences were issued to butchers Alfred Baker, 18 Downing Street, Samuel Beesley, 20/21 East Street, Frederick Cudley, 7 The Borough, George Edwards, 21 West Street, F. Pullinger, 32 West Street, Elizabeth Stewart, 82 West Street and Frank J. Stovold, 45 The Borough ... Plans for a house and shop in

South Street by George Robins–passed 'subject to the Surveyor being satisfied with the stability of the buildings'; it is still standing at No. 29.

The first of many major objectives in the conflict between the Local Board and the townspeople over the installation of sewerage was the acquisition of a sort of no-man's-land for the 'receipt of the sewerage matter'. The most practical way of inducing the flow of this was to have the pipes going gently downhill all the way to the sewage farm, so that this had to lie at the lowest point above sea-level. The most low-lying parts of Farnham were either to the west of the town, in the Coxbridge area, or at the other end of the valley, in the vicinity of Badshot Lea. That the latter site just had the edge on Coxbridge was no doubt proved by the fact that it was the natural tendency of the river to flow in an easterly direction, though a more popular reason for the choice of Badshot Lea was that the prevailing wind also had a tendency to blow in that direction and, with a sewage farm in the offing, the direction of the wind can be a matter of some importance.

Mr. Lemon, who had several prospective sites in mind, advocated the purchase of about 25 acres of land but Mr. Wonnacott persistently campaigned for half this area. The Estate Agent, Mr. A.J. Nash, was instructed to act for the Board and people living down-wind prepared themselves for battle. One could go so far as to say that nobody wanted to live next-door to a sewage farm. There were offers from G.V. Knight, John Henry Knight, William Kimber, J. Lazareck and Samuel Bide; Mr. Bateman also offered advice. The Board closed with Mr. Kimber for an acre of land in Guildford Road for £220, for the purpose of the pumping station; they were also attracted by the offer of J.H. Knight of 11½ acres at Hurlands, at £175 per acre. Contracts had been drawn up for signature when Mr. Bateman's solicitors, Messrs. Palmer, Eland & Nettleship (why not Mr. Potter?–because he was acting for Mr. J.H. Knight), wrote intimating that, in the event of the Board completing the purchase of J.H. Knight's land, steps would be taken to prevent it being used for the sewage farm on the grounds that such use would seriously affect property belonging to their client on the opposite side of Guildford Road. Mr. Bateman himself also wrote pointing out that Knight's price was far too high anyway and that he,

Mr. Bateman, knew of a much better site nearby at half the price, which he would be pleased to tell the Board about provided they would pledge themselves beforehand to accept his idea. When Mr. Potter pressed for the signing of the contract, the Board had to point out that the owner of adjoining land threatened litigation and therefore the deal with Mr. Knight was not on. They had to pay Knight £7 10s. 0d. compensation for withholding the ploughing of the land and also Mr. Potter's fees for preparing the abortive contract.

Ignoring Mr. Bateman's mysterious offer, the Board approached Mr. G.V. Knight. Mr. Knight's claim to distinction lies in the fact that he was christened George Vernon instead of John or James. His solicitors were Messrs. Knight & Ward. The piece of land he offered was adjacent to Bourne Mill and, as might be expected, William Simmonds objected on the grounds that the water in his mill pond would become polluted, though Mr. Lemon explained that the effluent water from the sewage farm would be conducted past the mill by means of a culvert under the road and so avoid the pond. But Mr. Simmonds was not satisfied and, through his solicitor Mr. Henry Potter, threatened to take action to prevent the acquisition of G.V. Knight's land.

It was now March 1884. Mr. Potter, on behalf of his former client, Mr. Bateman, reminded the Board that the County Court Order had come into operation on the previous 1 January and suggested that they should apply to the County Court for a further Order; he requested to be informed of the Board's intentions. To which the bewildered Board replied that they were making 'strenuous endeavours to obviate the evils which gave rise to the Action and hoped that Mr. Bateman would find no difficulty in seeing that no practical good would result from moving the Court as suggested'. Then, in absolute desperation, they chanced the wrath of Mr. Potter, acting for Mr. Simmonds, and signed the contract with G.V. Knight.

James Lemon, meanwhile, had been keeping out of the way and busy preparing detailed plans and estimates and these were approved by the Board on 18 March 1884. Application was then made to the Local Government Board for sanction to borrow the sum of £14,000; this was duly approved and the Loans Board, unable to think up any objections, agreed to advance the money, repayable over thirty years.

Mr. A.J. Bentall did not stand again at the 1884 Election; William Higgins, chemist of 49 The Borough took his place ... There were several cases of diphtheria due to unfit well water, and an enquiry from the Local Government Board concerning them ... Josiah Bentall died in July and his seat was taken by Alfred James Nash of 41 Castle Street ... Plans for solicitors' offices in South Street for James Stevens ... Mr. Potter acted for the Rural Highways Board in opposing the extension of the District; notwithstanding this, the Provisional Order was confirmed by Parliament with effect from 7 August 1884.

In July 1884, another phase broke out in the fighting–the individual complaints from persons aggrieved by the plans of the proposed sewers. These were mostly handed on to the Engineer to deal with and, mostly, the answer was a lemon. The first to arrive was a letter from the Medical Officer, Dr. S.G. Sloman and another from his father, Dr. S.G. Sloman, which drew attention to the annoyance that would certainly ensue from the proposal to carry a sewer through the gardens of houses in West Street. In the months to come, complaints came in from all along the streets, including that of Mrs. Paget of Lowlands, East Street (now Brightwells). This was a secondary sewer, serving areas such as Mead Lane and Babbs Mead at the back of West Street, the main sewer itself was to be laid beneath the centre line of the streets.

For Richard Mason J.P., the events of the past two years had exceeded the expectations of the Clerk of a local authority in a small, and deceptively peaceful, country town. It was a thoughtful gesture, therefore, on the part of the Board in voting him an additional reward. The Law Committe, on being referred to, recommended £50; Mr. Mason, in a nicely worded reaction, mixed politeness with sarcasm and was granted £100. It was not an ill wind–when it didn't blow from the east.

Whoso diggeth a pit shall fall therein

Proverbs

XV

CAUTION – ROAD UP

THERE WERE many pitfalls during the laying in of sewers in the mid-1880s. The installation of the town's entire network of drains in one huge operation was undoubtedly the largest, and most hazardous undertaking ever to hit Farnham. And although they engaged a Civil Engineer and a Contractor to carry out the works, the Board themselves were in the front trenches throughout in an administrative capacity, which is officialese for everything that failed to come within the province of either of those two gentlemen, and a lot besides which did. A major concern of any administrator is the finance. During the eighteen months from December 1884 to June 1886, the immense sum of £14,000 flowed into the Board's coffers in bi-monthly payments from the Loans Board of £1,500–and the whole town knew it. A big proportion of this money was passed on to the Contractor, the engineer and to suppliers, but there was a tidy bit left over and the hard-headed business-men in the town, like sharks to a corpse, rose to the occasion as one man.

Even before the first instalment arrived at Knights Bank, it was known that the Lord of the Manor himself had squeezed £82 from the Board as compensation for the enfranchisement of the land purchased from G.V. Knight; also that a Mr. Pritchard, the Board's Counsel at the Loans Board enquiry, had creamed off £56; then there was the Loans Board's own cut for legal costs. Perhaps it was ill-advised at this point to increase the Clerk's salary to £100 a year, and the Surveyor's by £20, for this action on the part of the Board signified that, whilst charity had not actually begun at home, what was left had now arrived on home ground.

There was, for instance, G.V. Knight's account for the land. The Board sent Messrs. Knight & Ward, his solicitors, a cheque for £2,145 7s. 1d., which included interest on the purchase price for the delay in completion. Under threat of calling off the deal, Knight & Ward conned another £21 from the Board for their services to G.V. Knight. Encouraged by this, they demanded a further sum of seven guineas, charged by Alfred William Mellersh, the Godalming Surveyor, for stumping out the limits of the land—the Board having funked this because it was next-door to Bourne Mill and the boundary was not clearly defined and the Board were a wee bit scared of William Simmonds. The Board refuted this, declaring it to be Mr. Knight's liability, and the battle waged to and fro until Richard Mason was served with a summons to appear in the County Court. Whereupon the Board instructed Messrs. Potter & Crundwell, who recommended Counsel's opinion, and finally five guineas were paid into the Court in full discharge of the debt, which, together with the Board's legal costs in the matter, must have come out at much more than seven guineas.

On Mr. Lemon's advice, tenders in respect of Contract No. 1—The Engines and Boilers—were now advertised for. Thirty-six engineering firms, mostly from the industrial midlands, put in quotations ranging from £1,119 to £2,270, and an agreement was reached with Messrs. W.R. Renshaw & Company of Union Foundry, Kidsgrove, Staffs., for delivery of the machinery when the buildings at the sewage farm were ready to receive it. Contract No. 2, which covered the constructional work of the farm, the pumping station, the laying of sewers and all other work in connection with the scheme, was then advertised. There were twenty tenders, from £9,342 to £14,888, the lowest—that of Richard Curtiss Trimm of Hersham, Walton-on-Thames—being accepted. The team was now established—Mr. Lemon as gaffer and the Board holding the nail whilst Mr. Trimm hit it. In April 1885 the 'ROAD-UP' signs were going up all over Farnham and the even tenor of the town was shattered to its very core.

Throughout these preliminaries the ordinary business of the Board was carried on, albeit with less enthusiasm; constituents are hard masters and their demands cannot wait. Mr. Lorimer was sent to a meeting at Croydon of the Boundary Commissioners in order to urge that Farnham should not be severed from the Guildford Parliamentary Division of the County (was Aldershot trying to take over this, too?) ... Samuel Bide of Alma Nurseries was reported to be encroaching on the highway near the railway junction bridge and the whole Board went out there on 11 March to view the locus and were satisfied with what they found. Mr. Bide, one-time Clerk of Hale Church and Sexton of the cemetery, was in process of establishing his remarkable empire at Runfold. This was an age of golden opportunities for those enterprising enough to grasp them ... The Railway people were threatened by the Board for causing 'nuisances arising from heaps and trucks of manure, putrid fish and decayed vegetable matter, collected in close proximity to the down platform at the Railway Station' and replied that additional sidings would be provided 'especially for the manure traffic' ... Mr. Bide was eager to rent land at the proposed sewage farm (was it to avoid having to come all the way to the station to buy manure for his nursery?), but it was too early to agree to this. It did however come to pass and, for a time, Bides were tenants at the Farm ... Mr. W.G. Forder of Westhampton was appointed Clerk of Works to Mr. Lemon at £3 per week, which was more than the Surveyor got ... At the 1885 Election, Mr. Wonnacott again lost his seat on the Board; his place was taken by John Sampson, hop-planter.

It was probably with relish that the Board served on the Railway Company Notice under the Public Health Act, 1875, of their intention to lay a sewer under the level-crossing; this was one matter in which the Company had no power of refusal. Notices were also sent to all owners of land through which sewers were to be laid. There were few objections, the public by now had grown accustomed to the upheaval, and probably welcomed the advent of proper sanitation; rates, moreover, as yet showed no signs of going up. The works of drainage–so far–were proceeding smoothly and on schedule.

There were cases of diphtheria in the Board's District, with which the Local Government Board in London were so concerned that they sent down an Inspector, Doctor Sweeting, to hold an enquiry. The Rural Sanitary Authority also attended and the subject of a joint hospital for infectious diseases was discussed ... In September 1885, George Trimmer had plans in for the new

Albion Hotel at the White Post. This pub had stood for many years nearby, on the north side of the street, probably where Trimmer built his Cottage Hospital nine years later ... There were plans, too, for R. & E. Beale's corn-merchants premises at the corner of South Street and Union Road.

Mr. A.J. Nash objected to the practice of fellow Members, who were also shareholders in the Gas or Water Companies, being allowed to vote in matters between the Board and those Companies. The Clerk advised that under Rule 64, Schedule 2 of the Public Health Act, 1875, application could be made to the Government for dispensation to enable such Members to vote, and a Member moved that application should be made. Then Mr. Goddard queried the right of the Members concerned to vote on this motion ... Samuel Andrews died in November and A.J. Bentall was invited back in ... Red Lion Lane was closed for the sewer to be put in; for those who lived in this long neglected road on the outskirts of the town, the appalling conditions were now about to end.

When the Local Government Board asked what action had been taken on Doctor Sweeting's Report on the diphtheria epidemic, the Local Board replied that 'they had more pressing matters to deal with'—which was quite true, though one must never speak like that to the gentlemen at Whitehall. In answer to a second, more irritated letter the Board peevishly announced that they were in process of installing a system of sewerage that would eradicate the causes of diseases in the future—the L.G.B. should have known this anyway; they put up the money.

That all embracing, monumental measure, the Public Health Act, 1875, included an adoptive section which gave local authorities powers to maintain water supplies in their Districts and, if considered advisable, to take over control of any existing Water Companies. For some time past, the Farnham Water Company had been stagnant. Its inadequate network of mains conveyed water only to the best people, so that many of the poorer streets in the town had to rely on wells, which, as we have seen, were frequently the cause of disease because of their contamination by nearby cesspits. The Board from time to time bullied the Company for not piping in water to the cottages. It is not recorded in any of the minutes that the Water Company retaliated by bullying the Board for not piping out the sewage. However the Act of 1875 gave the Board the right to intervene, and intervene they did. Had they been less busy, it is possible that they might have taken over the Company; as it was they played a big part in the Water Company's application to the Board of Trade for a Provisional Order for additional share capital of £10,000 for improvements to the water supply.

The Act, unfortunately, was less helpful over the supply of gas. Local authorities were empowered to supply gas in areas not already served by a Gas Company, but where one did exist the Board was not given the right to take it over, a fact which must have annoyed the Farnham Board beyond measure. In their running fight with the Gas Company ever since the 1830s, with the Company winning all the tricks, nothing would have given the Board greater pleasure than to storm the Gas Works in East Street and hurl copies of 38 & 39 Vict. c.55–all 300-odd sections of it–at Mr. Wells, the Secretary, and the Directors, four of whom were also on the Board. As it was, so great was their chagrin that the Board–with the exception of the four Members with divided allegiance–formed themselves into a Committee, and went berserk. In the face of yet another certain defeat, the Committee challenged the Company over the price of gas supplied to the street-lamps. The Company kept the Committee waiting and then sent their usual refusal to negotiate. Whereupon the Board, with dramatic effect, gave notice of their intention to terminate the Contract for Public Lighting as from 31 July 1886.

The situation was interesting. The Gas Company faced the prospect of losing a considerable source of income and in addition would find themselves the owners of a hundred or so disused lamp standards of little use to anyone without dogs. In the opposite corner, the Board sat wondering glumly what had become of the old oil-lamps, or whether they could use petroleum, as they did, apparently, in Wimbledon and Winchester. The Auditor did not help, either, in threatening to surcharge any item of expenditure on gas lighting without a Contract. As the 31 July approached, with no move from the Company, it was the Board who, aware of their statutory duty to light the town during the hours of darkness, pocketed their pride and tentatively asked whether the Company would receive the Committee to discuss the situation.

To which the Company replied that they would prefer to have the Board's observations in writing. The Board, seeing some slight advantage, offered to rent the lamps or even buy them. The Company finally agreed to let them at 4s. per annum per lamp, for the sole purpose of consuming the Company's gas, the supply of which would be measured by meter and at 3s. 9d. per 1,000 cubit feet, less 10 per cent discount. It was now December; how the town had been lit since July is not stated–perhaps the Gas Company were co-operative, after all it was their fight too. And so, on the Company's terms, though with minor financial concessions, the Contract was renewed.

Major-General Blair of Firgrove House wrote requesting a street-lamp outside his house but there being no gas main in that direction the Board were able to refuse. The next time the General wrote, he rattled his medals and, without further nonsense, both the Gas Company and the Board bent over backwards. James Blair had been in India during the Mutiny of 1857; his Victoria Cross must have been one of the very early ones.

It was decided to lay a pavement on the north side of Guildford Road from the *Albion Hotel* to Bourne Mill–that is to say if William Simmonds would consent to provide a strip of his front garden; if not, the pavement would be made as far as his hedge ... The Bentalls in The Borough had plans in for rebuilding their premises and the opportunity was taken by the Board to widen the bottleneck. The Bentalls had three separate businesses here–A.J. Bentall, W.K. Bentall and Messrs. A.J. & W.K. Bentall. Their exorbitant demands were watered down to £50 apiece and the Board were able to widen The Borough from Bentalls corner to the *Ship Inn* (No. 17) by some three feet ... The Railway at last consented to make the footpath across the station yard from the steps to join the pavement in Station Hill ... Doctor Sloman suggested some sort of supervision of the traffic in West Street during the road-up operations of Mr. Trimm ... Capital & Counties Bank had taken over Knights Bank in Castle Street and James Knight was personally retained as the Board's Treasurer ... Mr. Trimm's foreman assaulted Mr. Stevenson, Clerk of Works at the pumping station, and was prosecuted.

Throughout 1886 the work of laying the sewers continued; there were, however, undercurrents. Mr. Lemon was proving a

ate 26 *Bishop Morley, 1662-1684*

Plate 27 *Trimmer's Cottage Hospital, East Street; now Red Cross House*

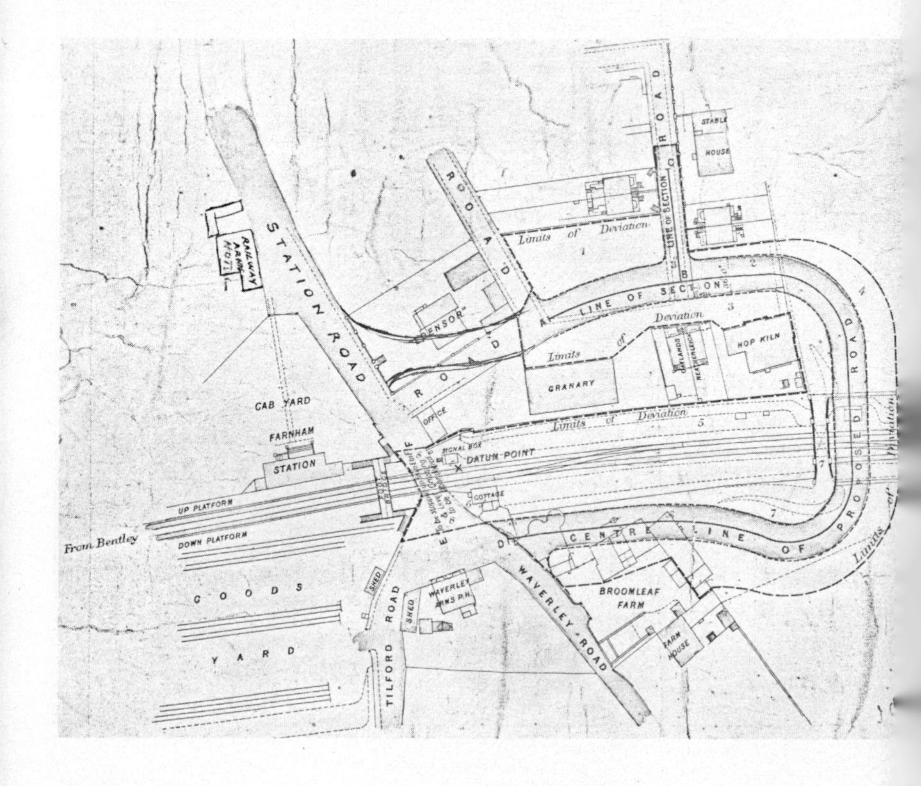

Plate 28 *When Farnham almost lost the level-crossing, 1892*

Plate 29 *Britain's first two-seater motor car; James Pullinger at the tiller, 1896*

Plate 30 *Volunteer Fire Brigade, 1896*
Left to right *(back row) John Hawkes, Harry Patrick, Alf Bailey, Tom Hudson, Harry Luffry, –, Albert Budd, Chris. Harrison;*
(front row) Capt. Elliott, James Hawkes, William Dalton, George Swan, 'Shoey' Varnes, George Windibank, –, John Chitty, Ernest Edwards, George Elliott

Plate 31 *Moor Park trouble, Sunday, 17 January 1897 – the townsmen besieged the gates*

capable and trustworthy engineer; the Board were doing their bit in holding the nail but Mr. Trimm, if he was not actually missing it, was in that position in which he could be expected to anytime. Mr. Lemon's monthly progress reports, though satisfactory and agreeable to the Contractor's fees being paid as instalments became due, seemed grudgingly so. Moreover the work was not being carried out in a spirit of friendly co-operation; there was bickering between the men on the spot. The quality of the work was not good and required constant supervision by the Clerk of Works and this was resented by Trimm's foreman. In July 1886 the Board did not hesitate to inform Mr. Trimm that, unless his future progress was more to the satisfaction of the engineer, his Contract would be determined. In the following October, Mr. Lemon was told to direct Mr. Mason, if considered necessary, to cancel the Contract.

Then a letter arrived from Messrs. Doulton & Company of the Lambeth Pottery, the suppliers of the sewerage pipes, enclosing a Notice of Assignment of Moneys due to Trimm under the Contract. And another letter of 30 November from a London firm of solicitors, enclosing an Order with a Summons attached, to the same purpose. In answer to the Summons, Mr. Mason's London agents attended the hearing and explained the Board's position in the matter. It looked rather as if there were trouble ahead.

And then Nature, adept in gauging the limit of man's endurance, staged a divertissement in the form of a mini-scale *opéra bouffe* which, though it was enacted in deadly seriousness by its producers, a voluntary body styled the 'Water Trough Committee', introduced a little light relief to the major worries of the Local Board. The Water Trough Committee was Mrs. La Marchant, a local lady do-gooder with a Cause. In this case the Cause took the form of drinking troughs for cattle. The Committee sought permission to erect one at the bottom of Bear Lane, but the Board considered this site unsuitable and invited alternative suggestions. These arrived, together with a Mr. Groom, aptly named Inspector of the Royal Society for Prevention of Cruelty to Animals, who explained the wishes of the Water Trough Committee on the subject and, the matter having been discussed at some length, he was informed by the Board that, in their opinion, a drinking trough in the Cattle Market on market days and a temporary one at the top of Castle Street on Fair days would meet the requirements of the case. There was no further development during the next month or two and then Mr. Groom wrote on behalf of the Water Trough Committee for permission to erect a trough opposite the Cemetery in West Street, but the Board failed to see the expediency of this. Mr. Groom retired from the scene, leaving the stage to Mrs. La Marchant, who tried again some weeks later for troughs in Castle Street. Not being required by the Public Health Act 1875 to assume the duties of the Water Trough Committee, the Board washed their hands of it altogether, but the incident, by its comparative triviality of purpose, did a lot towards keeping everyone on a level plane.

In December 1886, the Prince of Wales wrote to George Trimmer, the Chairman (and also, no doubt, to all the other Chairmen of Local Boards throughout the country), inviting the Board's co-operation in the formation of an Imperial Institute in commemoration of Her Majesty's Jubilee. The letter met with no formal resolution, the general opinion of the Board being that any celebration of the event should be more localised. It is only within living memory that the way of life in a small country town broadened out beyond its frontiers.

XIV

ON MAIN DRAINAGE

THE BANKRUPTCY in April 1887 of the Local Board's Contractor, Richard Curtiss Trimm, came late enough in the drainage works for a major disaster to be averted. Indeed Trimm himself was under the impression that his work in Farnham was completed; there was, however, still much to do in the way of extras and repairs of Trimm's faulty workmanship. The Board sacked the Contractor by Notice served on 7th June:—

> We, the Local Board for the District of Farnham in the County of Surrey, give you Notice that by reason of your having in several respects failed in the due performance of your Contract with us (dated the 7th day of April 1885) for the construction of certain works of Sewerage and Sewage Disposal therein referred to and also because you have become bankrupt, we have today pursuant to Article 27 thereof determined such Contract.

They asked Mr. Lemon to tell them the worst—one could never be sure with Mr. Trimm. People were stumbling into badly built sewers (fortunately not yet in use), such as John Matthews and James Amor who fell into the Castle Street one (this cost the Board £15 in compensation), and Ben Caesar's horse in Bridge Square (£5). When a dummy run had been made in March, here and there throughout the five miles of sewers, pipes were found to have been insecurely joined or laid at wrong levels and there were several leakages. With Mr. Lemon as spotter, the Surveyor and Clerk of Works grappled with these problems. Mr. Lemon was proving good value for his 5 per cent; his Contract with the Board was nearing completion, yet in their unforeseen difficulties he stood by the Board, even during a protracted aftermath. His hastily written notes to the Clerk (all the papers relating to the works exist intact) were in advance of his time and in contrast to the otherwise Victorian stiltedness of the file. They were handwritten–typed correspondence had not yet made its appearance–but Lemon's choice of words could compare with the clipped, sometimes witty phrases of business letters of the 1960s.

The Compensations Committee of the Board were at this time dealing with the several claims made by those through whose land the sewers had been laid. The claims varied according to the extent of damage and who it was making them. The game, which was played out in every case, had its recognised rules. The applicant doubled the value of the damage. The Board halved it; after a short rally, the players met somewhere in the middle and shook hands. If the stakes were high, an umpire was appointed. Mr. Barling, for instance, the East Street brewer, claimed £405 10s. 0d.; the Board offered him £50, which was declined; they raised their offer to £100, which was also declined; they both employed surveyors and an arbitrator was appointed; they finally settled at £196 10s. 0d. They were more successful with Mr. Lazareck of Aldershot, who owned hopfields in the District, in getting him to accept £92 against his claim of £400. Some people were more public-spirited–the Rev. Hoste waived his claim in respect of the Rectory; Samuel Bide (who had his eye on renting the sewage farm) went to great lengths to let the Board off with £2; Mr. Bateman claimed a nominal one shilling for several pieces of land, with a total of £1. Mr. Bateman's relationship with the Board since defeating them in the County Court was noticeably friendly and considerate, though his attitude over the site first proposed for the sewage farm had made it clear that he was still capable of protecting his interests.

In July 1887 Mr. Lemon reported that the Works were practically finished and, as the connections to sewer would soon start, advised the Board to set about framing regulations and drafting the necessary application forms and stationery for the purpose. He also pointed out that expenditure so far had exceeded his original estimate by over £1,000. In anticipation of more expenses to come, they decided upon a further loan of £2,000, but the Local Government Board gave leave to borrow £1,000 only and the rest later on if needs be. The October rate estimate, which increased the poundage to 2s., included an item of £393 repayment for the half-year on the £14,000 already borrowed.

At a Special Meeting on 19 July 1887, the Board proudly resolved 'that the first sewer to be brought into use for connections should be the low-level sewer extending from Babbs Mead to the Pumping Station'. It is fitting that the Board should have conferred on this particular sewer the honour of inaugurating the town's drainage. For this pipe ran through the meadows between the houses in the main street and the river, through the area of the erstwhile Bush and Gostrey Ditches and the no-man's-land of filthy open channels. Its course was parallel to the river and the twain would henceforth never meet again. Public notice inviting applications for connections was given and the regulations relating thereto:–

Public Health Act, 1875.
FARNHAM LOCAL BOARD
(Regulations relating to House Drains)

Every Owner or Occupier of any premises within the District who intends to cause his drains to empty into the Sewers of the Board shall sign (and give to the Surveyor) a notice undertaking and request, in the form hereunto annexed. Full information with Forms of Notice etc. may be obtained at the Surveyor's Office, East Street, Farnham.

Every drain and the branches thereof and all works and apparatus connected therewith as regards trapping, ventilation, size, level, fall, direction, form, materials and workmanship shall be made, laid and done to the satisfaction of the Surveyor of the Board.

No drain or any branches thereof or other connections therewith shall be covered in until they shall have been examined and approved by the Surveyor of the Board. No rain water (except with the consent in writing of the Board) shall be carried into the sewers.

In all cases where it shall be necessary to lay drains beneath the Public highway, the work will be done by the Board or their Contractors, at the expense of the applicant: the estimated cost to be deposited with the Surveyor prior to the works being commenced. In the event of the cost of the work being less than the deposit the balance will be returned, if more the extra cost will be charged to the applicant.

The soil from all existing cesspools must be removed and carted away and the cesspools then filled up with dry rubbish, preparatory to fixing the closet pans and traps, in such a manner as to provide a firm and solid foundation for the pan and trap.

(By order of the Board)
RICHARD MASON,
Clerk.

July 1887.

In January 1888, H.R.H. the Prince of Wales invited the Chairman (and also, no doubt, all the other Chairmen of Local Boards throughout the country) up to London for the forthcoming Jubilee. It was proposed that a public meeting should be held at the Town Hall on 16 February for the purpose of making local plans to celebrate the fiftieth year of the Queen's reign ... At the Election this year, Edward Barrett and William Higgins were replaced by Charles Austwick and Abraham Smith (he is described as builder of Long Garden Walk). William Simmonds came bottom with 103 votes ... Abraham Smith resigned as the town's dustman and Thomas Mitchell took on the job at 3s. 9d. per day 'for horse, cart and man' ... The Local Government Board asked what action the Board had taken on a Report by a Doctor Turner on the diphtheria epidemic. The Board looked but couldn't find it and asked for a copy. Whitehall wrote back stating that the Report in question had not yet been issued ... Major-General James Blair V.C. complained about the water supplied by the Water Company and also had another go about watering the road at Firgrove ... John Knight of Bentley had donated £100 to the Guildford Hospital with the request 'that Admission Papers be placed in the hands of the Chairman of the Farnham Local Board'; he was suitably thanked for his generous gift to the town.

An extensively signed memorial concerning 'a serious public nuisance, viz.–the frying of fish in The Borough'. There was nothing in the Offensive Trades Index about fish-frying and, indeed, the Courts had held that it was not an obnoxious trade, but Mr. Mason, evidently not a lover of fish and chips, hunted through the 1875 Act and found that it was possible to take steps to abate ... John Stevenson, Clerk of Works, resigned to go to Kensington Local Board and George Wareham, who had been Renshaw's man at the pumping station, was appointed at 22s. per week ... In July, the first crop grown on the sewage farm–barley–was sold to Samuel Bide for £20. They say to this day that vegetables grown at the farm tend to look like the pictures on the seed packets.

William Mason wrote on 22 August urgently requesting that his properties at 10–13 East Street be connected to the new sewer as the existing drains were in a dangerous situation; the Medical Officer confirmed this. The Board were not quite ready but agreed in the circumstances. These properties were thus probably the first in the town to go on main drainage and any claim to that distinction by the present owners would be unlikely to be challenged. Two weeks later, Mr. Lemon advised that, as connections had now started, care should be exercised in having the sewers properly flushed and water turned on at the flushing chambers.

They were only just in time; Mr. Bateman had become impatient again. Messrs. Potter & Crundwell wrote on his behalf asking 'how soon the Sewage Works would remove the sewage from the River and that Mr. Bateman was losing patience at the delay in complying with the Order made by the County Court'. The Surveyor pointed out that he was doing his best to cope but could not possibly deal with all the applications made, so a bigger team was taken on and a Mr. William Hockey to act as Mr. Hankins co-supervisor. In September, the Board started talking about their powers under section 23 of the 1875 Act to compel connections within three months of notice being served—it wasn't just the cost of the pipes, there was also the expense of the necessary furniture. The response of the townspeople was good and, apart from those who were saving up for it, the drains by December of 1887 were in full operation.

We know this because William Simmonds complained of the smell from next-door. So did his kinswoman, Mrs. Simmonds of Rock Cottage. Mr. Lemon investigated and found that they were right—there was a smell. A lot of the blame for it fell on Samuel Bide—who was now in occupation of the land; one gathers that his way of handling the providential source of fertiliser was open to improvement. Defects were also found in the sewerage equipment. All these matters were corrected as far as possible, though the smell from the sewage farm was to become a feature of Farnham, according to which way the wind blew. At an initial cost of over £15,000 smells had been transferred from just behind the *Bush Hotel,* from Moor Park and numerous other insalubrious zones and, with the added perfumes of lime, carbolic acid and other chemicals, concentrated all in one big stink on 12 acres of land behind Bourne Mill.

Consequent upon the dismissal of Mr. Trimm in June 1887, the Board became involved in a suit at the hands of Trimm's solicitors, Messrs. Bircham & Company of Parliament Street, London. By some strange circumstance, Birchams were also solicitors for the

London & South-western Railway Company and thus no strangers–indeed they were by way of being old sparring partners. Mr. Samuel Bircham was an able practitioner of the Law who enjoyed the cut and thrust of litigation and the case of Trimm *v.* Farnham Local Board was to provide him with enjoyment over the next eighteen months or so. On behalf of Trimm, he claimed the sum of £4,067 being remuneration due to his client for work done over and above the terms of his Contract with the Board. In view of the large amount involved, Mr. Bircham recommended that the matter should be referred to arbitration. Mr. Lemon, whilst commenting that, purely from the legal angle on which the case rested, the Board's position could be 'tricky', added that he 'knew Master Bircham' and advised them to fight the case.

Mr. James Mansergh C.E. was appointed as Arbitrator and the Board set about preparing their brief, containing a full and detailed account of Trimm's work, the depositions of Mr. Lemon, Mr. Forder and Mr. Stevenson, together with copies of all correspondence, which was anything but brief. The Trimm Reference was fixed for 5 and 6 April 1888 and all the papers were forwarded to the Board's Counsel in readiness. It was the Board who got cold feet first; in March they sought a compromise with Birchams, who replied that they could not advise their client to accept anything less than £2,750. The Board declined, so Birchams climbed down to £2,000. Encouraged by this, the Board made a firm offer of £1,250. Birchams' agents on the spot, Messrs. Knight, Saunders & Kempson, made a bid of £1,530 all in; still further encouraged, the Board stuck to their offer of £1,250. The hearing took place before Mr. Mansergh, who awarded £1,724 19s. 10d.

Then complaints began coming in from various parts of the town about smells issuing from the manholes. Mr. Lemon advised the Board to seal off the offending covers and erect ventilating shafts instead. These shafts, of 4-inch iron pipes costing 1s. 3d. per yard, raised the smells above nose level. In July 1888, the Board faced facts and published a statement of accounts so far:–

Renshaws' Contract		£1158 0 0	
	Extra Works	116 7 11	
	New Mortice Wheel	27 8 0	£1301 15 11

R.C. Trimm:	Paid to date	8996 0 0	
	Balance at termination of Contract	405 2 0	
	Arbitrator's Award	1724 19 10	
	Board's Costs	414 0 0	11540 1 10
Compensations to Owners of Land		393 7 3	
	Pending claim	400 0 0	793 7 3
Clerks of Works			433 10 0
Land:	Purchases	2460 0 0	
	Law Costs	181 11 2	
	Fences	63 9 6	2705 0 8
Engineer:	Fees	561 0 0	
	Travelling Expenses etc.	189 0 0	750 0 0
Sundries			50 0 0
Flushing Chambers, Vents (estimated)			250 0 0
			£17823 15 8

So far, a total of £15,000 had been borrowed, so they applied for an additional £3,000, which the Local Government Board pared down to £2,850.

The Lighting Committee reported jubilantly in February 1888 how clever they had been in wringing new terms from the Gas Company a year previously. The bill for street-lighting over the past year had dropped by £70 18s. 7d.—or 15s. 11d. per lamp, the cost of lighting the 89 lamps being £285. 1s. 5d. instead of £356 (or £3 4s. 0¾d. per lamp instead of £4). This was really something to boast about, though they should have kept quiet about it for the Gas Company, on being asked to renew the Contract on the same terms, found that they were unable to continue the discount of £20 5s. 11d., and also that additional meters were necessary. A minor scuffle ensued which the Company, as usual, won.

Superintendent of the Fire Brigade Edwards retired and G.F. Elliott took his place. Permission was granted to take the engine to Alton and Aldershot for demonstrations. Fire engines remained a source of fascination to the public until the County Council took them over, which suggests that the fascination lay not so much in the engines as in the crews that manned them ... Major-General James Blair V.C. finally got the Board round to watering the road outside his house. In keeping with its reputation, Firgrove sheltered yet another person of fame. James Blair was born on 27 January 1828. He joined the Bengal Cavalry in 1844, was made a

Captain in 1857 and was twice wounded during the Indian Mutiny of that year and the next. He was promoted Major in 1864, Lt. Colonel in 1870, Colonel 1875, Brigadier 1882, Major-General 1885, Lt. General with C.B.E. 1889 and General in 1894. He died, aged 77, on 14 January 1905 at Melrose in his native Scotland. Before coming to Farnham he was Political Resident in Aden from 1882 to 1885. The citation ran:

> Having on two occasions distinguished himself by gallant and daring conduct–Firstly on 12th August 1857 at Neemuch in volunteering to apprehend seven or eight mutineers who had shut themselves up in a house, the door of which he burst open, and forced them to escape through the roof, and, in spite of being severely wounded, pursued them but was unable to come up with them in the darkness. Secondly on 23rd October 1857 at Jeerum, in fighting his way most gallantly through a body of rebels who surrounded him. After breaking the end of his sword on one of their heads and receiving a severe cut on his arm, he rejoined his troops. In this wounded condition, and with no other weapon than the butt of his sword, he put himself at the head of his men and charged the rebels most efficiently and dispersed them.

At the 1888 Election, Edward Barrett regained his seat and Samuel Bide became a member. William Kingham was defeated ... A public enquiry was held at the Town Hall on 11 May in connection with the Boundary Commissioners' proposal to sever Aldershot from the Farnham Union area–an unpopular move, but better than transferring the lot to Aldershot.

Then a row developed over who should have the £1,794 19s. 0d. Award money, which Mr. Mansergh had directed should be paid to Mr. Trimm or to his Trustee in Bankruptcy, a Mr. Francis William Pixley. A third contestant had now entered the field in the person of Mr. Farley, an Assignee of Trimm's Contract. Each gave the Board notice not to release the money to the others. The Board had the money ready and all they wanted was a receipt for it–but only from the person legally entitled to it, for to part with the money to the wrong person and then be confronted by the rightful recipient could cause complications. As Mr. Lemon would have put it, the situation was 'tricky'.

The months went by with the four of them playing holding the hot brick in reverse. At one stage the astute Mr. Bircham threatened the Board with interest charges for the delay in handing over the money to his client but this, as Mr. Lemon would have put it, was 'just trying it on'. At a later stage in the proceedings, Mr. Mason summed the whole thing up–in a sentence—and wrote it all down in the Minute-book:—

> The Clerk having read a letter from Messrs Bircham & Co under date 31st October with reference to the payment of the amount awarded in the Trimm Arbitration and enclosing a copy of a letter from Messrs Saunders & Co, the Solicitors representing Mr. Pixley, the Trustee in Trimm's Bankruptcy, which stated that the Committee in the Bankruptcy proceedings had resolved that the Trustee should release the money awarded in favour of Mr. Farley and inquiring whether if they (Messrs Bircham & Co) produced the three authorities of Mr. Pixley, Mr. Trimm and Mr. Farley the Board would then be prepared to pay the money, and the Clerk having explained that from Messrs Bircham & Co's previous letters he looked upon the interest question as virtually settled, but that by adopting the course suggested by Messrs Bircham & Co's letter the Board would obtain the receipt of Messrs Bircham & Co only for the money, which as the Award gave specific directions for the payment to Mr. Pixley (who was a Trustee in Bankruptcy and could not in his, the Clerk's, opinion delegate his duties) he did not think would be sufficient to discharge the Board of liability under the Award and suggested the receipt of Mr. Pixley, countersigned by Messrs Trimm and Farley together with an authority to pay to Messrs Bircham & Co, signed and countersigned in a similar manner should be required by the Board before they paid the money over, a discussion ensued ...

Maybe—somewhere or other—Mr. Trimm, Mr. Pixley and Mr. Farley, like Goldsmith's village parson, are still arguing it out.

XVII

BIG BROTHER IS BORN

THE LOCAL Government Act, 1888, by creating County Councils, presented if not a threat to the sovereignty of the Local Boards then at least a potential rival in the field of local government. One moreover that, because of its greater administrative area, arrived with a status altogether higher than that of a mere District Authority. The attitude of the 23 year-old Boards towards this upstart in the early part of 1889 was much the same as that of a cat cursing its luck in a silent sulk upon being confronted on its home beat by a stray tom of more powerful physique. And although over the years some sort of *modus vivendi* has been hammered out, the undercurrent of resentment has remained–possibly not escaping the notice of Lord Redcliffe-Maud some eighty years later–notwithstanding the post-prandial compliments paid at successive Venison Dinners in Farnham and civic binges elsewhere.

It is true that County Councils were formed for the purpose of taking over those various services hitherto administered by the Justices or by unco-ordinated bodies vaguely referred to as 'the County authorities', which in the eyes of the Local Boards ranked little higher than a parish council. One of these bodies indeed reimbursed the Farnham Board with the expense of maintaining the main roads in their District. Perhaps it was the impact of Section 3 of the Act, which transferred to the new County Council the actual responsibility for such roads, that led the Board to fear other infringements of their copyright. One can sense a reaction at their meeting on the 2 April 1889 at which the Clerk presented his rate estimate for the ensuing half-year. Mr. Mason pointed out that he had as usual included the cost of main roads and sought the Members' instructions. Without so much as referring to the new County Council, it was resolved that, since main roads had ceased to be a local responsibility as from 1 April, the item should be expunged from the estimate.

At the Annual General Meeting on 10 April the Board considered a proposal from the County Council that the Local Board should continue to repair the main roads for a period of three years, thus giving County time to get established. Under the proposed contract, payment to be made to the Board would be based on the yearly average of the expenses incurred on main roads during the three years ended 25 March 1888, plus 5 per cent for establishment charges, which, said County, worked out at £289 per annum in Farnham. The Board had not been in business twenty-three years without learning a trick or two; they pointed out to the County Council that, during the year ended March 1886, little money had been spent on the roads owing to their having been broken up for the purpose of laying the sewers and that a more realistic figure should be adopted, such as the average of the three years ended March 1889, which worked out at £352 per annum. They also took the opportunity of slipping South Street, Castle Street and Downing Street into the schedule of main roads. First honours thus went to the Resident Cat.

It is the tendency in these situations to pity the underdog–or cat–and to condemn the intruder without a trial, especially if it happens to be on the big side. If one looks more closely into the circumstances leading up to the intrusion, one sometimes finds that these are unaccompanied by any wish on the newcomer's part to impose authority; indeed the visiting side is often more the sufferer than the home team, which has the crowd behind it. The Provisional Surrey County Council sensed the hostility of the natives even before it took office. There was trouble, for instance, over where County Headquarters should be set up. The Board of Guardians resolved that the place selected for the meetings of the County Council 'should be the administrative County of Surrey and that no portion of the public funds of the County should be expended on any place of meeting which is not within those limits'. The Local Board endorsed these feelings and went further in recommending that the County Offices should be in Guildford. Although the County Council, for reasons of their own, chose to be within the Metropolitan fringe of the County–and were to end their days outside Surrey altogether, Guildford's right to County Township has never been challenged in consequence; on the contrary and through no conscious effort it has grown even closer to the hearts of Surrey towns.

The Provisional County Council came bearing gifts. On 19 March they announced that they had delegated to Urban and Rural Sanitary Authorities as from April 1889 the granting of theatre licenses and also powers and duties under the Contagious Diseases (Animals) Act, 1878. Small presents, but it cannot be denied that the intruder was trying to be friendly.

. . . . .

In November 1888 the good relations between the Board and Mr. James Lemon were somewhat marred over an item in his final accounts of £119 9s. 2d. for his part in the Trimm Arbitration. It was held by the Board that much of the matter in the dispute had been caused by an error in Mr. Lemon's plans for the receiving tank at the sewage farm. On the other hand he had not charged his 5 per cent commission on the amount of the Award itself. The Clerk wrote to Lemon pointing out 'that part of the expenses which they were driven to incur in connection with the Trimm Arbitration was solely through some of his plans (and notably those relating to the Receiving Tanks) proving quite unfit for their purpose, they considered he should certainly modify his accounts'. Mr. Lemon attended the meeting on 1 January 1889 to plead his cause and as a result only a matter of £8 was deducted from the bill.

The 1889 Election saw William Kingham back on the Board, with a newcomer, John Stovold, grocer in The Borough; Dr. Lorimer stood down ... The Board took their new duty of granting theatre licenses very seriously. There was only one theatre in the town and that was the Corn Exchange, which was the inner big hall of the Town Hall. The Town Hall Company, whose Secretary was John Thorp, the Rate Collector, were informed that licences would only be granted on the condition that adequate means of emergency exit were provided. A clause was written into the Rules that 'all outer gates and doors during the hours of public performance shall stand opened and fastened back with chain and lock and all inner doors shall be made to open outwards'. The subdued manner in which this edict and others were accepted by the Company made up for a lot of the indignities suffered at the hands of that Company over the past ... The Board also appointed a Mr. C.W. Marshall as Inspector under the Contagious Diseases (Animals) Act. The animal population, in the days before horseless carriages and imported meat carcasses, was considerable ... A new water hydrant was installed for the convenience of the Fire Brigade in West Street by the entrance to Fenns Mineral Water Factory ... A new phrase makes its appearance in the Minute-book–'W.C.'

Mr. Wells of the Water Company complained that he had not been given notice of the use of water from the main by the Fire Brigade in order to extinguish a fire at Chuter & Green's premises in The Borough. The Brigade Officers were directed to acquaint the Water Company's Manager in future 'as soon as possible' ... In July a Member raised the question of the 'June Pleasure Fair, which no longer served any purpose and which was an abomination that ought to be abolished'. Mr. Mason explained the complicated process by which this might be achieved through the Magistrates Court under the Fairs Act of 1871, but advised the Board to await the publication of a Bill now before Parliament which would transfer powers to the County Council ... More smells from the sewage farm and suggestions offered to Member Samuel Bide that the sewage be more equally distributed over the whole of the farm ... Mr. Hankins was granted leave of absence to take a fortnight's holiday; the Englishman's annual seaside holiday was emerging.

In September they considered a numerously signed memorial complaining about the dustman. A dustman is one of the recognised whipping-boys of the local authority. His terms of reference were rendered down to an exact science by Section 42 of the Local Government Act, 1875, together with subsequent case-law. This defines 'House Refuse' as:

> Dirt, ashes, clinkers, rubbish, filth, sawdust, empty bottles and tins, straw, packing cases, tea leaves, coffee grounds, waste paper, egg shells, lemon peel, dust

> from rooms and staircases, newspaper, cabbage leaves, broken crockery, potato parings, scrapings from the sink, etc.

whereas

> Tots–e.g. broken white glass, bones, metal articles and knife handles, also 'ashes arising from coals burnt in the furnace of a steam engine used for the purpose of sawing and lifting timber and other materials for carrying on the business of a pianoforte manufacturer'

came within the range of 'Trade Refuse', which the dustman had the right to reject in the absence of special arrangements for removal. The definition of 'House' in Section 4 of the 1875 Act, moreover, was not to be read into Section 42, and premises might be a 'House' within the definition and yet their refuse might not be 'House Refuse' for the purpose of Section 42. One can see that Thomas Mitchell's man, going round Farnham with his horse and cart, watching the windows for D signs, was clearly a man with legal problems on his mind.

Also at the September 1889 meeting a decision to have the street-lamps lit on all nights of the year, for recently during a three-night full moon period clouds had gathered and the town was in total darkness throughout the night ... A report by the Surveyor that he had 'seized several pieces of Ostend Rabbit exposed for sale in the Market and which were unfit for human food and had taken same before a Magistrate who had condemned them'. The Board gave instructions for proceedings to be taken against the travelling provision merchant–one Silburn ... A letter from John Knight on behalf of his nephew, Mr. Bethune, asking permission to replace some trees in front of Vernon House, to which the Board agreed provided that the young trees were planted in the precise sites of the old ones and caused no additional obstruction to the public way ... More smells from the farm and Samuel Bide, who was absent from the meeting, written to in strong terms to 'endeavour to so work the land as to prevent any recurrence of the nuisance complained of'.

The Board were now serving Notices enforcing connections to the sewers. The difficulty was that in some cases it was a long way to the nearest sewer. James Knight, for instance, grumbled about having to bear the cost of 30 feet of piping for his houses at the *Six Bells* and 98 feet from his property in Bridge Square (the *Bridge House Inn*). The Board pointed out that 30 feet was nothing but extended their sewer in Bridge Square. The odd thing is that the Board, in July 1887, had minuted a resolution that they would be responsible for pipes as far as the boundaries of properties, a point which apparently escaped everybody's attention.

Among the pet aversions of the Board, as we have seen, the Fairs in Castle Street ranked high, the more so because the Board had little say in the matter since the Fairs were held on private land. Whilst Castle Street had not yet achieved the honour of being acclaimed the finest street in the south of England, it had started to attract a fashionable type of resident and its days of serving as Farnham's Petticoat Lane and Tin Pan Alley were numbered. The removal of the Fairs, and of a Mr. Matthews in particular, would accelerate the process. Mr. Matthews was the proprietor of a steam roundabout equipped with a steam organ. This would have been the equivalent of the electric roundabout, with an electric organ, of our childhood days, with the added fascination—and noise—of belching forth steam. The Board did not like Mr. Matthews and told the Town Hall Company so. The Company for once agreed and gave Mr. Matthews notice that they would not allow him to stand on their ground at the Fair to be held in November. On 3 December the Surveyor reported that, in company with Mr. Mason's clerk, he had attended the Fair and warned Mr. Matthews against playing his steam organ; but that such warning had been disregarded. With a little imagination one can picture this scene, set against a colossus that belched forth steam and 19 century pop music. Rather meekly the Board took no action, deciding that it was a matter that should be taken up by the inhabitants of the town—who probably liked it anyway.

A white canvas suit was supplied to the man engaged in cleaning out the sewer manholes ... Samuel Bide assured his fellow Members that he had done his best to work the farm without causing a nuisance, but the trouble was that the sewage was pumped onto the land on Sundays when his men were not there to dig it in ... The Local Government Board urged the Board to extend their system of refuse collection to include 'the contents of all filth receptacles', but the Board insisted that this was the responsibility of the householders concerned ... Plans for an 'Iron Office' in South Street; the hodge-podge of unrelated architecture in that street was well advanced.

On 7 January 1890, the Board joined the Epsom Board of Guardians in a protest against the County Council's appointment of a Medical Officer for the County at a—then fantastic—salary of £800 a year plus expenses ... A circular was read concerning the housing of the labouring classes under the Housing of the Working Classes Act, 1890, but Farnham's first Council Houses were not to come until 1902, when those in Adams Park Road were built ... Plans by John Griffith, chemist at 24 The Borough, for the rebuilding of his premises; these were set back 9 inches. Mr. James Alfred Eggar, architect of 10 West Street and founder of the present firm of Estate Agents, acted for him.

In February the Chairman submitted a letter received from a Mr. Stachelschier, calling attention 'to a system of giving commissions to the Board's Engineer and others by Bell's Asbestos Company and that the Director of the Company, having discovered that an Act against Bribery had become law, had instructed his representatives to visit all persons to whom commissions had been paid after the Act came into force and give them receipts to shew that the commissions had been repaid'.

Also at the February meeting was discussed one of the town's big fires, which had broken out on 30 January at the Stay Factory in Ivy Lane. The Board recorded their thanks to the Brigade for their valuable services in confining the blaze to the factory premises, apart from some slight damage to the nearby Conservative Club. Mr. Elliott, the Superintendent, took the opportunity to wheedle some more equipment. The fire so badly damaged the factory that the Board later served notice on the owner either to secure it or pull it down.

In April, George Heath, coachbuilder of South Street and co-founder of Heath & Wiltshire's Garage in later years, was elected to the Board in place of John Nash who had resigned owing to ill-health.

A final round-up was now being made of houses not yet connected to sewer, and Notices served on the owners. In some cases, the Board carried out the work and sent in the bill. You can take a horse to the trough but you can't make it drink. A fresh source of infectious diseases had arisen through the failure of several householders, though connected to sewer, to instal flushing apparatus in their water-closets. The Board viewed the Medical

Officer's reports with alarm and ordered the Surveyor to make inspections and bring to their notice all cases of inadequate flushing.

All through the summer of 1890 the Board struggled against a tide of petty offences. Their preoccupation with the drainage project over the past three years or so had to a large extent resulted in a relaxation of their policing of the District and the knaves of the town took full advantage of the situation. Perhaps the most useful service administered by a local authority during the past century has been the enforcement of bye-laws, until in the end the people got the message.

XVIII

NOR YET A DROP TO DRINK

ABOUT WATER. All that the theorists of Westminster wanted of the Suppliers, and they spelled it out loud and clear, was:—

> to see that every occupied dwelling house within their district has within a reasonable distance an available supply of wholesome water sufficient for the consumption and use for domestic purposes of the inmates of the house

But there is often a wide gap between theory and practice and the application of a law, bedevilled as it is by public apathy and sales resistance, is a much more complicated procedure than its drafting. Sometimes this can lead to a danger to health. Water from contaminated wells had long been a problem for the Local Board and since the 1875 Act they had put pressure on the Water Company to extend their mains. Now the Company's water itself came under suspicion. In response to a memorial signed by residents in South Street and Union Road, samples of water were taken from the mains and sent to the County Analyst. Doctor Stevenson's report, which was accorded an Extraordinary Meeting on 26 August 1890, ran:

> the waters were turbid and unsightly and insufficient care had been taken either in the collection or distribution of the water supply after clarification. Satisfactory degree of freedom from organic impurities; might be used with safety for domestic purposes but could not be considered satisfactory town supplies

This the Water Company watered down by regretting that the water 'had been somewhat discoloured of late' and they were taking steps to prevent this in the future.

The unappetising appearance of Farnham's water was by no means exclusive to Victoria's reign. It persisted as late as the 1930s when on occasions a brown rusty-looking fluid used to issue forth from the taps which, although not injurious to health, was enough to cause one to think again about using it for any other purpose than watering the garden—and even then one didn't fancy the cabbages.

Another matter that perturbed the Board was the failure on the part of many householders to pipe water to the closet and thus convert it into a water-closet—a purpose for which the brackish water would have been ideal. This reluctance to pull the chain made nonsense of the costly provision of sewers and the householders' enforced and expensive connection thereto. A bucket of water was the usual alternative, and indeed canpails were recognised by the Local Government Board in London; in some cases they used to ram it down with a stick. The consequent illnesses were a complication unforeseen by the theorists on drainage systems.

It irritated the Board, and they got tough. They had just passed through a period of hardening up and were now a more mature government. Also the growing practice of Whitehall of interfering in local affairs, together with Big Brother, now up at Kingston, had put the Board on their mettle. In course of time they established locally an absolute authority which they could then afford to temper with indulgence.

With no big undertaking currently on the slate they decided to return to the repaving of the iron-stone pitched footways with Victoria Stone or blue bricks, which they had started back in 1882 with the north side of East Street. Bricks were chosen for the south side of East Street from Mr. Dolley's to the *Royal Deer,* West Street from Babbs Mead to the end, Downing Street and Longbridge, and Abbey Street as far as the *Railway Arms.* In places stretches of this blue bricked pavement remain—as easy to walk on as the *grachts* of Amsterdam and safe from the sole-destroying edges of flagstones. For the Golden Mile, and Castle Street, from Ransom's corner to Babbs Mead and Bentall's corner to Mr. Barnett's house, Victoria Stone at double the price was adopted. Total estimated cost, £2,317. There was a row about it.

Wareham, the engine driver at the pumping station, got the sack for carelessness; the last straw was when he let the safety plug blow out of one of the boilers. A Mr. A. Diplock was appointed in his place at 24s. a week ... Mrs. Nash was refused financial help towards the cost of £119 11s. 3d. for connecting her cottage in Church Passage to the sewer–a distance of 209 feet ... A fatal case of diphtheria in South View and outbreaks in the Waverley Estate, where tubs of offal were discovered in a field ... Plans for a new Institute in South Street (now the Central Club) ... A deputation of townspeople attended the October 1890 meeting to campaign for an improvement in the accommodation at the railway station for passengers and goods, 'great inconvenience and danger arising from the insufficiency of the present accommodation' ... An application from Balfour & Company to affix automatic delivery machines at suitable places in the town for the sale of postage stamps etc.

In 1890 Sir William Rose, Bart, bought Moor Park. Sir William (1846–1902), second baronet, was head of Govett, Sons & Company of the Stock Exchange. During the reign of Victoria there were no less than four owners of Moor Park–Charles Basil Bacon, of Sir William Temple's family, until 1858, John Frederick la Trobe Bateman from 1858 to 1890, Sir William Rose from 1890 to 1899 and, from 1899, Mrs. Hannah Johnston-Foster. In each case relations with the local authority were marred by incidents and the Local Board may be excused for adopting a wary attitude when Sir William Rose wrote on 6 October 1890 requesting permission to erect a signpost at the junction of the roads to Guildford and Moor Park just by the Bourne Mill, and inscribed GUILDFORD and MOOR PARK ONLY. There was a catch about this somewhere, so the Board played for time to think it over, sending Mr. Hankins along on the pretext of ascertaining the exact position of the post–and anything else he could find out.

The narrow road through the Park, from the entrance off Guildford Road to Waverley by Stella's Cottage, was a public right of way. There was also a perfectly good highway from the town to Waverley, but that was neither here nor there–a public footpath was sacrosanct. The annoying feature about this one, from the Squire's point of view, was the public's point of view. The road passed right up close to the mansion in the middle of the Park. It was worst at weekends, when an almost continuous procession of local bumpkins dressed in their Sunday best filed by, pausing on their way and gawking in. One cannot stifle a feeling of sympathy towards Sir William Rose, even though the closure of Moor Park would have robbed Farnham of one of its more glorious amenities. The addition of the word 'only' on the indication board had a sinister significance which the Board interpreted as a move to discourage this established Sunday recreation of the townspeople and they agreed to the signpost only on condition that the word was deleted.

Whatever success he enjoyed on the Exchange, and this must have been considerable, Sir William Rose discovered that in this Surrey stockbrokers' belt he just couldn't put a foot right. For the Surveyor, when visiting the locus, caught him out building a lodge without having submitted plans. Sir William pleaded ignorance of the bye-laws and got his architect, Mr. Watson, to see to it. This was presumably Paxton Watson, a local architect of some renown who had taken up where Wonnacott left off. He should have known better.

On 29 October 1890, Thomas Mitchell determined his contract for refuse collection and the Board decided to take the job on themselves for a trial period of one month. Ashes were to be carted to the pumping station and the cinders used on the boiler fires; other rubbish was to be sold. It cannot be denied that the Board were thrifty ... The Local Government Board called a public meeting over the proposed expenditure on repaving the footways for 13 November. The Clerk told Members that 'he had been convinced that that date would prove inconvenient to almost every person involved' (he did not give the reason—unless it had something to do with the date), so he had got the L.G.B. to make it the 14th ... The Allotments Act, 1890, which gave Boards the power of 'providing small plots of land for the working classes so as to enable them to indulge in the profitable recreation or industry of horticulture' (one never thinks of it in that light), was discussed and adjourned in the usual manner.

They joined the national Local Boards Association, at an annual subscription of one guinea, in return for which they received the Association's monthly circular, an exchange of know-how between Boards that, in those days of poor communications, must have been invaluable. During the next eighty years the number of associations covering almost all aspects of local government—there is as yet no association for the Associations–has grown to an absurd proportion. Much as the swopping of ideas is desirable, and three days at the seaside not to be sneezed at by conference delegates, the whole thing has got rather out of hand.

In an attempt to reduce the smells that arose from the sewers, ventilation shafts were going up all over the town. The difficulty lay in getting people in the vicinity to agree to having them. The South View Smell was taken care of by a shaft up a tree in the nearby Farnham Park. The Bishop of Winchester assured the Board that he and the Bishop of Rochester had no objection provided the shaft was painted an indistinguishable colour. There was currently an interchange of Bishops with the See of Rochester–it did not necessarily mean that the South View Smell had reached Rochester.

The Rural Highways Board tried to get the Local Board interested in an improvement scheme costing £500 for Farnham Lane, offering to find one-third of the money and hoping the Board would contribute the rest. As only a few yards of the road were within the Board's District, the invitation was declined. Farnham Lane was developed during the nineties by George Robins and others and later renamed Firgrove Hill. It ran through the middle of the former Firgrove Estate, now the property of the son of the late Rev. E.J. Ward, John Martyr Ward, who was cashing in on his inheritance. The whole of the area rising from the valley on the south side of the town was about equally divided by the road to Tilford between the two great estates of Firgrove and Waverley. The former was the first to fall to the builders and in the next twenty years or so doubled the size of the town. Waverley followed in the 1930s and brought the population up to the twenty thousand mark.

For some time that progressive member, Samuel Bide, had been campaigning for a steam road roller. Amongst the accoutrements of a local authority the steamroller has a very special place. It is, in fact, an object of beauty, discovered in later years by artists who associate beauty with attractiveness. The Board's horse roller was considered out of date and it was decided to sell it, for not less than £30. Whereupon Mr. Bide repeated his proposal for a steamroller and they had a special meeting on 16 December to consider it. In the end, the horse was retained. Horses continued to serve the town until the early 1930s; there was a horse named Drummer that never failed to capture an audience from the nearby office windows when, its driver having unharnessed it at the end of the day's work, it found its own way across the depot yard to its stable door.

The Christmas of 1890 was white. At a special meeting on 22 December it was resolved 'that where practicable the snow be cleared from the streets of the Town' ... On 6 January 1891, it was announced that, after a long fight with the Local Government Board over who did what with the footways in the County Council's main roads, the Board were sanctioned a loan of £2,131 for their repaving project. Richard Chamberlain of Farnham won the contract and began the work of tearing up the iron-stone ... Colonel Edward Barrett, who had sold the Red Lion Brewery to George Trimmer, to form the Farnham United Brewery, had moved from The Fairfield to beyond the limit set by the Public Health Act, 1875, and thus forfeited his seat on the Board ... Plans were made for additions to Guildford House, Castle Hill–that much messed about with, and later restored residence.

In March 1891, a circular from the Surrey County Council concerning the provision of Technical Education in the District was greeted with an enthusiasm not usually apparent in the Board's reception of new-fangled ideas, and due possibly to the fact that with it came promises of a grant from County to finance any reasonable scheme the town might care to submit. A local committee was formed consisting of six members of the Board together with Charles Stroud, Headmaster of the Grammar School, R.W. Mason for the School of Art, Admiral Sir T. Brandreth for the National Schools, W.T. Simmonds of the British School, Robert D. Kingham representing the Farnham Institute and E. Jackson the Working Men's Institute. They built a laboratory at the rear of the Grammar School.

There was an argument over the building line of Potter & Crundwell's new offices in South Street, which were finally built level with the next-door Institute. Why these two buildings stick out in relation to other properties on this side of the street is a secret that died with the Local Board ... Samuel Bide topped the 1891 Election; a newcomer, in the place of Edward Barrett, was Surgeon-Major William Henry Hayes of The Fairfield. Unsuccessful candidates were Ernest Crundwell and Edgar Kempson, solicitors, and Charles Smith, saddler and corn-dealer of 72 Castle Street. Mr. Trimmer thanked the Board for having chosen him as Chairman for the past eleven years but preferred not to act again—he was then 67 and his lifetime of public service to the town was drawing to its close. The Chairmanship went to Daniel Goddard, the builder of East Street.

The Medical Officer's report for May included three fatal cases of diphtheria in Castle View and two in Guildford Road—not a bad bag for one month. It led to rumblings from Whitehall and to the adoption of the Infectious Diseases (Notification) Act, 1889, which provided for the notification to the Medical Officer by the head of a family or nearest relative where an inmate of any dwelling was suffering from an infectious disease. The M.O. then took all necessary action to isolate the diseased person and carriers ... The Bishop of Winchester decided to change the drainage system at the Castle, carrying all drains into the town sewer, and made formal application to the Board to extend their sewer to within the statutory 100 feet of the castle, which Henry Patrick did for £20 15s. 0d. This was not a cottage in Church Passage.

Mr. Crundwell, as Clerk to the Board of Guardians, suggested a public mortuary for Farnham; they certainly needed one .. Mr. Bide presented a large quantity of trees for landscaping the sewage farm; in return the Board expressed their satisfaction with the way in which the smells at the farm were being kept down .. In June the Surveyor was instructed to make house-to-house inspections and report all inadequate flushing devices in closet and water supplies generally ... A fresh source of nuisance wa checked, that of people carting gas lime through the streets from the Gas Company in East Street.

Mrs. Hankins wrote that her husband had 'flu and that he ha arranged for Henry Patrick to act as Surveyor *pro tem.* Hankin had fallen foul of a Mr. Higgins in East Street, who had refuse him access for the purpose of checking drainage; Mr. Higgins ha used threatening language. In reply to a letter from the Clerk, h stated that he was 'quite willing to admit any gentleman the Boar might appoint to inspect his connection with the sewer, but nc Mr. Hankins' ... A letter dated 29 June was acknowledged, an stored away for future reference perhaps, from the Secretary of the Provincial Electric Light and Power Supply Limited, giving notice of their intention to apply in due course for a Provisional Order to authorise them to supply electricity within the area of the District of the Local Board. Electricity for public lighting had been experimental since 1882 and subsequent legislation had brought it closer.

Plans in August for Colonel Marsden's new house in Castle Hill, replacing the old one which stuck out like a sore thumb in front of the Castle in any view up Castle Street ... The Board complained to their landlords about the defective lighting and ventilation of the Board Room at the Town Hall ... Mr. Nichols, the Postmaster, wrote pointing out 'the saving of time which would be effected in the delivery of letters if everyone had a letterbox affixed to their premises' and asking the Board help ... The County Council urged the Board to join the Rural Authority in providing an Isolation Hospital. The Local Government Board joined in. The Rural people stated that they had limited powers to compel persons to use hospitals and in any case had the use of the ward at the Workhouse, so the Board declared that they could not bear the expense alone.

The Surveyor's report in December 1891 included an item about ten cottages in Bridge Square with two water-closets between them and the owner was told to provide an additional three closets. In time the number of little sheds at the bottom of the gardens was to grow to one per cottage ... In January the Medical Officer reported that his attention had been drawn to a cottage in South Street in the occupation of one Henry Hopkins, which from the lack of a proper water supply and drainage, he did not think anyone would consider fit for human habitation. The property, which made first column news in the January minutes, belonged to George Trimmer, who was present at the meeting and promised that the cottage would be put in a fit state. He also stated that 'it was not correct to say there was no water supply because the property was bounded by the river on one side'.

The house of every one is to him as his castle and fortress, as well for his defence against injury and violence as for his repose.

Sir Edward Coke

XIX

A PICTURE OF RUDE HEALTH

BENEATH THE gay veneer of the nineties lurked a number of the ills the flesh is heir to. The governments of the day, both central and local, whilst not unconscious of the charms of Marie Lloyd, were gravely concerned with the frightening increase in infectious and epidemic diseases sweeping the country, and the available means of eliminating them. The successive Public Health Acts and a plethora of related legislation had introduced wide powers of intrusion into the private lives of the people for the purpose of cleaning them up. For it is in the nature of people to be dirty and left to themselves the human race would perish, as it very nearly has on more than one occasion.

Progress was slow; indeed in the early 1890s it almost seemed as if the local authorities, in their efforts to apply the Health Acts, were fighting a losing battle. They were fighting with inferior weapons. Their pipe-dreams of two essentials for good health, piping in wholesome water and piping out waste matter, were far from being a reality in each and every home. They were only in the toying stage with the idea of providing isolation hospitals. They had efficient, but overworked, cemeteries, but at the other end of the pipeline it seemed rather impudent to exercise the right to enter an Englishman's castle to whitewash and disinfect it with the object of tackling disease at its source. Illnesses which beset Farnham at this time—the Medical Officer produced a long list of them each month—included Diphtheria, Typhoid, Scarlatina, Erysipelas, Scarlet Fever, Smallpox and Croup; there was even a Cholera scare.

In February 1892 the Charity Commissioners invited the views of the Local Board on the formation of a Board of Governors for the future administration of the Grammar School. Most of them being old boys, the Board put themselves at the top with three, with two from the County Council, two from the Rural Authority and one nominated by the Bishop. Whereupon it was pointed out that as the Local Board had played no part in the endowment of the School, it was only by courtesy that they were represented at all. Their share was cut to two and the County Council's increased to four. The final recommendations had to go for approval to Her Majesty in Council.

The County Council renewed the contract for the upkeep of main roads for a period of two years at £539 per annum, an increase of £187. The Board, wondering what to do with this unexpected windfall, decided to use Victoria Stone at 5s. 3d. per yard, instead of bricks, for the footway on the south side of East Street. There was in addition a grant from County of £500 towards the cost of repaving the main road footways and the Board could not believe their luck.

The residents in the new Waverley Estate petitioned for the estate roads to be taken over. These were named as Albert Road, St. Georges Road and William Road; the first-named, presumably after the Prince Regent, was soon renamed Alfred Road. The estate had been developed by the Robins brothers, George and Alfred, of The Fairfield, and their brother-in-law William Foot. Being the leader, George it seems distinguished himself by assuming the rank of Saint. The Robins were an extremely prolific family who played a big part in the development of Farnham from the 1870s onwards, not only in building but also gravel digging, farming and commercial enterprises, some of which exist today. William Road was the stretch of road from the top of St. Georges Road to Tilford Road, which was absorbed into Morley Road when that road came in 1906 with the new Grammar School. It was decided not to adopt William Road as no houses fronted on to it.

A local authority does not declare a road to be repairable by the inhabitants at large until it has first been made up to required standards by the frontagers. In practice it has become the procedure for the authority to move in initially, make a really good job of it (the more lasting the effect, the cheaper it will be for the inhabitants) and charge it up to the frontagers. But with the Waverley Estate the Board quaintly played through the folk-law, serving notices on the owners requiring them to make up the two roads according to specifications, then waited for the notices to expire and, in the default of the owners, taking it on themselves. Or would have done if it had not been for the delaying tactics on the part of the Local Government Board when asked to sanction a loan of £400.

In April 1892 the Board again pressed the Railway Company to improve the platform accommodation at the station and the Company again replied that this was a good way down their list of priorities and that the Board were exaggerating anyway. The Board took the matter to the Board of Trade but this got them nowhere of course and so the Clerk compiled another memorial that was signed by the Bishop of Winchester, 'which he thought would carry great weight with the Company', and Richard Combe of Pierrepont, Frensham, Esquire, head of a famous Brewery, and extensively signed by the Magistrates, Merchants, Traders and other prominent persons in the town–some of these memorials make good autograph books. This got them nowhere of course and the passengers had to continue to put up with the inadequate platforms, though in what respects is not stated.

That year William Kingham lost his seat to Ernest Crundwell, Mr. Potter's partner ... County wrote about the condition of finger-posts and milestones in the District and it was decided to erect two new posts in Crondall Lane and to touch up the two milestones ... Some of the stone delivered by the Victoria Stone Company was not up to the sample and a representative of the Company came down to inspect. The Company, he said, had a record of the age of every stone issued but went on to say that the stones complained of might not be so fine in texture as the sample 'but the intrinsic value of both was equal' ... The Surveyor reported that there was one water-closet only at the Post Office, shared by thirty employees, both male and female, and no water laid on to it. Mr. Nichols was told to provide at least two closets properly connected to water. In the meantime it was arranged for the ladies on the staff to use the toilet in the Postmaster's house. Really–the things these minutes throw up! ... The sewer in Abbey

Street was blocked up by a 'quantity of rags and hair matted together', which was as good as anything for blocking up a sewer, and Abbey Street just the sort of place to do it ... Alton Local Board invited Farnham to join in a protest to the L. & S-W.R. for a better service, suggesting that one train in the morning should run non-stop from Aldershot to London, returning non-stop as far as Aldershot in the evening. We are still waiting for this train.

The Medical Officer's report for July 1892 blamed a Diphtheria case in Beavers Yard on the fact that twenty cottages there shared five closets, two very dirty. He also mentioned a nuisance at a cottage in Park Row at the rear of the *Nelson Arms*—the house was extremely dirty, in bad repair and ashpit in scullery'. Miss Cranstone, the tenant, was 'very strange in her manner, committing many nuisances' ... Mr. R.D. Mason, owner of the Board's depot in East Street, stopped the Board's men using water from a pump serving the two cottages in the yard, this being objected to by his tenants. R.D. Mason suggested that as the Board had a closet in the yard, they should get the Water Company to lay water on ... Mrs. Bethune asked permission to plant Virginian Creepers outside her house at 88 West Street—there was no doubt something in the 1875 Act to cover this.

John Henry Knight of Barfield, Runfold, Esquire, lodged a complaint about the smells from the sewage farm and, in keeping with his inventive genius, suggested a remedy, namely the deodorizing of the sewage matter before pumping it on to the land. Mr. Bide again assured his fellow members that all possible care was taken by his men but the work came during the daytime, when the neighbours were up and about and it was difficult to avoid spreading some of the smell around. So they laid it on for the Surveyor to pump at five o'clock in the morning before people got up. Knight was one of the lesser squires, so the Board wrote back obsequiously that they were applying every possible remedial measure in their power to abate the nuisance. A few days later Knight wrote again asking when they were going to start.

The roads had not been watered on Bank Holiday and at the August meeting the Surveyor explained that it was customary for the Board's men to do a little cleaning up in the morning of Bank Holidays and then have the rest of the day off. A long discussion ensued and it was resolved that in future the Surveyor 'do not recognise Bank Holidays in reference to street-watering and the employment of the Board's workmen' ... Regulations from the Local Government Board regarding Cholera from the importation of rags from France and Black Sea ports. As the Board were not in the habit of trading with those countries, no action was taken ... Letter dated 5 July from Colonel Windham, complaining of 'persons bathing in the river in Bishops Meadows in an indecent manner' ... There was a special report from the M.O. on accommodation for hop-pickers, which would have delighted the late Mr. Wonnacott. Doctor Sloman and the County Medical Officer, Doctor Seaton, had carried out an inspection. Barracks in Red Lion Lane belonging to J.R. Nash had defective water supply and privy accommodation and the same owner's establishment at Weydon Mill also had bad water and filthy privies. After all, the members of the Board were themselves only human and could not be expected to set a shining example to the public on whom they were forcing better conditions ... Doctor Sloman also gave a grave warning about the serious risk of Cholera in Red Lion Lane because of polluted water from shallow wells. Samples tested by the County Analyst were found to be 'sewage polluted, dangerous water quite unfit for drinking purposes'. But it did lead to a water main being laid along Red Lion Lane.

Defeated in their attempts to enforce a built-in flushing apparatus in closets, the Board sought the opinion of the Local Government Board. Whitehall considered that bye-laws on the subject would be satisfactory if they merely stipulated the use of water in closets without particularising the method of flushing. But the advantage of a cistern was that one did not have to keep refilling the bucket.

Mr. Bentall called the Board's attention to the nuisance often caused by traction engines when passing through the town and gave as an example an engine, belonging to Mr. Frank Knight of Yarnhams, which had passed through the town recently. What the driver had said or done is not stated, but it was enough for the Police to be informed and for the 'insolent conduct of the man' to be brought to the notice of his master.

In October 1892 there was a letter from Mr. Potter, acting on behalf of Mr. John Henry Knight of Barfield, threatening legal action if the sewage farm smells were not abated. It caused a panic

Plate 32 *Diamond Jubilee – Scene in Castle Street*

Plate 23 The Fair in Castle Street in the 1880's

Plate 34 *Robert Cass, Surveyor*

late 35 *Bridge Square before improvements*

Plate 36 *Mr. Aylwin's butchery at 8 West Street*

Plate 37 *Jubilee swimming bath*

in the Board Room and it was decided to recall Mr. Lemon for his advice generally as to the better working of the sewerage system. There was, at the same time, another disaster. On 21 September there had been a violent storm and flood damage had resulted. The sewers had literally overflowed, washing sewage into peoples' houses. Lemon's immediate proposals were for additional storm outlets to carry surface water direct to the river. Many were the claims for compensation in respect of damage caused by the storm but the Board accepted no responsibility. They announced that 'owing to the severity of the storm the sewers had overflowed and that, acting under the advice of their Engineer, they were proposing to make certain alterations in the sewerage system which they hoped would prevent the recurrence of the cause of complaint'.

To abate the smells from the farm, Mr. Lemon recommended carriers for more evenly distributing the sludge over the land. He then looked at the matter more closely and advised the Board that the trouble came from the turning into the sewers of refuse from the breweries, this causing fermentation of the sewage. As brewing was the main industry of the town, this was an unforeseen complication that called for urgent attention. The Clerk wrote to twenty-four other towns enquiring whether they had similar problems; six had–Shepton Mallet, Croydon, Stratford-on-Avon, Richmond, Churtsey and Romford. On being approached their breweries had either discontinued sending their 'hot liquors' down the drain or had just rendered them unobjectionable. The Board invited the local brewers to a conference ... A circular from the Local Government Board asking the Board to find jobs if possible for the unemployed during the winter. With a view to taking on extra men, the widening of Crondall Lane was discussed. Charles Smith suggested using some for breaking up the iron-stone into little pieces for use on the roads. For the perusal of the Local Government, a letter was sent saying that it would have been possible to employ labourers in the making-up of two roads in the District but for the delay in obtaining sanction to borrow the money.

There was a letter dated 17 September 1892 from Mr. Jordison, the Assistant District Auditor, which said that the accounts of the Rate Collector, Mr. John Thorp, had been found to be in a very unsatisfactory state. Mr. Thorp explained to the Board that certain matters had fallen behind owing to ill health. Thorp was now an old man; had he lived in the following century, he would have been retired years earlier. It was not given to the Board to show consideration towards their staff but surprisingly, on this occasion, they did. They suggested changes in the system to make things easier and, what is more, defended Mr. Thorp when the Local Government Board enquired into the irregularities reported to them by Jordison, who, one assumes, never grew old himself or suffered from ill health.

George Trimmer was the first of them to die. On 15 November 1892, a Special Meeting was held at which the Chairman, Mr. Goddard, explained 'that he had called this meeting owing to the great loss the Board had sustained by the death of Mr. Trimmer, who had been a Member of the Board ever since the formation in 1866 and had occupied the position of Chairman from 1880 to 1891, during which time several important businesses had occupied the attention of the Board'. They wrote to his two sons, Robert and Charles, offering sincere sympathy, and arranged to meet at Mr. Mason's house at 2.45 p.m. on 18 November to precede the funeral cortege.

George Trimmer first finds mention in this chronicle as a member of a Police Committee in 1849. For forty-three years of his life he had regularly attended meetings of voluntary bodies in the town, his last attendance being at the meeting of the Board on 1 November just before he died. During that time he had made a fortune; instead of spending it in some millionaire's playground, he gave unstinted service to the town that helped him make it.

A month later the Board mourned the death of Abraham Smith, whose funeral they attended on 10 December. Smith had been the builder in Long Garden Walk before Arthur Figg. On 13 December, they paid their respects to the late Mr. John Thorp and in a letter to the family expressed their deep appreciation of the many excellent qualities displayed by him during the time he held the appointment of Collector of Rates. Alfred Thorp informed the Board that his father had signed, only a day or two before his death, a letter resigning his appointment owing to ill health and tending his thanks to the Board for the kindness and consideration shown him during the time he had held the appointment.

XX

BUSINESS AS USUAL

ON CHRISTMAS day 1892 occurred one of those fires that left a scar on the town. No. 96 West Street was so badly gutted that the dangerous shell had to be replaced. The Water Company afterwards complained that the Brigade had failed to notify the Company's Engineer of their use of the hydrants; had they known, the Company said, they would have been able to increase the water pressure. One reads in this a possibility that 96 West Street might have been spared demolition. The scar that replaced it became Toop's butcher's shop, a building in the worst Victorian idiom and a dreadful companion to the old bookshop at 97, of which the original 96 had been a worthy partner. Both buildings were replaced in 1968 by Maxwell Aylwin's tasteful office block, but old-timers will continue to mourn the old bookshop.

The Board appreciated the Water Company's need to know what was going on and they formed a committee to study ways of quick communication between the Fire Brigade and the Company's engineer. They considered offers from John Henry Knight and James Tily of Castle Street of 'telephonic communication'. It was only to be expected that that genius of mechanical contrivances, J.H. Knight, should be on the phone–he probably helped to invent it. There was, however, a body going about the town called the National Telephone Company, formed for the uphill task of getting the masses interested–for what was the use of being on the telephone if hardly anyone else was? Gradually another innovation was entering peoples' homes. The two gentlemen were thanked for their offers, which were declined–the old-fashioned messenger boy was quite good enough. It was not until 30 June 1908 that the National Telephone Company persuaded the Fire Brigade.

The Board's resolution was 'that on the outbreak of fire in the District, a messenger be at once dispatched to the Waterworks to inform the Official there of the fact and to state that the Board would be glad to be informed what hose etc. he thought would be required to render the Brigade efficient'. Perhaps this passion for polite observance of social etiquette, together with other leisurely processes of a Brigade turnout in the last century, cost the town other gems of ancient architecture, thus accounting for the Victorian replacements dotted here and there.

The Medical Officer discovered cases of Scarlet Fever and Scarlatina in Lower Church Lane and packed them off to the Workhouse Infirmary. Investigating, the Surveyor found that in one of the cottages the sink water had been connected to the sewer, but not the privy ... The Rural Highways Board offered to hire one of their steamrollers at 35s. per day, inclusive of the driver. The swank displayed by the country cousins over having more than one steamroller, whereas the town-dwellers possessed none at all, should be offset by the fact that the much larger rural area was all roads and hardly any buildings, whereas the smaller urban district was all buildings and hardly any roads.

On 3 January 1893, Alfred Ernest Thorp was confirmed in his appointment as Rate Collector, on the same salary as his late father. Thirty-six years later, the writer was to become a junior on his staff and thus able to study this remarkable man at close quarters. Alfred Thorp was what is commonly known as one of the old school. He bridged the gap between history and what is, for older readers, nowadays. His knowledge of the people and events now featuring in this chronicle–he should, of course, have written it–was first-hand and profound; it died, unfortunately, with him.

As a young man, Thorp was a great local sportsman. On the wall of his office at 9 Downing Street (Farnham), there hung a rifle, ready to hand should any shooting friend drop in with an invitation, but more often supposed to be either an instrument of persuasion for reluctant ratepayers or a means of defence against their fury. He was almost completely stone-deaf; the combined operation of a phone call, with Thorp manning the mouthpiece and the writer on the receiving end, was a moving experience. His stock jokes, at which he laughed even more heartily than his audience, included the one about a letter which ran 'Dear Alf–Please find enclosed cheque for rates because I can't'. He delighted, too, in telling of his early days of collecting rates–particularly in the then notorious Upper Hale area, where the news of his arrival would be flashed through the village by some never discovered means, with the result that he found everybody out, and where he and a constable used to collect rates from a certain defaulter by holding him upside down so that the money fell from his pockets, then picking up what they wanted and issuing a receipt for it.

With the advent of electricity the Board bought half-a-dozen oil lamps for use if the gas-lamps failed from the effects of frost. Noticing these in use one frosty night a short time later, the Gas Company, aware also of the advent of electricity, couldn't have been nicer. Let us know, they told the Board, and we'll have the gas burning again in no time ... Plans for the late George Trimmer's Almshouses in West Street approved ... They conferred with Charles Trimmer about the discharge from the Brewery into the sewer but got nowhere, even though they pointed out that the threat of litigation hung over their heads–including Charles Trimmer's ... There was a rare instance of friction when Daniel Goddard and John Robert Nash were nominated as the Board's two Grammar School Governors. Alfred James Nash, the auctioneer, objected to his kinsman's nomination and Mr. Mason, the Clerk, who had been made a Governor by the Surrey County Council, threatened to resign. Mr. J.R. Nash stated that, after what had been said, he would not stand as a Governor and moved that Mr. A.J. Bentall be appointed instead. The Board then expressed their hope that Mr. Mason would reconsider his intention and all ended well–except that Mr. J.R. Nash's name does not appear in any further attendance lists of the Board's meetings.

At the March Meeting, the Surveyor produced a plan of a house to be built at the rear of East Street on part of the late Fords' Hopgrounds. It looked also as if a new road was intended, though this was not mentioned in the application. Above all, the Board did like to know about any new roads. So they called the attention of Henry Patrick, the builder, to it and in due course came a letter from Mr. James Stevens, acting on behalf of the owner of the land, Mr. M.O. Stevens, saying that the proposed road had been set out before the introduction of the Board's bye-laws relating to new streets. Further that Mr. M.O. Stevens was quite ready to give the necessary land for the road, would comply with the bye-laws and generally do his bit towards laying out a new street, if the other landowners involved would do the same. And Alfred James Nash, as one of the owners, could not very well refuse. The road became High Park Road.

Charles Austwick gave notice that he did not intend to seek re-election. With the deaths of Trimmer and Smith, there were three seats on the Board beckoning to newcomers and on 7 April 1893 election fever seized the town. There was a field of fourteen, from which Barling, Crosby, Jackson, William Kingham and Robert Trimmer withdrew. Charles Edwin Trimmer led easily with 966 votes; then came Daniel Goddard (757), James Alfred Eggar, auctioneer of Swanthorpe, Crondall (702), Frederick Hart, ironmonger of 117 West Street (582), George Barnett, brewer of West Street (547). Unsuccessful candidates were John Griffith, the chemist of 24 The Borough (465), James Brett, hop-planter Firgrove (416), George Elphick, draper, 13 West Street (409) and, way down bottom, William Simmonds, described as ratepayer, the Ferns, Fairfield, with 32. Mr. Goddard was returned as Chairman.

Mr. Eggar was also an architect—an architect is a useful person to have as a member of any authority with the important function of approving building plans. At his first meeting he took an active part in forming future policy in that plans should first be considered in detail by a committee of the Board.

At a special meeting on 23 May, from which Charles Trimmer was absent, they studied a report prepared by a Mr. Start, acting for the Farnham United Brewery in connection with the drainage system and the Brewery's contribution thereto in particular. The Board sent it on to Mr. Lemon who attended another special meeting a week later and confirmed his opinion that the Brewery was responsible for the nuisance despite Mr. Start's theory. A meeting was arranged between the two engineers. It was another idea of Lemon's that the sludge should not be pumped over the land at the farm for Mr. Bide's men to dig in but should be dealt with inside the pumping station where it could be turned into manure by mixing it with ashes. They tried this and found it satisfactory though this minor triumph was marred by a memorial from Guildford Road residents complaining of 'stenches arising from the present method of dealing with the sewage'. On 14 and 16 August there were further complaints of a similar nature but it was pointed out that on these two days no mixing had taken place owing to the mud pump having broken down, also that the engineer had visited the pumping station and pronounced the manure made from the sludge to be entirely inodorous, though there was a slight smell from the tanks. Mr. Eggar made the suggestion that brimstone should be burnt during operations.

It was not often that the L. & S-W.R. wanted anything from the Board, but in May they wrote saying that the station area was difficult to drain in wet weather owing to inadequate surface water drainage and would the Board mind laying in a larger pipe from the station yard to the river. The Board took advantage of the situation, replying 'that in the circumstances of the present insufficient accommodation at the Farnham railway station, the Board do not see their way to incur any expenditure in reference to the surface water drainage there'.

A grant was claimable from the County Council in respect of upkeep of roads other than main roads provided that the 'foreign traffic' over them was not less than 40 per cent of all vehicles. A traffic census disappointingly revealed more than 60 per cent local users, until the Board thought of counting in the gravel carts that shuttled to and fro between the station and points outside the District .. The 'Sports Committee' were granted the use of the water cart after hours ... The Postmaster asked if the Board had any objections to the East Street Post Office being closed for the royal wedding day on 6 July 1893. The Board's workmen too were given a half-day's holiday. The wedding was that of Queen Victoria's grandson, George—crowned King George V in 1910—to Princess Mary of Teck.

The Local Government Board at last sanctioned the loan of £400 for making up Alfred and St. Georges Roads. William Cox was given the job at £405. Alfred Road was not straightforward, the road was one-sided and, at a distance of less than 30 feet, a hedge ran in front of the houses, screening the railway land opposite, and to provide the required width this hedge had to be removed. The water main had to be lowered and gas laid on. All the operations were arranged simultaneously for the sake of convenience; with all of them at it at the same time, the unemployment figures must have fallen through the bottom.

On 1 July the Local Government Board prodded the Board to consider the provision of an isolation hospital, either by themselves or in conjunction with adjoining authorities. The Board approached the Rural people, doubtless expecting the answer as before, but they had changed their mind and appointed a committee of six in the matter, and could Mr. A.C. Pain, who was Chairman of the Frimley Parochial Committee, also come along? The representatives met on 17 August and reported back to their authorities that (1) it was considered desirable that an isolation hospital be provided and (2) in the opinion of the meeting, Aldershot and Hartley Wintney Sanitary Authorities should be invited to join. The Joint Isolation Hospital Committee thus established met on 28 September 1893 and passed the following resolutions:–

> (1) That it is desirable that an Isolation Hospital be provided for the Joint District of the four Authorities.
>
> (2) That the representatives from the various authorities be requested to lay before their Boards the foregoing resolution and in the event of their agreeing thereto that each authority should be asked to nominate two members of a sub-committee to be formed for the purpose of drawing up a report as to the site for the hospital and its probable cost, such sub-committee to have the power to spend not exceeding £5 for each authority nominating members, and to report to the Joint Committee in the first instance.

Mrs. Henrietta Halton of the *Waverley Arms* wrote on 24 August stating that she had been seriously ill from blood poisoning attributed to the stenches arising from the unloading, on 5 and 7 August, at the railway station opposite of concentrated fish and blood manure. The Railway Company were asked to issue orders for all such manures in future to be 'unloaded outside the Board's District' ... A circular from the Board of Agriculture asking Boards to notify the Director-General of Ordnance Surveys of the formation of any new highways or alterations in existing ones ... County requested the Board's observations upon the alleged encroachments on the rights of the public by the inclosure of a piece of waste land near the Bourne Mill. The encroachment had been made to prevent squatting by gipsy hoppers, but Mr. Bide promised to remove the fence ... In October the Surveyor reported the completion of Alfred Road at a cost of £123 12s. 6d., of which the Railway paid £59 14s. 7d., and St. Georges Road, £281 16s. 8d. The charge to individual frontagers worked out at about 4s. per foot ... Leonard Parratt, Harry Parratt and Arthur Eade were summoned under the Towns Police Clauses Act for 'using obscene language in The Borough on the 22 October'.

Mr. Start's revised scheme for the disposal of the Brewery's waste products was sent on to Mr. Lemon, who advised minor alterations; these were adopted and the plans approved. Then the Directors wrote saying that they did not consider themselves liable but were willing to pay one-half of the cost of £350, provided the Board would find the rest. The meeting, at which Mr. Trimmer was present, regretted there was no money available for the purpose and trusted that the Directors would reconsider the matter and proceed with the works, which were intended to abate a nuisance created by themselves.

Mr. Barnett proposed that representations be made to the L. & S-W.R. to obtain cheap return tickets to Farnham on Market Days from other towns in the area. In a rare instance of good relations, the Traffic Manager replied on 22 December, stating that he had introduced Market Tickets for Farnham's Thursday markets, the return fares to be from, Alresford 2s., Ropley 1s. 8d., Medstead 1s. 5d., Alton 11d., Woking 1s. 5d., Godalming 1s. 5d., Worplesdon 1s. 5d., Guildford 1s. 1d., Bagshot 1s. 6d. and Camberley 1s. 2d. The Board thanked him profusely and asked him to do the same with Basingstoke, Hook, Winchfield, Fleet and Farnborough. In the thick of things at Waterloo, the town had found a friend; the market tickets for those places were reduced to 2s. 11d., 2s. 6d., 2s. 2d., 1s. 11d., and 1s. 7d. respectively.

I have fought a good fight, I have finished my course, I have kept the faith

2 Timothy iv 7

XXI

THE LAST MONTHS OF THE LOCAL BOARD

THE PUMP at the bottom of Bear Lane was finally removed and the well filled in; it is a pity about this pump, it would have had such a sobering influence on the new shopping centre. But the days of parish pump politics were over, local government was now sophisticated, and already there was talk of more strength to come. Like the Market House in 1866, these out-of-date things just didn't fit in any more ... Mr. Frisby of 32 The Borough almost got a summons for obstructing the footway, despite his manager's plea that it would not happen again. One of the firms still in occupation of the same premises today, Frisbys' were advertising shoes from 1s. 6d. to 2s. 11d. a pair.

The Medical Officer had given a warning about the bad state of the river bed between the Bishops Meadows and Longbridge and the unfortunate frontagers had been made to clean it out. They had all complied except in a stretch belonging to the Rector. Farnham was temporarily out of vicars. Canon Hoste had left for Meonstoke. He had been very popular in the town and in 1897 a new pulpit costing £250 was installed in the Church by public subscriptions, inscribed 'In memory of Philip Hoste, a faithful servant of the Lord's poor, Rector 1875–1893'. The welcome now extended to his successor, the Rev. C.H. Simpkinson included a notice to clean out the river. He stopped three and a half years, moving on to Stoke-on-Trent, where the living was reputedly worth over £2,000 a year gross. Farnham always was a good jumping-off place, especially for the clergy–possibly because of the influence of the Bishop of Winchester, who had a good say in who should be Vicar.

The Bishop had something to say, too, about the ventilation shaft at The Cedars, Castle Hill, where the street sewer ended. This shaft was in a strategic position to carry the Castle Street Smell upwards to where the Castle loomed above on its steeply rising mound. At a cost of £25, the Board extended the sewer up the hill to the 'site of the old Pound' and put up their shaft against a tree in the Park 'near the site of the old Toll Gate'—which are pre-Victorian matters, though the Pound was no doubt where stray cattle had been lodged at the order of the Highways Board dated March 1836. Also of earlier history was the Conduit with its pump at the corner of the Town Hall, once Farnham's only piped water supply, presented to the town by Bishop Morley in the 17th century. The pump was running short of water. Ownership could not be traced, beyond a vague reference to it being 'vested in the Trustees for the use of the Inhabitants of the Parish'. It was decided that, as such trustees were also long since dead, the same, by virtue of the Public Health Act, 1875, could now be deemed to be vested in the Local Board. A stoppage was found half-way up the street which called for a new stretch of piping.

A form of return came in February 1894 from Mr. F.G. Howell, the County Surveyor, requesting the Board's estimate of expenditure over the next two years on main roads. Messrs. Bide and Trimmer, with the Clerk, were detailed to cope with it. With memories of past financial triumphs over the County Council, they went to it, one can sense, with gusto and included everything they could think of, like watering and scavenging, and put in a return of £750 per annum. Howell requested an interview, attended by the Surveyor and Mr. Mason's assistant from 93 West Street, and pointed out that, whilst he could not advise his Council to pay more than the old rate, £532 per annum, perhaps the Board would be good enough to reconsider their estimate and quote the lowest figure they would be prepared to accept. They stuck at £750. Then the County Clerk invited the Board's Chairman, Clerk and Surveyor to Kingston to attend a sub-committee. They came back with £700 in their pockets and were accorded 'the best thanks of the Board'.

In March, the M.O.'s report included a case of typhoid caught by the temporary caretaker of the ladies waiting-room at the station, where sanitary arrangements were found to be defective ... There was a claim by Herbert Sloman of the Benevolent Society for £2 11s. 0d., being the cost of two bundles of clothes lent by the Society to homes where Scarlatina had broken out, and afterwards destroyed ... Mr. Chiverton, Relieving Officer of the Board of Guardians had taken to reporting on the living conditions of persons taken into the care of the Guardians. One concerned the effect on adjoining cottages of the manure heap at the *Jolly Farmer* in Bridge Square and the owners were made to remove this to a fresh site. The manure heap was an accepted feature; most houses had one ... The discovery of an accumulation of manure, as well as defective drainage, at the premises of one B. Wicks of West Street, dairyman, startled the Board into checking on the town's suppliers of milk, who were supposed to register their premises and thus render them open to inspection. People often carried on more than one trade and it was easy for some to be overlooked because of the traders' main occupations. Enquiries brought to light the following unregistered Cowkeepers, Dairymen and Purveyors of Milk—Samuel Bide, Hatch Hill and The Borough; A. Robins, Station Road; T. Mitchell, Waverley Estate; B. Baigent, Old Brewhouse Yard; F. Turk, Red Lion Lane; H. Sims, and B. Wicks, of West Street and E. Coxe, Downing Street. Yet another potential source of infectious diseases had been uncovered.

A letter dated 20 February 1894 from the Clerk of the County Council enclosing a print of proposed bye-laws 'for the good rule and government of the County', and inviting observations. The Board had no comments beyond objecting to the one relating to lights on vehicles which in their opinion was not only undesirable but impracticable. With fewer night soil carts, traffic on the roads during the hours of darkness was negligible ... Mr. Charles Smith moved that 'a public urinal be provided in the town' but the motion was lost by four votes to five ... The horse roller was sold for £40 ... The rating assessment of the railway rose from £332 to £558, a nice little windfall at 1s. 10d. in the pound per half-year.

Mr. Lewis, Headmaster of the West Street School, complained of nuisances in and about the school premises adjoining the churchyard and asked for the yard to be lit at nights. The School Board had just acquired a new site for the West Street School in

Potters Gate. A section of footpath short-cutting a public right of way from West Street to Crondall Lane crossed the site and the School Board asked the Board to use their powers to stop this stretch of path in order that the building of the new school might proceed. Application was accordingly made to two Justices of the Peace. The School Board agreed to give up 15 feet of frontage on the north-east flank of their plot and this was added to the footpath and became the wider section of Potters Gate ... In April the Board joined the Parish Officers, Waywardens, the Burial Board and other interested bodies in a concerted action to oppose the County Council's proposal to transfer the village of Tilford from the Parish of Farnham to the Parish of Waverley. Four months later an Order of the County Council united the Parish of Waverley with the Parish of Farnham. But somewhere down the line, when the old Farnham Parish once again came under one roof, the lovely village of Tilford had somehow been lost to Farnham.

The Farnham United Brewery notified the Board–some six months after being asked–that they would reduce by one-half the quantity of refuse turned into the sewer. They were told 'not only to reduce the quantity, but the quality, so as not to prove a nuisance at the pumping station' ... In reply to a letter dated 18 April from the County Clerk, in reference to section 36 of the new Local Government Act, the Board intimated that they had no present intention of applying for an extension of the boundaries of their District. In the light of present-day greed for territorial gain, the Local Board seemed peculiarly loth to enlarge their area ... They noted with approval–but without much enthusiasm –that Big Brother had powers to lend money to District Authorities in the County ... The Railway People had lately been particularly trying. In addition to closing the level-crossing gates for scheduled passenger trains, an abomination when one did not happen to be on one, they were keeping them shut during shunting operations. Why they were carrying out shunting operations on this side of the station, when they had a perfectly good shunting yard on the other side, is not stated–perhaps it was retaliation for the higher assessment. Mr. Mason turned up his law books but could find nothing suitable to the occasion; it was wondered whether to seek counsel's opinion. In answer to the

Board's spirited protest, the General Manager of the Railway himself wrote that he was 'assured that the detentions at the level-crossing seldom exceeded a few minutes and that the Company's servants had been strictly enjoined to use every effort to minimise the detention of vehicles at the crossing, but some delay under the circumstances was unavoidable'. The Surveyor was told to engage a person to watch the gates for a week and report on closings. The Board should have learnt by this time that in anything to do with the railway, it was best to pretend it wasn't happening.

Plans for a malthouse at the Red Lion Brewery; also for a factory in Darvills Lane for a Mr. Ball ... On 1 May, Mr. Goddard was re-appointed Chairman 'for the remainder of the term of office of the Board', i.e. 31 December 1894. There was no election this year, the electorate would next go to the poll in order to elect a new authority ... Representations were made to the County Council for the division of the District into two wards–Eastern Ward and Western Ward, with six members in each, but County were not interested ... The Police were asked to take action to abate nuisances arising from the behaviour of certain boys on Sunday evenings in Darvills Lane ... There was smallpox at the Workhouse and the Board recommended sealing off the tramps' quarters, which evoked an emphatic refusal from the Guardians who, one gathers, couldn't upset the guests ... Plans for the late George Trimmer's Cottage Hospital in East Street. It cost about £15,000 and, as Farnham's first purpose-built hospital, has been of immense value to the town ever since.

The Sanitary Committee reported as follows on an inspection of cottages in the *Wheatsheaf* Yard, West Street:–

> Your Committee visited the premises in this Yard and found three houses there without any water supply. Two of these houses were drained into the main sewer, the remaining house (in the occupation of Mr. Parratt) had a common privy, the contents of which, they were informed by the tenant, were emptied into a manure pit adjoining. The sink and slops water went into a cesspool a few yards from the house; the contents of the cesspool, according to the tenant, soaked away he did not know how or where. Your Committee did not think these arrangements sufficient for effectual drainage of the house and premises and directed the Clerk to serve Mr. Penfold (the owner) with notice to drain same into the main sewer and to provide water supply to all three houses.

On 4 September 1894 they considered plans for the building of the Liberal Club in South Street and resolved 'that the same be approved subject to its being in accordance with the Board's bye-law, viz. that the walls of the first storey be increased to 14 inches in thickness and that separate surface water drainage be provided'. The plans went back to the architect, who complied. He was Edwin Lutyens–later Sir Edwin Lutyens K.C.I.E., R.A.–of 6 Grays Inn Road, London, and lately of his parents' house (now Lutyens House) at Thursley. He was 21, just established in London and on the road to fame. When still in his teens he had designed the Thursley village shop; in 1889 he built Crooksbury House, which he rebuilt on a grander scale six years later. The Liberal Club was his first essay in town architecture. It was originally roofed with heavy Roman tiles, which gave the building a slightly Italian look; their replacement later with slates robbed the Club of its initial glory and one would pass it by without a second glance. It was missed in Lutyen's listed works; the omission has since been pointed out. In any future face-lift in South Street, a plaque would go a long way.

In contrast with the normal monthly bag, the M.O.s report for December 1894 carried the boast that 'no deaths from zymotic disease' had occurred during November. There was also a letter from the Registrar of Births and Deaths to the same effect, 'save six fatal cases in the Union Workhouse', which presumably did not count.

At the close of an adjourned meeting on 11 December 1894

> a presentation was made by the Members of the Board to the Chairman, consisting of a silver inkstand and blotting-pad, together with an illuminated address expressive of their appreciation of his services as Chairman. The Chairman in a few suitable words acknowledged the compliment and expressed his pleasure at the kindly feeling evinced by the Board towards him. At the same time the Members of the Board presented the Clerk with a silver salver and a similar illuminated address expressive of their appreciation of his services during the whole of the Board's existence of 28 years. The Clerk in turn thanked the Board for this mark of their favour and expressed himself deeply indebted to the Members past and present of the Board for their uniform courtesy, kindness and forbearance extended to him and that he should very highly prize those tokens of their esteem.

Words–but one can sense their sincerity. The Farnham Local Board met for the last time at a special meeting on Friday, 28 December 1894, to consider an application by the Postmaster General to erect telegraph poles from near the railway bridge to the Board's boundary near the Hale Church. The matter was referred to the new Farnham Urban District Council.

. . . . .

The Local Government Act, 1894 (56 & 57 Vict. c.73) was passed on 5 March of that year 'to make further provision for Local Government in England and Wales'. It added strength to the elbows of local authorities, more particularly in rural areas, where it transferred powers from the Church Vestry to the Parish Council, or Meeting, and set up Rural District Councils. Urban Sanitary Authorities, except for boroughs, which retained their status, became Urban District Councils and their districts were called Urban Districts. It was rather more than renaming the rose. Although the Act said most of the old things over again, it said them in more definite terms and passed many additional duties to the new Councils. It was one of the major reshuffles and had the desired effect over the next seventy-five years with undoubted success. As a form of government of the townspeople by their peers–and in local affairs that is the only way for people to be governed–it will probably never be equalled.

PART THREE

What's in a name? That which we call a rose
By any other name would smell as sweet.

William Shakespeare

XXII

UNDER NEW MANAGEMENT

AT A lively poll on 18 December 1894, all twelve members of the new Farnham Urban District Council were elected as follows:

BARNETT George Henry	58 West Street	169	not elected
BENTALL Alfred Josiah	Hillcrest, Farnham	454	
BIDE Samuel	Alma Nurseries	361	
COLEMAN William Thomas	90 West Street	412	
EGGAR James Alfred	Swanthorpe, Crondall	214	
FRY Charles	9 Castle View	329	
GODDARD Daniel	East Street	436	
HART Frederick	117 West Street	150	not elected
HAYES William Henry	Fairfield Lodge	537	
HEATH George	South Street	151	not elected
KEMPSON Edgar	61 Castle Street	293	
KINGHAM Robert Dixon	Parkleigh, Fairfield	353	
RANSOM George	Beechcroft, Fairfield	260	
SMITH Charles	72 Castle Street	203	not elected
TRIMMER Charles Edwin	69 West Street	334	
WELLS George	96 East Street	133	not elected
WILLIAMS William Welsby	122 West Street	204	

Members of the former Local Board who either lost their seats or did not stand were George Barnett, Frederick Hart, Charles Smith, Alfred James Nash and Ernest Crundwell. Newcomers to local politics were William Coleman, George Ransom the baker, William Williams the wine merchant, Edgar Kempson solicitor, and Charles Fry.

The first meeting of the Council, held in the Council Room at the Town Hall on Tuesday, 1 January 1895, was mainly devoted to domestic affairs. Daniel Goddard was voted Chairman, though it was resolved that in future the Chairman would be elected annually from those members who had not already occupied the

Chair. Councillors (they had a title now) were appointed to serve on the various standing committees–Finance, Sanitary & General Purposes, Lighting, Highways & Paving. Four were named for retirement on 15 April in each of the three years 1896, 1897 and 1898. There would be a fine of 40s. for non-acceptance of office or resignation. It went without minuting that Richard Mason became Clerk and R.F. Hankins Surveyor. They unwrapped their presents; the 1894 Act had terminated the activities of that energetic body, the Farnham Burial Board and transferred their powers and duties to a joint committee of the Urban District Council and the Parish Council of Rural Farnham, whose Clerk, Mr. A.J. Nash, had written in to say that five of his members were all ready to go–a step that would have looked better had it come from the senior service. Mr. Mason explained other additional powers which the Local Government Board could confer upon the Council under the Act and they sent in an order forthwith. The Directors of the Town Hall Company were invited to be so good as to provide furniture 'suitable to the new Council Room', particularly chairs for the exclusive use of that room, and to provide lavatory and W/C accommodation, ventilation and warming. There were two board rooms, one on each side of the entrance to the Town Hall; one assumes that the newly constituted Council had moved across the hall to a place of their own. The Company agreed to see to all these things provided the Council signed a lease for three years at £12 per annum. The ordinary monthly meetings were fixed for the first Tuesday in each month at 7.15 p.m. They paid the monthly bills (they had taken over the debts as well) and adjourned the meeting until 8 January.

Councillors Goddard, Bentall, Coleman, Kempson and Kingham had made contact with their country cousins and set up a Joint Burial Committee. The Surveyor was instructed to prepare a plan of the town on an enlarged ordnance scale, showing the drainage system, including both sewage and surface water disposal and connections thereto, and mark in all buildings up to date. This map, which is in the present Surveyor's office, is an authentic bird's eye view of Farnham in the mid-1890s. The Union Assessment Committee (Ernest Crundwell, Clerk) wanted to know how the Council proposed to go about the revaluation of the

Urban District for rating purposes–whether they would share in the services of a valuer to be appointed in the Union or whether they preferred to go it alone with the aid of the Surveyor of Taxes' schedule A assessments. The Council chose the latter course and a new valuation list appeared in 1896. This list, which is in the present Rate Collector's office, is an authentic record of the occupiers and owners of all the buildings depicted on Hankins' map.

The Surveyor reported at the February meeting that two Thames Conservatory Board Inspectors had called at the sewage farm and stated, rather ominously, that they would in future be taking samples of the effluent from time to time. It was not because of this that Mr. Hankins handed in his resignation, it was because he had been appointed Surveyor to the Walton Urban District Council. His vacancy was advertised at a salary of £160 per annum in the *Local Government Chronicle,* the *Surrey Advertiser, The Times, Surrey & Hants. News* and the *Reading Mercury.* There were eighty-six applications, which the Selection Committee whittled down to a short-list of six. On the first Tuesday in March, the Council blotted their brand new copybook –'an ordinary meeting of the Council was duly convened for Tuesday, 5 March 1895, but there not being sufficient members present to form a quorum, the same was adjourned to Thursday, 7 March.' On that day, Mr. Herbert Frost, Assistant Borough Surveyor of Wolverhampton, was engaged as Surveyor to the Farnham Urban District Council.

The Water Company had been invited to reduce their charges for water supplied for street-watering purposes from 1s. to 6d. per 1,000 gallons. This is new, this use of the verb 'invite' in place of the former 'ask'; it marks a superiority of status over that of their predecessors. It impressed the Water Company so much that they offered 'the same terms as their most favoured customers', viz. 1s. per 1,000 gallons for the first million gallons, 11d. per 1,000 gallons for the second million and so on down to a minimum of 6d. The Council bid 10d. down to 6d., pointing out that the water was used for public purposes and remarking that the continual breaking up of the roads by the Company caused not a little addition to the expense of their maintenance. This was more like old times, and the Water People dug their heels in. The Farnham

Rural District Council (Ernest Crundwell, Clerk) expressed their opinion–as if pioneering something–that an isolation hospital should be provided and invited the Council's co-operation.

The wife of the Medical Officer excused his absence from the March meeting because of influenza and informed the Council that Doctor Sloman had nothing to report for February except that there was a widespread epidemic of influenza ... Complaints were coming in about Mr. Ball's factory in Darvills Lane, which manufactured carbonic acid gas. Anyone who can remember back to the bicycle lamps of the 1920s will understand why. Mr. Ball gave an undertaking that fumes would not be allowed to escape in future ... Plans for new schools in East Street and West Street. The School Board were asked to leave space on the north side of the West Street School for road widening; this became Beavers Road ... The Council became involved in one of those protracted schemes for widening the footway which started off in a fit of enthusiasm and more than often ended in frustration–this time on the north side of East Street from the *Seven Stars* to Zingari Terrace at the end. Interfering with a pavement sets off a chain reaction all along its length, and when it comes to its weakest link it snaps. The Brewery agreed to set back the projecting portion of the *Seven Stars* by two feet and Mr. Sturt consented to remove the front door steps of some houses in his ownership. The Trustees of Trimmers Hospital, now being built, offered two feet provided the Council would build a retaining wall, and quickly, but there was trouble with the owners of Zingari Terrace, so they took two feet of Trimmer's frontage on the west side and tapered to nothing on the east, where it joined the Zingari frontage. And this is why in old towns one can sometimes walk three abreast on the pavement, then suddenly have to break into Indian file formation.

A letter came in March from the Thames Conservancy Board to the effect that the River Wey was being polluted by drainage from Bourne Mill and Bone Mill Cottage on the opposite side of the road. Although Mr. Alfred Simmond's properties were next door to the sewage farm, they were a long way from the nearest sewer, which the Council extended especially for the purpose of–as the Conservancy people put it–preventing any pollution reaching the Thames or its tributaries ... Mr. Frost reported difficulty in obtaining office accommodation and asked the Council to consider the provision of a permanent office for the Surveyor. Two rooms above Holden's shoe shop at 44 The Borough were leased at £10 per annum, and the Council decided to pay the rent themselves ... Damage had been caused to the pitching in the market place by the standing thereon of Mr. Cox's traction engine. Either the Council or the Town Hall Company–they never could decide which–chased him off, for a month later he and his traction engine left The Fairfield; with a third of the councillors living there, Mr. Cox could not have chosen a worse spot ... On being prodded, the Local Government Board regretfully stated that the Council's application for additional powers under the 1894 Act had been mislaid and would they send another. Whereupon the L.G.B. asked–were the Council serious, perhaps they would think it over?

Plans in May for new offices on Station Hill for the Farnham Flint, Gravel & Sand Company, of which Alfred Robins, of the adjoining nest of Robins, was a co-founder with Tom Mitchell, John Knight and William Cox. The Company offered to set the building back nine feet if the Council would buy the frontage for £10 and pave it with Victoria stone. This accounts for the extra wide bit of road on the town side of the level-crossing gates. The office was later merged with A. Robins & Sons' premises next door ... It was proposed by Cllr. Kingham, further proposed by Cllr. Hayes and seconded by Cllr. Ransom, that the roads in The Fairfield be made up and taken over; all three councillors lived in The Fairfield.

In June the Superintendent of the Fire Brigade reported that the No. 1 Fire Engine was in a very defective condition. A committee was formed to confer with the rural parish on the purchase of a new one and in due course it was resolved to buy a new manual engine for about £130, the Council finding two-thirds of the money ... Twelve cottages in Lower Church Lane were found to be sharing three closets without water laid on, and, for water supply, one pump for the whole row. This was only seventy-four years away from a technical perfection that put man on the moon ... The Council's workmen were given a day's holiday on 13 July 'to join the excursion to Brighton' ... Mr. Eggar moved 'that the duties of the Clerk being greatly increased, his salary be raised to such a sum as will be equivalent to the increased work'.

The Finance Committee raised Mr. Mason's salary from £100 to £150 from the 24 June and he was given a bonus of £25 for extra duties from 1 January 1895 ... They were now embarked on a footway along Hale Road, which was filling up between the East Street School and the *Six Bells* public house. Edgar Kempson, as Clerk to the School Board, expressed his Board's willingness to concede frontage providing the Council would erect a retaining wall to the satisfaction of Mr. J.A. Eggar, the School Board's architect. Finally a motion, seconded by Councillor Eggar, decided on giving the School £50 to set back the wall themselves, though there was an amendment, voted against by Councillor Kempson, to abandon the whole project ... The Thames Conservancy Board again; the County Analyst's test also showed an unsatisfactory sample from the sewage farm. Mr. Lemon's advice was that Mr. Bide's tenancy of the farm should cease and that the Council should farm the land themselves. This was put into effect the following November and a Farm Committee was formed, consisting of Cllrs. Coleman, Eggar, Fry, Trimmer–and Bide.

It was decided to repave Church Passage with two strips of blue bricks, 18 inches wide, with an ironstone centre and sides, at a cost of £30. This passage is so paved today; one's pleasure in walking over it is tacit but real, it is this kind of gesture that sets Farnham above its neighbours ... Mr. Kingham moved that 'it is desirable for the convenience and advantage of the public that steps be taken for the abolition of the Fairs held in the town'. He handed in a memorial in support. A copy of the resolution was sent to the Town Hall Company, who were invited to receive a deputation of the Council, but the Company did not consider it desirable to abolish the Fairs ... Mr. Bentall called attention to the great waste of time inflicted upon business men by the calling of a far greater number of jurors at a recent Quarter Sessions than would have sufficed.

At a special meeting on 29 July, 'the Clerk explained that, it having been suggested that the town should show some mark of regard for the memory of the late Bishop of Winchester on the passing of his funeral cortege from the Castle to the railway station, he had sent out a card inviting townsmen to line the footways and, having by visits to the Castle yesterday ascertained that it would be agreeable to the wishes of his late Lordship's family if the Council took some more prominent part, it was resolved that the Council do meet at 11.45 at the Council Room and precede the funeral procession from there to the railway station. That the Clerk do write and offer the sincere sympathy of the Council to the family of the late Bishop in the loss they had sustained, and express their conviction that in the Bishop's death the town had lost a sincere friend ...' When Bishop Thorold came in 1891, he had found the Castle a dark and gloomy place. It was one of those occasions that have arisen from time to time in its long history when the Castle has emerged as a white elephant. In 1890 reformers had advocated its sale but Bishop Thorold decided to save it; he prolonged its life as the residence of the Bishops of Winchester and, later, of Guildford. There have been other saviours of the castle, amongst them Bishops Fox, Morley, Brownlow North, Mew and Sumner, and Mrs. Rupert Anderson of Waverley Abbey.

There was more trouble with the cottages in Factory Yard. The M.O. discovered one in a filthy condition, without ventilation, a bedroom completely dark and the whole generally unfit for habitation. This rather sad yard with its no longer relevant name was once the home of a thriving industry. In 1827, John Stevens, maker of waggon cloths, had brought his looms from Reading to premises behind the *Bell & Crown* in Castle Street (later pulled down to provide an entrance to Watneys brewery). The business was acquired by John Leadbeater (or Lidbetter) of 5 Castle Street, who removed it in 1831 to the factory at the rear of West Street. Here he continued to manufacture waggon cloths, or rick cloths, and sarpliers for the hop industry, his produce going by road twice a week to be sold in London. Leadbeater died in 1843. The Grammar School, on its revival in 1848, used the factory for a time before moving to the other side of West Street. Factory Yard has been little changed and poses as a good example of Victorian industrial architecture on a small scale.

In August, the Joint Isolation Hospital Committee, consisting at the moment of Farnham, Urban and Rural, and Frimley, announced 'that a hospital be provided by a voluntary combination of the three authorities under section 131 of the Public Health Act, 1875'. The committee was empowered to purchase the necessary land to carry such recommendation into effect ... Several of the houses in Castle View, but not No. 9 where Councillor Fry lived, were without flushing apparatus or water supply. This dismal row of small houses off Abbey Street disappeared in the mid-1950s to make room for the by-pass road ... The Council's insurance policy covered 1 horse, 4 iron tank watering carts, 1 iron tank waggon, 9 wheelbarrows, 2 handcarts and 5 ladders, of a total value of £200 ... Plans for St. Polycarps School, next to the Roman Catholic Church in Bear Lane. It followed the Church to Waverley Lane in 1964 ... Accidents caused through shunting at the level-crossing, and a contrite Railway Company ... Letter from a Mr. Rand calling attention to the danger to perambulators through the bars of a grating outside the *Ship Inn* in The Borough running parallel instead of at rightangles to the path ... The Police reported obscene language at the public footbridge at the station, and were asked to deal with 'young fellows and others loitering on and obstructing footways in the town, particularly at street corners' ... The Fire Brigade Joint Committee had changed their minds about a manual engine and recommended the purchase of a Steam Fire Engine, and that public subscriptions be raised to cover the difference in cost–approximately £300.

In October 1895, the Council led the townspeople in a lavish welcome at the Town Hall for Doctor Randall T. Davidson, the new Bishop of Winchester, formerly of Rochester. Although the days of the Bishop as sovereign overlord were long since passed and he was like any other ratepayer, the feudal attitude never died. In the nicely balanced relationships between Englishmen, there was no good reason why it should. The townspeople were manifest in their respect for the Bishops, who earned that respect–if only by having to endure on occasions hours of being fulsomely respected in the Town Hall.

XXIII

OPPORTUNITY KNOCKS BUT ONCE

THERE IS about Farnham very little that jars upon the senses. Indeed, as everybody knows, the town has preserved intact much of its character and charm, despite its proximity to (as one of its more famous sons would have put it) the wen of London. But if there is one cloud on the horizon it is the level-crossing at the station, which has been with us–though more often against us–now for a hundred and twenty years. Yet there was a fleeting moment back in 1896 when it almost seemed as if we were going to lose it. A truce had broken out between the Railway Company and the Farnham Council, the reason being that the Company, who normally held most of the ammunition, found themselves for a change in the invidious position of wanting a favour of the Council; it had to do with the surface water in the station yard. On 24 March 1896 Mr. Samuel Bircham hoisted the white flag and proceeded to do a deal with Mr. Mason. If the Council, he said, would receive the railway's surface water into the town's surface water drainage system, and also take over the repair of the road over the bridge at Firgrove, his Company would probably pay £50 and would concede a strip of land near the level-crossing for road widening. The two generals met and arranged a summit meeting at the station on 17 April between Councillors Goddard, Eggar and Trimmer on the one part and Mr. Andrews and Mr. Hood, Railway Engineers, on the other.

The special meeting of the Council on 24 April was one of triumph. Mr. Mason reported that Mr. Bircham had increased the monetary offer to £70. The members of the deputation announced that they had discussed the drainage matter with the engineers, and also the question of whether it was possible to remove the level-crossing by diverting the road through–it was suggested–The Fairfield and Broomleaf Farm. Mr. Andrews and Mr. Hood had promised to give the scheme their support if the Council would approach the Company's Directors. It was resolved (1) that the Company's offer be accepted, and (2) that a letter be written to the Railway Company enquiring whether it would not be possible to do away with the level-crossing and if so to beg the favour of the Directors submitting a plan of any scheme to that end to the Council. Mr. Samuel Bircham replied on 16 October stating 'that the Company were prepared to abolish the level-crossing and to make and carry a road through The Fairfield over a new bridge which they would build some one hundred and fifty yards east of the present crossing gates, such road to be continued through Broomleaf and rejoining the present highway opposite the *Waverley Arms,* provided the Council would find all the land required for that purpose and indemnify the Company from all claims in respect to the diversion of the old and the making of the new road'. This letter and the accompanying plan were studied at a special meeting on 9 November. Mr. Mason gave a brief history of the level-crossing from the first reference to it in the minutes in 1890 (he was wrong–it was 1848) down to the present time. The Chairman then produced a memorial signed by some two hundred persons in opposition to the scheme.

A committee was formed consisting of the Chairman and Councillors Coleman, Eggar, Kingham and Trimmer, to approach all parties concerned. They reported on 18 December 1896:–

> Your Committee having considered this matter directed the Clerk to approach the owners of the Waverley Estate, the owners of the bulk of the buildings and land included in the Scheme and which lands, with others, the Railway Company make it a condition shall be provided by the Council, with the result that they have interviewed Mr. Anderson upon the subject and have since received from him the terms upon which he is prepared to advise the Trustees of the Waverley Estate to sell the land and buildings required of them for the Scheme. Your Committee find that these terms are so high as to place the Scheme out of further consideration by the Council and they have not therefore considered it necessary to approach the remaining owners, but recommend that the Council inform the Railway Company that they are unable to entertain the proposal contained in their letter of the 16 October last.

It was again considered in detail by a committee of the whole

Council at the close of the meeting but in the end the report was adopted. The Clerk was directed to write and 'thank Mr. Rupert D. Anderson for his courtesy in the matter and inform him that the terms mentioned had placed it beyond the power of the Council to proceed further therein'. They also wrote to Mr. Bircham, who replied on 21 December expressing regret that the Council did not see their way to proceed with the requisition of land necessary for the new road and bridge, and enquiring to what extent the Council would be prepared to assist the Scheme. Mr. Bircham and Mr. Andrews were invited to meet the Council at an early date to discuss the matter and, together with Mr. Shortt, an assistant engineer, they attended a special meeting of the Council on 23 January 1897, at which a full and frank exchange of views took place which included (1) the bringing back of the heavy goods traffic to the south of the line, (2) the provision of subways, (3) making Farnham a distributing centre, and (4) the provision of a gravel siding at the junction near Badshot bridge. On the 2 February a proposal by Mr. Kempson that a public meeting of the ratepayers should be held to consider the proposal of the Railway Company for abolishing the level-crossing was defeated by five votes to six. Then came a requisition from the ratepayers themselves for a public meeting.

The Railway Company, who seldom did anything big without getting the approval of Parliament, had written the Farnham project into the London & South-Western Railway Company (Various Powers) Bill which was already before the House, and the deadline for any objections thereto was 16 February 1897. The Council, eight days earlier, decided that their own attitude should be neutral whilst it remained a straight fight between the ratepayers and the Railway. The public meeting on 12 February resolved:–

(1) That this Meeting of Ratepayers of Farnham are opposed to the proposal of the London & South-western Railway Company for stopping up the Level-crossing near the Farnham Railway Station as described in the London & South-western Railway Company (Various Powers) Bill now before Parliament.
Proposed by Mr. E. Jackson, seconded by Mr. R.G. Trimmer and carried *nem.dis.*

(2) That in the opinion of this Meeting it is not desirable that any of the Ratepayers' money should be expended in the purchase of land or otherwise in respect of the same matter as suggested by the Directors of the London & South-western Railway Company.
Proposed by Mr. A.J. Nash, seconded by Mr. G. Ransom, and carried *nem.dis.*

(3) That in the opinion of this Meeting that unless the Railway Company can be

> induced to withdraw their proposals, the Urban District Council be requested to lodge a Petition against and oppose the Scheme to the utmost of their power.
> Proposed by Mr. E. Crundwell, seconded by Mr. Hart, and carried *nem.dis.*

On 9 March 1897 Mr. Bircham attended a special meeting of the Council and made a statement at some length in reference to the Railway Company's position in regard to the proposal to abolish the level-crossing and stated that, in view of the petition presented against the Company's Bill by some 300 to 400 ratepayers, the Directors had instructed him to say that they would withdraw that portion of their Bill relating to the level-crossing 'which they did with regret'. They thanked Mr. Bircham; if it achieved nothing else, the fiasco had brought about a closer understanding. What is certain is that the Railway Company could no longer be blamed for the continued existence of the level-crossing; the fault now lay with the townspeople themselves.

. . . . .

In his January 1896 report, the Medical Officer submitted his routine list of infectious diseases, bad sanitary conditions and the like, and stressed the great need for an isolation hospital. It was about time that the donkey caught up with the carrot, so Mr. Mason was instructed to write to Mr. Crundwell and suggest whether he could not possibly revive the interest of the Joint Committee upon the subject of the provision of an isolation hospital for the District and whether the present was not a favourable time to urge the Aldershot and Frimley Authorities to reconsider their determination with the view to their joining in the movement. In April the Local Government Board wanted to know what progress was being made, so the pressure was increased on the Rural Council to hold a meeting as soon as possible. On 15 May Mr. Crundwell wrote that Mr. Roumieu, Colonel Annand and Mr. Gardner of the R.D.C. had been nominated to serve on the Joint Committee; they met with Councillors Bentall, Goddard and Eggar and announced in July that they had purchased 11¼ acres of land known as High Elms in Weydon Lane and wanted the money to pay for it.

A reward of 40s. was offered for the arrest of the person who, on New Year's Eve, had toppled the coping of one of the piers of the bridge in South Street into the river ... Kingham & Sons were thanked for adding, in matching blue brick, the surface water channel at the side of the paving in Church Passage ... Plans for Mr. W.R. Worsam's new shop and bakery in Downing Street ... Mr. Holden gave the Surveyor notice to quit 44 The Borough and offices were rented above the Savings Bank in East Street ... It was discovered that The Conservative Club—that unofficial council chamber in Ivy Lane—was not connected to the sewer ... The Engineer at the pumping station was told to keep a logbook and note anything of a special nature 'such as any unusual discharge into the tanks' ... Mr. A.R. Bide's estimate of two guineas was accepted for 300 trees to plant at the farm.

John Henry Knight of Barfields complained about the condition of the roads in the Guildford Road area; to Farnham's first motorist, this was a matter of some importance. It was only to be expected that that genius of mechanical contrivances, J.H. Knight, should own a car; he invented it. George Parfitt built it at his workshop at 50 West Street. The car, if not the first to be made in Britain, was, it has been said, the first two-seater. It went on show at the Crystal Palace in 1896 and is now in almost mint condition at Beaulieu. The car's speed of 8 miles an hour put a severe strain on the man with the red flag who was required by the Locomotive Acts to precede it, so Mr. Knight often dispensed with his services and instead put a severe strain on his peers sitting on the Bench. The County Council, too, picked him up in Castle Street for 'permitting a locomotive, other than a locomotive for repairing the roads, to be used without a licence'. That motorists' charter—the Motor Car Act, 1903—was forced by men like Knight who did not mind paying the fines.

James Knight, manager of the Capital & Counties Bank, and the Council's Treasurer, died in February. The new manager, Edward Eaton Richmond, was appointed as Treasurer, rather than change banks, though Henry Goujon, manager of the London & County since 1862 and a very well known figure in Farnham, also applied ... M. & J. Tily of Castle Street had a plan in for a workshop in Long Garden Walk; it did not conform with the bye-laws and was disapproved. In March the Council asked them how it was they had built it when the plan had not been passed.

This was an awkward question to answer, and there is no record of it being answered. A motion to make Tilys pull it down was lost by a small majority; they were allowed to keep it for ten years. The affair toughened the Council's attitude towards planning approvals ... A provisional order dated 25 March 1896 from the Local Government Board conferred upon the Council the power of appointing Overseers of the Poor for the Parish of Farnham. This was one of the things the L.G.B. had asked whether the Council were serious about; Overseers were appointed by the Justices unless application was made by Councils under the 1894 Act–there did not seem much point in it unless it was one of prestige. Overseers chosen for the ensuing year were Charles Smith, George Ransom, Henry Patrick and Charles Borelli ... In their proud role as farmers, the Council met at the sewage farm on 8 April to inspect the crop of rye grass, which was later sold for £12.

They had again counted in everything that they could possibly think of in submitting an estimate for main roads for the year ending 31 March 1897, amounting to £804. The County Surveyor stated that 'nearly every item in the schedule proposed by the Council was too high'; he sent an amended schedule which came to £604. They had a special meeting on 14 April to consider this outrage and called the County Surveyor's attention to the heavy traffic on the roads, that his revised estimate had not included provisions for channelling and that the roads required this from end to end, that he had not allowed a sufficient sum for legitimate repair of footways which on the outskirts of the main roads were in a bad condition and finally 'that unless the amount mentioned by the County Surveyor was very considerably increased, the Council would prefer that the County Council should themselves take over the repair of the main roads'. In July the County called their bluff and gave notice of taking over the roads as from 1 August; the Council grudgingly pruned their estimate and accepted the £604.

The retiring members this year were Eggar and Kempson, who were re-elected, and Williams and Ransom, who lost their seats to Charles Smith and Samuel Beesley, the grocer in East Street. A.J. Bentall became Chairman ... A Mrs. Clinton wrote on 28 April concerning the damage caused to her dress by the negligent

Plate 38 *The Borough, with former Town Hall*

Plate 39 *84-85 East Street, pulled down to make room for St. Cross Road. Sturt's wheelwright shop is on the right*

Plate 40 *John Henry Knight and his wife in a Benz motor car, 1901*

Plate 41 *The* Sun *and* Bird-in-Hand, *Downing Street*

Plate 42 *Site of Council Offices built in 1903*

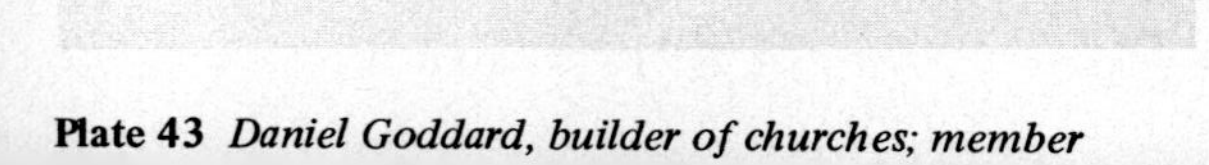

Plate 43 *Daniel Goddard, builder of churches; member*

Plate 44 *Randall T. Davidson, bishop of Winchester,*

behaviour of one of the water cart drivers. The Council profusely apologised and told the contractor 'to employ upon the water cart in question only intelligent and reliable men' ... The Bishop of Winchester complained of the stoppage of a drain at the Castle caused by the fault of the Council's workmen and claimed compensation of £1 2s. 6d. for having it put right. The Surveyor explained that an accident had occurred in removing a drain plug in an inspection chamber at the Castle; the plug, said Mr. Frost, had 'got washed into the drain', but thinking it had fallen through into the sewer, he had taken no further action. Fulsome apologies to the Bishop and a severe reprimand for the Surveyor ... The Water Company wanted to lay a new main across the railway bridge at Firgrove but there was no depth in the road in which to bury it. The Company's Engineer, Mr. Pain, suggested raising a 3-foot wide footway on the west side of the road over the bridge and burying the pipe in that. There wasn't much width on the bridge to spare and that accounts for the single file formation necessary when walking across ... The Liberal Club were given permission to erect a flagstaff outside the Club ... Plans for Mr. Heath's showrooms in South Street, with workshops in Union Road ... The Hale Road area was being developed rapidly; Park Road and Winton Road were sewered ... The L. & S-W.R. were persuaded to improve the entrance from the road at Firgrove into the proposed new road for gravel traffic leading to the station yard.

At a special meeting on 28 July, Mr. Goddard, as Chairman of the Fire Brigade Joint Committee, proudly announced the Committee's proposal to purchase a Merryweather 300-gallon, double-cylinder, horizontal steam fire engine, with accessories and hose, at a cost of £479, and that his Committee had collected over £300 towards it. It has been told that, at its inauguration ceremony, presided over by Mrs. Fitzroy of Hale Place, it was urgently summoned to a big fire in the district and in the morning the resplendant new engine limped home, a battered veteran with its paintwork blistered off ... The five cottages taken over by the Burial Board when extending the Farnham cemetery in 1883 had 'two privies only which were full and very foul; the drain was stopped and the drinking water was from a well and did not appear to be very good', so they were demolished and the site taken into the cemetery ... Mr. Kingham moved 'that overtures be made with the view to the purchase of the property of the Farnham Market House & Town Hall Company'. Mr. Crundwell, described as Honorary Secretary of the Company, intimated that his Directors were prepared to consider any offer the Council might make. They studied balance sheets for the past five years and bid £4,200. Mr. Crundwell replied that not less than £4 per share could be accepted, making a total of £5,600, and that there could be no separate sale of the fair site in Castle Street–which was what the Council was really after. There the matter ended, another of those good ideas which never materialised ... The Council took over the administration of the various parochial charities ... The Secretary of State for War was invited to make a grant towards the upkeep of the roads by reason of the extraordinary traffic thereon caused by the Military of Aldershot.

In the autumn of 1896 there was a bad epidemic of measles, causing several deaths, and the schools were closed for some weeks ... In October the meter lamp at the bottom of Castle Street exploded whilst being lit, injuring Baker, the lamplighter, who was granted three guineas by way of compensation; Doctor Coffey claimed £3 17s. 6d. for attending him ... The foreman at the sewage farm was given a rise of 2s. 6d. a week for pumping the sludge at four o'clock in the morning during the summer. £77 was realised for the farm's crop of mangel-wurzels ... The County Medical Officer, reporting on water supplies, said that Farnham had the worst record in the County for typhoid, which was caused 'by the shallow, polluted wells allowed to continue by the Council–an example of how a good water supply was allowed to suffer from bad sanitary arrangements' ... Obscene language in South Street from Frederick Siftern, George Nutbean and Henry Martin ... Mr. Gould Q.C. and another resident complained of the firing of guns in a show at a recent fair in Castle Street ... The Local Government Board sanctioned a loan of £270 to purchase the site for the isolation hospital in Weydon Lane. Why it was later called 'Green Lane Hospital' is neither here nor there–the hospital certainly isn't there ... John Nash of the old Local Board died ... In the middle of discussing the month's bag of illnesses at the December meeting 'several ratepayers entered the Council Chamber'. Voting was even on whether they should be allowed to stay and the Chairman gave his casting vote against this, whereupon the intruders explained their reason for gate-crashing– not stated, though it might have had something to do with the offer to the Town Hall Company, for large items of expenditure never failed to arouse the ratepayers, and on second thoughts they were allowed to remain. The incident perhaps might have been responsible for the transfer in 1903 of the seat of local government in Farnham from its proper place at the corner of Castle Street and The Borough to an inferior site in South Street.

Queen, that from Spring to Autumn of thy reign,
Has taught thy people how 'tis queenlier far
Than any golden pomp of peace or war,
Simply to be a woman without stain.
Queen whom we love, who lovest us again.

W. Watson

XXIV

DIAMOND JUBILEE

SIR WILLIAM Rose, Bart. of Moor Park did not, surprisingly, renew his bid for privacy in his expensive home until 4 January 1897, when his solicitors, Messrs. Bompas & Co., wrote to the Council enclosing a copy of a notice which they were inserting in the local press, stating that their client intended to close the lodge gates of Moor Park and not allow any person to enter without written authority. The Council informed Messrs. Bompas & Co. that 'they had no doubt as to the rights of way over Moor Park and were resolved at whatever cost to use all proper means to preserve such rights'.

The affair escalated rapidly. At a special meeting on 15 January, Mr. Mason read correspondence from which it appeared that Sir William Rose adhered to his intention to close the gates, and to do so on the following Sunday, 17 January. The Council instructed Mr. Frost to be present with some of the workmen and 'if any obstructions to the right of way be then found, that he do remove same'. Public notice of the Council's intention was given, with the request that the inhabitants refrain from any conduct which might lead to a breach of the peace. On the following day a joint meeting of the Urban and Rural Councils was held, chaired by Colonel Windham of the latter council, who explained that the meeting had been called in consequence of Sir William's express determination to close the gates of Moor Park on Sunday in spite of efforts made by their Clerks to induce him 'to select some other day and to fasten the gates in some manner that they might be broken open technically by Council representatives, so raising the question as to the right of way through the Park'. Colonel Windham also announced that Sir William had enlisted the services of some ex-Metropolitan policemen and others to secure the gates by force and that, in the present state of feeling in the matter, a serious disturbance might well arise, the consequence of which would rest with Sir William Rose.

It is seldom, in the relationships between English gentlemen, that disputes are settled otherwise than by the dignified processes of litigation, but this was fighting talk. Three proposals were considered by the councils on the eve of battle, namely:

> That no action be taken by the Councils tomorrow (Sunday) in the matter, but that the Councils' Surveyors do attend on the next day (Monday) and endeavour to remove any obstructions to the highways in question and continue their efforts until they were successful.
>
> That the Councils take no action in the matter tomorrow (Sunday) but wait until it was seen what course of action the public would take.
>
> That the Councils' Surveyors do attend at Moor Park tomorrow (Sunday) to remove any obstructions to the highways in question and that, if they were met with force, they should retire and take such steps as they were able for the removal of such obstructions whenever the opportunity for so doing arose.

Number 3 was passed by the twelve votes to six. One should not criticise the strategists in the field, but it is conceivable that had the second proposal been adopted the course of Farnham local government history might have been considerably brightened. As it was the events of Sunday, 17 January 1897, at the Bourne Place entrance to Moor Park were hardly in keeping with the traditional Victorian passion for observing the Sabbath.

Farnham's miniature battle was fought out in the cold January weather. Sir William's men duly closed and chained the gates early on Sunday morning and a crowd of some four or five hundred townsmen, and a sprinkling of women, gathered outside. The snow lay on the ground; this came in useful as ammunition for those who were not armed with sticks, crowbars, sledgehammers and other assorted ironmongery. Herbert Frost and his rural colleague, John Stedman, were cheered as they forced the chains with crowbars. The defenders, consisting of a handful of lodgekeepers and other servants, though reinforced by the six ex-City policemen, were clearly no match for the superior strength of the attackers, who by sheer weight of numbers breached the gates and won for the town a victory that has never since been challenged.

Herbert Frost was given a hero's welcome at the Council meeting on 2 February. News had spread; the Secretary of the Commons Preservation Society wrote congratulating the Council upon their action and promising support if needed. And so what came to be known as 'The Battle of Moor Park' passed into local history; there were, as has been said earlier, two ways of evaluating the outcome.

. . . . .

Two cases of enteric fever at the Workhouse, probably caused by overcrowding of the infectious wards because of an epidemic of diphtheria at Hale ... The Surveyor reported that it was impossible to keep Frensham Road in good order because of the extraordinary number of vehicles on the road carting gravel. Mr. C.A. Pearson of Frensham Place (now Edgeborough School), who used the road frequently, complained about the bad surface. Later Sir Cyril Pearson, he was the owner of *Pearsons Weekly* and other periodicals of the time. The Frensham Road was described as running from the Council's boundary as far as the railway and did not include the steep stretch down into Bridge Square, known variously in the past as Sir Nelsons Hill or Barlows Hill ... The Council applied to the Local Government Board for joint custody with the Rural District Council of all non-ecclesiastical maps, books and documents belonging to the ancient parish of Farnham, the same to be deposited in a proper receptacle to be kept in the Council Chamber, which was the common meeting place of both Councils. Apart from purposes of reference one senses that the Councillors, who in their turn are characters in a history book, had a love of old records ... £270 was borrowed from Bolton Corporation over fifty years at 3¼ per cent to pay for the site of the proposed isolation hospital ... They went to a great deal of trouble to act as hosts to the Surrey Volunteer Brigade at Easter, writing round to likely people in the town who owned large buildings suitable as temporary billets and, having arranged these, sent an invitation to Lord Belhaven, the Commanding Officer, who thanked them but declined ... The Urban District Councils Association sent a copy of a Bill extending the provisions of the Poor Law Officers Superannuation Act 1896 to officers and servants of other local authorities ... The attention of the police was drawn to the excessive speed at which some locomotives travelled through the town ... An enquiry was held on 26 January in reference to the proposed severence of Aldershot from the Farnham Union. Aldershot had now grown up and was ready to leave home; the town has since been trying to get the old people to come back and live with them ... Father Gerin was asked to change the position of his dung pit in Bear Lane ... Incandescent gas mantles were now being tried out as an experiment as an answer to dirty lamp glasses.

In March they purchased a new street sweeper and an additional horse and mud cart for £93 ... On 15 March they were invited to the opening of the new waterworks in Darvills Lane. The Water Company had installed filters and Doctor Stevenson, reporting on a sample, said that it was excellent water for drinking and all domestic purposes ... Plans in April for Taylor & Anderson's new offices in South Street, and next door for Nash & Sons, the auctioneers ... A printed list of Members' attendances at meetings during the year to March 1897 was inserted in the minute-book. Of a possible total number of Council meetings–ordinary, adjourned and special, Mr. Bentall was at all thirty-five. Charles Trimmer was at the bottom of the class with only eighteen. The notice also states, as if a matter of some surprise, that during the year 1,231 letters were written and 1,364 circulars issued.

Mr. McDonald's application to erect a fountain in Castle Street, in commemoration doubtless of Queen Victoria and Mr. McDonald, was greeted with enthusiasm, provided that no expense fell on the Council and that they were indemnified against any possible claim for damages, etc., and that a committee would fix the site, and so on–anyway, Mr. McDonald, whose fountain it really was, abandoned the idea altogether ... At the 1897 Election, Charles Trimmer did not stand, but his brother, Robert George, upheld the family tradition by taking his place. Charles Fry lost to George Ransom, who regained his seat with top marks of 439. Surgeon-Major William Henry Hayes of The Fairfield was appointed Chairman and Mr. W.T. Coleman Vice-chairman.

In May, the Guardians gave notice that no more cases of infectious diseases would be admitted to the Workhouse wards after the end of 1897. That left eight months for the Joint

Isolation Hospital Committee, who were as yet in the negotiation stages with the Mayor, Aldermen and Burgesses of the Bolton Corporation over the site money, to complete the deal, get their buildings up and make the beds. They were asked for a progress report and in July Mr. Crundwell was able to announce Mr. Stapley's plans for the hospital, estimated to cost £4,997, and to suggest that the Urban Council should go about getting sanction to borrow their proportion of it without delay. Somewhat dismayed, the Council asked for a meeting with the Rural Council in order to discuss the whole matter. The special meeting on 15 July was attended by Mr. Baldwyn Fleming, an inspector from the Local Government Board, and Doctor Seaton, the County Medical Officer, and it was probably due to these two gentlemen that the project went through, for there was a lot of huffing and puffing and some attempt to prune the estimate.

Herbert Frost resigned in June, having been appointed Surveyor to the Gosport and Alverstoke Urban District Council. On 13 July Mr. Robert William Cass of Pudsey, Yorkshire, was chosen to replace him. Unlike his predecessor, Mr. Cass was to stay in Farnham for the rest of his life; his sons also ... Plans for a shop in South Street for Charles Smith and a new school in Castle Street for Mrs. Swayne ... A new entrance to Farnham Park was made at the top of St. James Avenue and a cordial vote of thanks to the Lord Bishop of Winchester 'for conferring a boon upon the inhabitants of the District by granting a new approach to the Park' ... An extract from the *Weekly Herald* of 5 June was entered upon the minutes, entitled 'A Narrow Shave':–

> Just before the 10.45 Guildford train steamed into Farnham Station on Monday, considerable excitement was manifested in the neighbourhood of the level-crossing. The gates were not opened when expected and porters and others hurrying to see what had occurred, found that a pony attached to a chaise coming down the hill and slipped and fallen just outside the gate. Fortunately the accident had occurred a few yards out of danger, and after a minute's delay the gates were opened and the train was able to pass through. Neither the pony nor the occupants of the chaise were injured.

By far the most important event of 1897 was the Queen's Diamond Jubilee, though it was heralded in Farnham by a mere flicker of interest when Charles Smith proposed, at the February meeting, 'that the Council do consider what steps, if any, shall be taken by the Council to commemorate the long reign of the Queen and that the Parish Council be invited to confer with this Council as to the joint action in the matter'. It was decided, however, at a joint meeting of the two councils, to go their separate ways, apart from a treat for the schoolchildren on Commemoration Day. A public meeting was held at the National Schools at the end of March, at which such events were arranged as a tea for the children, a dinner for the old people, a bonfire and fireworks. Whitehall sanctioned any reasonable expenditure and the Council voted a sum not exceeding £50. As representative of Farnham, it was resolved 'that a humble address of congratulations under the seal of the Council be presented to Her Most Gracious Majesty upon the attainment and completion of the Sixtieth Year of her Reign'. This was worded as follows:–

> To Her Most Gracious Majesty the Queen,
>
> We, the Urban District Council of Farnham, representing all classes of Your Majesty's subjects in the ancient Town of Farnham, Surrey, do humbly approach and offer with sincere loyalty and affection to Your Majesty our heartfelt congratulations upon the attainment and completion of the Sixtieth Year of Your Majesty's Reign.
>
> We earnestly pray that Almighty God may vouchsafe unto Your Majesty a continuance of His blessing and ensure to Your Majesty all peace and happiness.

The Chairman's scheme for the public celebration by the Council was:–

> (1) for the planting of three trees, presented by Samuel Bide, opposite Windsors Almshouses in Castle Street, one opposite the centre, the others 30 feet distant on either side, each 9 feet from the kerb.
> (2) two seats to be placed between these trees
> (3) a third seat at the corner of St. James Avenue by the School wall
> (4) a fourth seat near the entrance to the Castle upon a site that the Bishop would be invited to fix at or near Lovers Walk
> (5) a fifth seat with the consent of the Brewery by the cemetery
> (6) a sixth seat as near to the site of the old tree which used to stand by The Cedars, Castle Hill, as may be after consultation with Mr. Andrews and Colonel Marsden.
>
> The Council's employees to be given a holiday with double pay on Jubilee Day–22nd June, the drivers of water-carts included. The inhabitants to be encouraged to decorate their houses and business premises.

The Council, since Mr. Smith's reference to 'what steps, if any' had got a little carried away and their enthusiasm was watered down in the days that followed the glorious 22 June. It is true that a letter arrived from the Home Secretary stating that the Address of the Council had been laid before the Queen, 'who had been pleased to receive the same very graciously'. The Rev. C.H.

Simkinson and the Churchwardens, too, had shown them a courteous consideration at the Special Thanksgiving Service at the Parish Church on 20 June. But the Farnham United Brewery were unable to offer a site for the fifth seat and the Bishop was only willing to allow seat No. 4 in Lovers Walk 'in the hope that definite instructions would be given to the Police to prevent the seat becoming a nuisance and that the Council would remove if it it did'. Colonel Marsden of The Cedars thought the situation of seat No. 6 would be 'unwise and objectionable', though he did present seven trees for planting on the bank between The Cedars and the foot of the castle steps. And the Town Hall Company expressed surprise that the Council had planted trees and two seats in Castle Street without consulting them, that it infringed the Town Hall Company's Market and Fair Rights and would the Council remove them. To which the Council replied that they were 'extremely surprised to receive such a communication and could not believe the Company to be serious in making the request and that the Council were unanimously resolved to decline to remove either the trees or the seats and that they could not admit the right of the Company to dictate to them what they should do or not do in the exercise of their statutory powers'. To which the Company pointed out that they did not at present ask the Council to remove the trees and that if the Council were willing to make a payment of 7s. 6d. for each fair in respect of the space occupied by the seats, they would let the matter rest, otherwise they would have them removed. The Council did not answer this letter.

The seat in Lovers Walk at the top of the Castle steps, almost certainly the venue of many a betrothal, has not so far caused a nuisance, though this may be due to lack of vigilance on the part of the police, who were young themselves once. And Mr. Bide's three plane trees remained; they have grown into a lovely feature of their noble setting.

This Bath was built to commemorate the Sixtieth
Year of Her Majesty Victoria 1st. Reign, 1837-1897.

Inscribed by Harold Falkner above entrance to
old Swimming Bath, Farnham

XXV

ROBERT WILLIAM CASS, SURVEYOR

AND NOW the Victorians knew that they had entered the closing phases of the reign, that the splendour of the Diamond Jubilee had marked the approaching finale of what, after a period of sixty years, they recognised as an era in the social life of the country. The celebrations commemorated the past and held little promise for the future; the ageing Queen, nearing her eightieth year, had retired to her reclusion at Osborne and, together with her subjects, awaited the next ceremonial occasion of the reign—the state funeral ... Little, if any, melancholy settled on the surface of local affairs which, as needs be, were carried on in Farnham as usual; there were in fact noticeable improvements, attributable to the new Surveyor, Mr. Robert William Cass.

Mr. Cass heralded the importation of a new breed of local government officers, who were knowledgeable in their profession and competent to give advice to rather than execute the theories of a secular body of brewers, builders, grocers, tailors, bakers, nurserymen, doctors, saddlers, solicitors and other gentlemen of the town who, with the best will in the world, could not be expected to be experienced in the practical business of repairing roads, coaxing intractable drains, coping with nuisance-mongers and the hundred-and-one other jobs that Cass, as a qualified surveyor, took in his stride. This Yorkshireman strode through Farnham discovering its weaknesses and, with recommendations of remedies that were usually accepted, obtained his employers' permission to put them right.

There was trouble, for instance, with the smells again from the sewage works, which meant recalling Mr. Lemon, and also visits to Dorking, Alton and Sutton to see how they managed. Dorking used a chemical precipitation system, coupled with filtration of the effluent. Alton and Sutton were experimenting with biological or bacteria filters. Such equipment was expensive to install and the results not certain. Mr. Lemon made suggestions, but the Council 'had the benefit of an exhaustive report by Mr. Cass which practically agrees with Mr. Lemon but going further in recommending remedial measures of much value'. They gave him the go-ahead to try them out. Mr. Cass also sorted out the street lighting situation, suggesting that a man be employed full-time to cleanse, examine, paint and glaze the lamps, replace burners, etc., and two men for lighting and extinguishing them. Mr. G. Fitzpatrick was appointed as Lamp Examiner and Lighter at £1 a week. It is said that Cass later pioneered the repair of road surfaces by tar-spraying, a system first attributed officially to J.A. Brodie, City Engineer of Liverpool, in 1904. The report-book claims earlier experiments in Farnham streets, in one instance referred to as 'my patent tar process', and Cass records on 7 July 1903 that 'some time ago' he had tried out tar-spraying in the passage that leads from Station Hill to The Fairfield. He formed a company with Richard Preston which operated for a time in the neighbourhood of Farnham before coming to an untimely end.

The Bishop Morley Stone features off and on in the minutes between June 1897, when Colonel Marsden, who had dislodged it from its former resting place when rebuilding The Cedars and was wondering what to do with it, passed his embarrassment on to the Council, suggesting that the Stone should be resited with a suitable inscription on the wall alongside the footpath leading to the castle steps, and May 1898, when it was finally laid to rest on the wall in the entrance courtyard of the Castle. It is said that the Morley Stone, which is dated 1677 and bears the mitre and arms of the Bishop, was once set in the wall of the reservoir that supplied water to the Conduit, though Mr. Goddard, in a letter to Mr. Mason, doubted this. The Council wrote to Bishop Randall Davidson that 'it appearing to be somewhat difficult to discover the previous history of the Stone, it had been unanimously agreed that it would be best preserved if his Lordship could find a place for it somewhere on the Castle walls where it could be seen by the public, and allow a short inscription to be placed beneath it to record the fact of its recent removal and adding the date thereof' The Bishop disagreed but was willing to place the Stone somewhere inside the Castle for its permanent protection, though out of sight of the public. The Council thanked the Bishop and resolved to replace it at the spot from which it had been removed; an amendment that it be put on the outside wall of the Grammar School was defeated. Then it was decided to have another go at Bishop Randall Davidson and, at the end of a year's palaver, they settled on the best place for it, where it is safe from vandals, though it lacks an inscription whereby visitors to the castle could learn something of its history and relate the Stone to the town's first channelled water supply.

There was a letter from Mr. Austwick dated 27 July 1897, which complained of the furious riding by cyclists. Whereas motorists were restricted to walking pace, the speed of cycles was entirely unchecked, though the Chief Constable promised to watch out for dangerous riding. As if by way of retaliation, the Cyclists Touring Club put in a complaint about hedge cuttings being left on the roads ... The Local Government Board stipulated that the proposed isolation hospital should itself be isolated from the surrounding world by a corrugated iron fence at least 6½ feet in height. The Council agreed, if only the Board would sanction the loan of £6,000 so that they could get on with the job. The Joint Committee had accepted the tender of Messrs. Tompsett & Co. of £5,668 for building two wards, each to contain ten beds (instead of three wards with ten, eight and four beds, as originally planned), and the total cost, excluding furniture, worked out at £6,118. The Guardians' deadline for non-admission to the Workhouse after the end of 1897 came and passed, with the Councils frantically trying to borrow £300 to erect an iron building on the site to serve as a temporary ward until the hospital was built ... In September 1897, an opportunity arose to improve Bridge Square when Mr. Stacey rebuilt his premises on the corner of Abbey Street and Longbridge. He parted with a width of 8 feet in Abbey Street and 5 feet in Longbridge for £120; Reid & Co., brewers for the *Bridge House Inn* also sold a strip to continue the new frontage line. Bridge Square, potentially one of Farnham's more attractive features, has its promise, seventy years later, of achieving that distinction ... The Rt. Hon. St. John Brodrick, M.P. promised Councillor Bide that he would do everything in his power to obtain a grant from the War Department to help pay for the damage caused by military traffic on the roads ... The Council expressed their sympathy to the Royal Family on the death of the Duchess of Teck ... Doctor Stevenson adversely reported on the condition of the water supplying the Conduit. Windsors Almshouses, which still used this supply, were now connected to Company's mains and Bishop Morley's water undertaking finally went out of business.

A nuisance was reported at the dairy at Hatch Mill in Darvills Lane where there was 'an offensive manure heap and a pool of filthy matter, also that there was on the premises a privy which was hand-flushed and discharged directly into the river'. Doctor Sloman was told that, in cases like this, he should 'take photos' of the premises involved ... Name plates were ordered, costing £5, for St. James Avenue, St. James Terrace, South View, Park Lane (vice Bear Lane), Factory Yard, Beavers Yard, Babs Mead, Mount Pleasant, West End Estate, Alfred Road, St. Georges Road, Hale Road, Guildford Road and Union Road–an indication of how the town had grown in the last few years ... It was the butchers who were the chief offenders when it came to obstructing the footways in the shopping streets. Their curious practice of hanging out their wares all over the front of their shops, where they were exposed to the dust and dirt, persisted well into the next century. The police were asked to keep an eye on it; Fletcher & Co. were singled out by the Council for a special warning.

Mr. Cass got a £10 rise on condition that he provided himself with a bicycle 'or other means of locomotion' to assist him in carrying out his duties ... The custody in conjunction with the Rural District Council, of non-ecclesiastical records of the old Parish was confirmed by the Local Government Board. The two Councils met the Rector and Churchwardens on 11 February and inspected the chests in the Church only to find nothing of any value save the Rate-books, which were not complete. It was resolved to gather them all up and keep them in the Council Chamber. These books today are mouldering away in a damp store, once a mortuary; in 1897 they received the respect such old books deserve.

When the Town Hall Company raised the rent of the Council Chamber to £15 per annum as from 25 March 1898, a committee was formed to study ways and means of acquiring permanent accommodation of their own to house councillors, officers and equipment. Of all buildings in a town the Council Offices should be owned by the occupiers; in Farnham the Council were the mere tenants of a commercial company, whose secretary, forsooth, was their Rate Collector, Alfred Thorp—it was a galling situation. They were to move to a place of their own in South Street in 1903; it was opened by the Archbishop of Canterbury.

Messrs. Potter & Crundwell, acting on behalf of the owners of properties in Tilford Road just the other side of the District boundary, asked whether by some special arrangement their clients could be brought into the town's sewerage system. The Sanitary Committee were not in favour but recommended an extension of the boundaries to bring in various developments around the town. A Committee of the whole Council considered the question and their recommendation 'that the Council do take immediate steps for the extension of their District' was subsequently studied by the Council who, by seven votes to three, adjourned it sine die ... There was a circular from the New Mutual Telephone Syndicate Limited which the Council considered and, somewhat pompously, resolved:—

> That in the interests of Trade, Industry and Social Convenience it is essential that the fullest possible development of the Telephone Service in this country should be promoted. That in order to effect such development the charge must be considerably reduced. That the best and cheapest service can only be secured by competition. That as the Treasury Minute of 23 May 1892 provides as a matter of general policy that competition shall not be prevented, this Council earnestly requests the Postmaster General do grant licenses to any municipality or companies which comply with the requirements of the Treasury Minute.

Having sorted out the nation's telephone problem they next wrote to the Secretary of the Board of Agriculture informing him 'that in the opinion of the Council, the existing regulations in reference to the muzzling of dogs are unnecessary and should be removed'.

In the spring of 1898 arose that curious phenomenon of the St. Cross Estate—its two narrow, half-width entrance roads, from the west leading to Beaufort Road and the approach from East Street into Sumner Road, which make of that Victorian enclave a sort of residential fastness; one expects to find drawbridges. A

Mr. C.E. Moore had submitted a plan for a house in Wykeham Road which showed a road not of the width of 30 feet required by bye-laws. A committee met on the site with the Estate owners' solicitor, Mr. Crundwell, who contended that the proposed road was in fact in accordance with the bye-laws. By some mischance he was right and the Council had to give way; Mr. Moore's plan was approved, together with others for two houses for Mr. Fostekew in Wykeham Road, four villas in Beaufort Road and four for Mrs. Kelly in St. James Terrace. The pockets of building land were filling up fast.

In April 1898 Mr. A.J. Bentall (257 votes) lost his seat to James Henry Wilcox (425), the South Street outfitter. Mr. Coleman (459), Doctor Hayes (448) and Mr. Goddard (273) were returned. Charles Fry staged a comeback but lost with 218. Mr. Coleman succeeded Doctor Hayes as Chairman ... They expressed sympathy to the widow on the death of William Neal, who had for many years attended meetings as the representative of the *Surrey & Hants. News* ... They called the attention of the Thames Conservancy Board to 'the unsightly and objectionable state of the water in the river', which was sort of reversing the normal process ... Notices warning cyclists of dangerous conditions on the roads were set up Castle Hill, Firgrove Hill and Bourne Mill Hill.

At a special meeting on 18 May 1897, the Chairman asked what steps 'if any' it was proposed to take to accord a public welcome to Her Royal Highness the Duchess of Albany on the occasion of her visit on 30 May in order to open the new Swimming Bath. This was one of the projects of the townspeople, acting through a Commemorative Committee, whose Chairman was Doctor Charles Tanner of Downing Street and Secretaries were Mr. R.W. Mason and Mr. George Murrell, to mark the Diamond Jubilee. Swimming had always been a popular sport in the town, first in a disorderly way in the river and the nude, then as a Swimming Club, with Mr. E.W. Langham as Secretary and a fenced-off stretch of the river complete with dressing-boxes and, presumably, swim-suits. Doctor Tanner collected £600 from his wealthier patients and Mr. Harold Falkner, in addition to acting as Hon. Architect, contributed the required balance of £100. When it came to the opening, Bishop Randall Davidson, who was one of Doctor Tanner's patients, invited the Duchess of Albany to lunch at the castle and got her to perform the ceremony. She was presented by Mr. Falkner with an illuminated address from the Commemmorative Committee and a gilt key cast by Mr. Borelli which, to everyone's relief, turned in the lock. The Council's part in the ceremony was small; the Bath was not their's–it was not taken over until the 1920's, when the Club could no longer afford to run it. It was, on the other hand, incumbent upon the town's governors to show an interest. Their own address of welcome was a masterpiece of verbosity:–

> May it please Your Royal Highness, we, the Urban District Council of Farnham gladly avail ourselves of the opportunity which Your Royal Highness's visit to our ancient and historical town offers, to tender to you a cordial welcome and on behalf of ourselves and our fellow Townsmen to testify the pleasure we experience in the honour which Your Royal Highness is conferring upon us.
>
> We cannot but be aware that Your Royal Highness's visit is to perform certain functions, the one which cannot fail to result in much good to the Town in that it will contribute both to the health and recreation of its inhabitants, the other to promote the religious and moral culture of lads, the fruit of which the old Town must in due course reap, and we trust that the name of Your Royal Highness will so be perpetuated amongst us.
>
> We venture, though it may be unnecessary, to remind Your Royal Highness that we are justified in referring to the Town as 'ancient' and 'historical' in that it dates at least a thousand years back, when its inhabitants gallantly fought for Christianity against Paganism and that, with the Castle, the home for so many centuries now of successive Bishops of Winchester, it directly shared many of the stirring events of bygone days.
>
> We would finally beg to offer to Your Royal Highness our sincere thanks for your presence today which is accepted as a token of the interest always taken by the Royal Family in every effort which contributes to the Welfare of Her Majesty's subjects.

They thanked the ladies and gentlemen in the town who had taken part in organising the ceremony–the Misses Banks, Preston, Andrews, Mathews, Cooper, Longhurst, Mason, Bentall, Mrs. R.W. Mason, Miss C. Mason, Miss M. Mason, the Bishop, Mr. Richard Mason, Mr. Robert Sampson, Mr. Simmonds, the Police Superintendent, and Mr. Elliott of the Fire Brigade. The Local Volunteers, who had been booked to provide a guard of honour, had failed to materialise and the Council expressed their disappointment to their Commanding Officer, Captain the Hon. H. Cubitt. The Local Volunteers, it seemed, were loth to volunteer for local duties.

Peaceably if we can, forcibly if we must.
Henry Clay–1813

XXVI

BLOODY, BOLD AND RESOLUTE

ABOUT THE time when stirring things were happening in the Soudan the Farnham Council exhibited a new aggressiveness in their attitude towards old adversaries, an attitude inspired perhaps not so much by Major-General Kitchener as by Mr. Robert William Cass, who stalked or cycled through the streets, the embodiment of local power and the complement of that equally astute though more gentle lawyer, Mr. Richard Mason. And, in turn, their adversaries displayed a new wiliness, so that honours were about even and in the ultimate result the Council made no significant gains. But the good fight changed the course of history in one respect to the Council's advantage in that they rid themselves of their landlords and acquired a place of their own. Which is why the Town Hall is in Castle Steet and the Council meets in South Street, a point that often puzzles strangers.

The Town Hall Company, who had repeatedly declined the Council's invitation to provide W.C. and lavatory accommodation for the users of the Council Chamber, were now admonished for a similar lack of hospitality towards the professional men, prisoners, witnesses and others attending the sittings of the Courts held in the Hall. When the Company next applied for the annual renewal of the theatre licence, they were told–no toilets, no licence. The Council were also campaigning for one outside. Negotiations had been reopened for the purchase of the Town Hall, and more particularly the market and fair rights in the street outside, and although the Company would not budge from their figure of £7,000, they were willing to lease a site for £7 a year at the rear of the Hall in The Borough and the Council set about planning a public convenience, in the face of a protest from the outraged residents in the immediate vicinity. There was also an alternative suggestion of a site in South Street, and this is where it was built some five years later, with Council Offices attached.

They were not above taking part in Parliamentary affairs. Over the Vaccination Bill they made known their views through the medium of the Rt. Hon. St. John Brodrick M.P.:–

> That this Council is most strongly of the opinion that clause 3 of the Bill now before the House of Commons entitled 'A Bill to amend the Law with respect to Vaccination' is a direct infringement of the liberties of the people and also of the liberties and powers which should be exercised by the Poor Law Guardians of this country, and therefore expresses its strong and emphatic disapproval of such proposed legislation. The Council also respectfully, but firmly, calls upon the House of Commons to refuse its sanction to this or any similar measure unless provision is made in the Bill that any Rules and Regulations thereby proposed to be made by the Local Government Board shall not come into operation until they had been laid upon the table of the House of Commons for forty days and have received the sanction of the House.

They also petitioned Parliament in support of the Local Authorities Officers Superannuation Bill, which provided for pensions based on contributions from salaries.

They were at loggerheads with the Railway Company over a number of matters in addition to the level-crossing, which they soft-peddled nowadays. The demand was repeated for just one fast train 'to town' in the early morning and another back in the evening. Waterloo responded with a train leaving Farnham at 10.5 a.m. which would in future run non-stop from North Camp and arrive in London at 11.13 a.m., and that an additional train would leave Farnham at 1.50 p.m., calling at North Camp and Brookwood and arrive at Waterloo at 2.58 p.m., both doing the journey in 68 minutes. But they couldn't promise one back. This was of no particular advantage to business men and an action committee was formed with Alton and Aldershot, which got them nowhere. So they sent an invitation to the Great Western Railway Company to extend their system to Aldershot and Farnham. Meanwhile the L. & S-W.R. were making improvements to the line which entailed the widening of the bridges at Firgrove and Weydon (one fails to see an advantage in this to the railway), an operation full of possibilities for the Council, who demanded adequate accommodation for foot-passengers, and gas and water mains, at Firgrove, and then changed their minds to one footway only. Pauling & Co., the Railway's Contractors, requested leave to close the road at Weydon during the work. The Council said no and were told that the Rural Council had raised no objection so they agreed, on payment of £25 compensation, for a period not exceeding one month. The £25 they divided between religious charities in the town, the Church of England getting the lion's share. At Firgrove it was not so simple. The engineer asked the Council to put up half the cost of £800 and, although the scheme commended itself to the Council, they jibbed, got the local contribution reduced to £300, with a third recoverable from the Rural Council, as an interested party, and informed the Railway people that they wanted iron spikes on top of the girders at the sides of the bridge.

Mr. Crundwell wrote in June 'that in future the Guardians would not be prepared to receive dead bodies into the mortuary at the Workhouse as they considered that a public mortuary should be provided by the Council'. This communication was passed back to Mr. Crundwell, as Clerk of the Joint Isolation Hospital Committee. Infectious diseases were already being dealt with in the temporary ward, the charge for each patient fixed at £1 per week ... At a special meeting on 12 July a letter from Mr. Crundwell, as Clerk of the Rural District Council, threatened legal action if the sewage farm smells were not abated. At the time the Council had a fairly clear conscience about the farm and replied that they were prepared to defend any action brought against them. In the course of discussion it transpired that the Gas Company were in the habit of making a smell, and the blame was put on them ... Mr. A.J. Nash gave notice of his intention to apply for a provisional order to introduce electric lighting to the town ... Mr. Mason, on the occasion of his daughter's forthcoming marriage to Mr. Gordon Tompsett, was asked to accept a silver salver on her behalf. The Clerk expressed himself as taken quite by surprise and cordially thanked the Members ... Hearty congratulations were tendered through the Commander-in-Chief to the Sirdar of the Egyptian Army, and the Officers and men engaged under him, upon the brilliant victory over the Dervishes at Omdurman. They were acknowledged by Lord Wolseley and, a month later, in a letter from Major-General Sir Herbert Kitchener himself.

Proceedings were taken against John Lord of Downing Street for causing a nuisance by the frying of fish 'without taking the best practicable means of counteracting or preventing the effluvia arising therefrom' ... The National Telephone Company were given permission to erect a line of telephone poles in Tilford Road, at a rent of 1s. per pole per annum ... The Farnham United Brewery were still discharging their hot liquor into the sewer at one end of the town and the Council getting blamed for the smell at the other end. At anything up to 190 degrees at the Brewery end, by the time it had worked its way through the pipes to the sewerage works, the effect on the more normal traffic was pungent. Mr. Thomas Tovey, the Brewery's Secretary, wrote on 16 September in reply to the Council that, whilst denying that the discharge was of a chemical nature and illegal under the Public Health Acts, his Directors were willing to consider any suggestion. Then Mr. Crundwell of the Rural Council complained that recent illnesses, one fatal, in the Badshot Lea area had been attributed by Doctor Tanner to the smells from the farm. The Council engaged an expert chemist to investigate and the Brewery put up their Mr. Start, the argument went on and the smells continued.

It was recommended that, because of 'the excellent services rendered by the Surveyor during the past twelve months, resulting in a considerable saving in the labour account of the Council', Mr. Cass' salary should be increased. He had already been given a £10 rise, and a further £10 cycle allowance, now he went up £20 ... As the result of lobbying in Parliamentary circles by Mr. Bide, Mr. Vincent Griffiths C.B. of the Treasury offered a grant of £15 per annum for road repairs owing to military traffic; the Council accepted with thanks, but asked for it to be made retrospective two or three years ... The Urban Council's share of the Isolation Hospital furniture came to £200 ... Mr. Borelli, owner of 47 Castle Street, complained of a nuisance next door at 46. Mr. Cass was authorised under the 1875 Act to enter and inspect the drains ... Plans in November for a new infirmary at the Workhouse, and the conversion of hop-pickers barracks in Red Lion Lane to a dwelling for Mr. Wells ... The newly formed Wey Valley Water Company, operating outside the Urban area, applied to lay a main near the *Six Bells.* The strings attached to the Council's permission were so harsh that Mr. F.C. Potter the

Company's Secretary, objected. Mr. Potter was with the Wey Valley for over forty years ... The Councillors, in their corporate capacity, attended the Parish Church on 11 November 1898 for the dedication of the Hoste Memorial pulpit.

They passed into the year 1899 with more on their minds than it is fair to expect of men who were not being paid for it ... They allowed Reid & Co. to cut through the iron fence in Longbridge to provide a 'rolling way' to the *Bridge House Inn* ... The Chairman stated that he had been approached upon the subject of calling a town's meeting in support of the Tzar's Rescript, but this was considered undesirable at the present time ... In February, the owners of the *Queen Street Tavern* at 125 East Street were served with a notice to put the same into a habitable condition. Alone of Farnham's many vanished pubs, the legend of this tavern at the bottom of Bear Lane has remained, for two reasons–at one time it was called the *Fourteen-penny House,* for one could pay that sum and drink as much as one liked; also it recalls an attempt, following the Queen's visit in 1857, to rename East Street 'Queen Street' ... In March plans from George Sturt were considered for a new workshop in South View. The Council took the chance of negotiating for room in which to provide a 30-feet road from East Street to the St. Cross Estate and Mr. A.J. Stedman, Sturt's architect, made certain proposals which were followed up at a special meeting on the site on 11 March. Two cottages, Nos. 84 and 85 East Street, were acquired so that, with the passage way between them and Sturt's wheelwrights' shop, a road could be constructed. In contemporary records the new road was called Sturts Road; later on it became known as St. Cross Road. With the disappearance of the wheelwrights' shop, Farnham's only monument to George Sturt is to be found on the shelves in the public library, the common grave of those who write about Farnham.

But the really big guns were pointed at their arch-enemies, the Farnham Gas Company. This time it was the Council who fired the first shots, in September 1898, with a provoking resolution to apply to the Board of Trade for a Provisional Order enabling them to supply electricity within the District for all public or private purposes in accordance with section 3 of the Electric Lighting Act, 1882–like the telephone, electricity was a long time coming. It was decided to engage a Mr. Warden Stevens, an 'Electric Engineer' currently advising the Dorking Urban Council, to make a report on the matter, for a fee of 25 guineas. Mr. A.J. Nash gave notice of his intention not to apply for a Provisional Order.

In the new year the Gas Company had an application before the Board of Trade for an Order enabling them to increase capital, limit dividends, revise the price of gas and other domestic matters, and the Council instructed a firm of Parliamentary Agents, Baker, Lees & Company, to represent them in opposition to the draft order. The occasion was taken for a resolution 'that, in the opinion of the Council, the supply of gas to the Urban District of Farnham should be in the hands of the Urban District Council' and that a clause should be inserted in the Provisional Order enabling the Council to purchase the Undertaking. Fully determined in their course, but wishing to avoid expense, a committee of Councillors Eggar, Kempson, Kingham and Wilcox was detailed to overture to the Gas Company for the purchase. Potter & Crundwell, acting for the Company, wrote on 31 January 1899 stating that the Directors were not prepared to confer upon the subject of the purchase of their Undertaking but would be pleased to meet the Council's representatives to discuss the other points of difference mentioned in the opposition to their draft Provisional Order.

On 28 February 'a general discussion took place upon the question of purchasing the Farnham Gas Company's Undertaking or of providing Electric Lighting Works for the town, and various figures having been considered, it was on the motion of Mr. Bide, seconded by Mr. Smith, resolved that, in order to obviate the expense of an appeal to Parliament on the Farnham Gas Company's Provisional Order, this Council do direct their Clerk to make to the Company an explicit offer of £20,000 for their Undertaking, such offer to be made subject to the following conditions, viz.–(1) that the sanction of the Local Government Board be obtained thereto, and (2) that such offer shall under no circumstances prejudice the position of the Council in the event of its non-acceptance and of the Council being driven to obtain and proceed upon power to purchase the Undertaking compulsorily'. At the same time it was arranged to be represented at the Board of Trade enquiry and, if the purchase clause was not inserted, then the Council should be represented by Counsel before Parliament.

In a letter dated 3 March, Potter & Crundwell complained of the Council's manner of making the offer and of the condition imposed, but asked what the sum of £20,000 covered. They were informed that, included in the term 'Undertaking', were the following:—

(1) Freehold Works
(2) Mains
(3) Meters, gas-stoves, lamp columns, tools, barrows, other fixed and movable plant and other articles and things *ejusdem generis* used in the business, and nothing more. That the Council will be prepared to take by valuation in the usual way, any stock of coal, coke, gas and residual products, and that they had no such ulterior motives in making the offer as suggested.

XXVII

A GAME OF MONOPOLY

THE GAS Company were granted their Provisional Order at the Board of Trade Enquiry without the insertion of the cause enabling the Council to purchase the Undertaking. At a special meeting on 28 April 1899 it was resolved 'that the Council do take all necessary proceedings to secure the insertion of the purchase clause'; at the same time, in order to avoid the expense of Parliamentary proceedings, they increased their offer to £13 for each of the 1,920 shares if the Company would withdraw their Order and not oppose any Bill introduced by the Council. This offer, too, was declined, so the Council went ahead with a petition to the House of Lords which cost £371 0s. 11d. fees but had the desired effect of getting the enabling clause inserted. The next step was to get the approval of the inhabitants.

Mr. A.J. Nash gave notice of his intention to apply for a Provisional Order to supply the Urban District with electricity. Mr. Nash's proposals for a one-man Electricity Undertaking had a way of switching on and off and of reminding the Council that, notwithstanding their obsession with gas, there was another method of lighting–one, moreover, they themselves had a good opportunity of getting into on the ground floor. They considered Mr. Nash's latest proclamation on 26 September, together with a report from Mr. Warden Stevens, the Electric Engineer, and resolved 'that the Council do take all necessary steps to obtain a Provisional Order enabling them to supply their District with Electricity for lighting and other purposes'. A letter dated 1 November from Potter & Crundwell enquired whether it was the definite intention of the Council to apply for an Electricity Order as their client, Mr. Nash, wanted to know whether or not to proceed with his application. The Council replied that it certainly was and thus put their competitor out of the running. At the same meeting on 26 September it was resolved 'that the Council do take all necessary steps to introduce a Bill into Parliament and promote the same in the next Session of Parliament to empower them to purchase the Undertaking of the Farnham Gas Company Limited and incur all necessary costs, charges and expenses in relation thereto'. Having thus committed themselves on two fronts, they sat back to see what would happen.

Another matter which rekindled during the summer and autumn of 1899 was the level-crossing problem. In April Mr. Cass reported two recent accidents, the gates each time being broken down by an engine running into them. The Railway Company were urged to remove this enormous risk of accident and their Secretary replied 'reminding the Council of the Company's proposal for the abolition of the crossing in 1897, which was opposed by the Council, and stating that his Directors thought any further suggestion should come from the Council'. This took the form of stressing the necessity for building a new station at Farnham which would eliminate a considerable part of the danger. Later in the year the Railway, when asked to surrender a strip of land for improvements in Tilford Road, refused to do so unless in connection with a scheme for the abolition of the crossing–one gathers that opening and shutting the gates had become just as irksome to the Railway as to the members of the public who stood by shouting encouragement. And so the argument passed into the 20th century.

The 1899 Election brought in Charles Monk of West Street with 285 votes and A.J. Bentall regained his seat with 354; Samuel Beesley (166) and J.A. Eggar (237) made room for them–'The freeman casting with unpurchased hand, the vote that shakes the turrets of the land'. Edgar Kempson (368) and Charles Smith (249) were returned. Mr. Kempson became the new Chairman ... A public meeting was convened to consider a programme for the visit of the Hampshire Yeomanry for annual training ... Mr. George Elliott of West Street was caught out with the erection of a building before submitting plans. The plans were disapproved because of unacceptable materials and they made his life miserable until he complied ... The houses on the other side of the boundary in Tilford Road were allowed on the sewer provided the Rural Council laid the necessary mains to connect up and agreed to pay 1s. 6d. per year in the pound on the rateable values of such properties. The country cousins were pleased to accept this arrangement; it is unfortunate therefore that they should at this time have fallen out with the Urban Council over the sewerage works. Mr. Crundwell sent an extract from a report by the Rural District's Medical Officer to the effect that on 23 May he had at the request of the County Medical Officer accompanied him to the sewage farm, where conditions were found to be so bad that they created a serious nuisance. Mr. Crundwell ventured to suggest that nothing had been done to abate the nuisance since his Council had last complained. The Council, who were currently quite proud of the way things were going in the circumstances, indignantly pointed out that lots of things had been done, such as threatening the Brewery with legal action, and went on to say that it would have been courteous if the Rural and County Surveyors had informed the Council of their visit to the farm. Mr. Crundwell wrote again asking what exactly the Council had done in the matter; the reply was rather evasive but insisted that the steps taken were considered sufficient. To make sure, the Council thoroughly inspected the farm on 6 July, during a pumping session and, although the evening was very close and oppressive, the working of the farm, in their opinion, was very satisfactory. The Rural Council, who engaged an expert to watch the farm, declared that, if no improvement was made, they would be reluctantly compelled to take legal proceedings against the Urban Council. This really annoyed the Council who replied that they were quite prepared to defend themselves.

The Council's workmen were given their usual holidays on 8 July—the 's' on the end of holiday is because of the plural pronoun ... There was a complaint from a Mr. Patterson of Castle View about a report in the *Herald* of Court proceedings against him which inferred that Council Officers had said in evidence that 'his house was in such a dirty state as to be a nuisance'. Doctor Sloman and Mr. Cass were questioned on the matter and Mr. Patterson was informed that 'the Officers' reports in the Court did not appear to exactly correspond with what he alleged was the Newspaper's report' ... Mr. Eyre and Mr. Fryer complained about nuisances in the Goats Head Yard and the police were begged to prevent persons committing such nuisances in this and other yards ... There was a petition signed by twenty-six ratepayers grumbling about the fish-frying at Clarke's premises at 37 Downing Street. Mr. Clarke attended the meeting and expressed his willingness to do all in his power to stop the nuisance, but the Council took proceedings and Mr. Clarke was fined 10s. ... Someone wrote in about the noise of the steam roundabout on fair days in the meadow by South Street.

These fairs! Damage was reported by Mr. Cass, at the June meeting, to the road surface in Castle Street, caused by stall-holders at recent fairs. The culprits were W. Davis, no address; L. Davies, Woking; C. Odoin, Farnborough; Morris Ayres, Farnham; G. Gale, Byfleet; R. Mathews, Woking and James Mathews, Epsom. A strong protest was sent to the Town Hall Company calling attention to 'the intolerable nuisance to the inhabitants of Castle Street caused by the fairs'. Mr. Crundwell, for the Company, admitted that, on the occasion complained of, 'there were unusual circumstances and that the Company were not the masters of the situation'. He also made the interesting suggestion that 'if the Town were desirous of acquiring the fair rights and had any proposal to make for the purchase of the Company's interest in the tolls, his Directors would be prepared to consider same'. Mr. Crundwell also referred to the Council's enquiry about a site for a public convenience at the rear of the Town Hall and asked whether they had made up their minds yet. The Council offered £300 for the fair and market rights; this was refused, accounts being produced which showed an average of over £25 per annum over the past three years, with the recommendation that a sum which would produce a similar income would be of more interest to the Directors. Negotiations for the site for the convenience fared better and it was agreed to take it on a 99-year lease. But in November, Mr. Crundwell wrote saying 'that pressure having been brought to bear upon the Directors of the Company in the matter, they could not see their way to grant the Council a lease of any part of their premises for the purposes of a public convenience'. The neighbours, no doubt, had been getting at them.

Mr. Moore of the St. Cross Estate called attention to the necessity for sewering the estate because of the nuisance caused by the emptying of cesspools–'in effect asking the Council to carry out such sewerage works at the ratepayers' expense'. It was decided to lay sewers but at the estate residents' expense. Mr. Moore was informed of this; it was also pointed out to him that he had emptied his own cesspool at 9.30 p.m. on 11 July, 'thereby causing the nuisance of which he complained ... Ex-Councillor Eggar wrote about the 'enormous quantity of paper scattered about in all directions in the Park, evidently the remains of picnic parties'. Mr. Eggar was reminded that the Park was outside the Urban District and the Council had no power to act ... The Clerk was absent from the September meeting and reported 'far from well'. Mr. Mason's dedication to numerous activities in Farnham was all the more remarkable because of his refusal to allow indifferent health to interrupt. His right-hand man at the offices of Hollest, Mason & Nash in West Street, as well as in his Council business, was James William Wright. Mr. Wright's neat handwriting in the minute-books, from a long time back in the Local Board days, eases the task of the researcher. As Acting Clerk, he took the meeting in September 1899. He succeeded Mr. Mason as Clerk of the Council in 1910.

Mr. W.T. Coleman was congratulated on being made a Magistrate ... The Bishop of Winchester urgently begged the Council to take all possible action to secure 'the decent housing of the hop-pickers coming into the town'. The pickers, who in their hundreds annually invaded Farnham to harvest the rich abundance of hops, were a rough lot. After a busy day in the fields, and a busier evening sampling the products of the previous year's picking, they were content to doss down in the sleazy accommodation provided by those landlords who made a side living from the town's great industry. Now the Council had a blitz on the lodging-houses that would have gladdened the heart of the late Mr. Wonnacott. Notices were served, mainly in respect of inadequate sanitation, though other causes were darkly hinted at, on such establishments as *The Sun* and *Bird-in-Hand,* both of Downing Street, at Weydon Mill and Beavers Kilns, and a cottage in Harts Yard 'to cause a certain room there over a privy to cease to be occupied' ... G.H. Hawkins of East Street and T. Stratford,

West street, were two butchers made to stop draining their waste liquids into the sewers ... A man who stopped a runaway horse belonging to the Council was rewarded with 10s. ... Mr. Ransom spoke of recent accidents to passengers in the streets caused by the reckless riding of cyclists, and Police Superintendent Simmonds was asked to act ... The *Bush Hotel* dung-pit was still a source of nuisance. Notice had been served on the landlord, Mr. Hunt, but there had since been a change of tenants, referred to a few years later as 'The Bush Syndicate', and the notice was re-issued, together with a demand that 'the use of the back of the *Bush* gates as a urinal' should cease ... In a list of unpaid accounts on which the Collector sought instructions appeared an item of 12s. owing by Lord George Sanger ... The County Council invited views on Light Railways and the Council thought these would be most useful

> (1) from Farnham to Crondall in the County of Hants–between each place there is considerable and increasing traffic, both of passengers and goods–and thence to Odiham and Basingstoke, and (2) Farnham to Frensham, Churt and so on to Haslemere.

The Boer War, which broke out on 10 October 1899, kindled a Kiplingesque fever of patriotism. At a public meeting at the Town Hall on 2 November a fund was raised in aid of the wives and families of men serving in South Africa; five days later it had topped the £200 mark. Many of those wives became widows. The conflict had caught the Government unprepared and lacking in military intelligence. What they had estimated as nothing greater than a police action against the Boers, or at the worst something on the scale of the Khartoum affair, developed into full-blooded warfare. In the first three months or so the Boers had it all their own way and the country was shocked to the core ... Mr. Mason was congratulated on being appointed Chairman of the Board of Governors of the Grammar School ... Colonel Torkington of Willey Place, Alton Road wrote on 18 November that a horse belonging to his son had recently died from injuries received through shying at some water pipes by the side of the road at the West End of the town, which pipes had remained by the side of the highway an unconscionably long time, and leaving the matter of compensation in the hands of the Council.

Meanwhile the Councillors had been looking for a place of their own. The first recorded move came in June, when Mr. Bide offered to sell them Hatch Mill in Darvills Lane for £2,000. The Council inspected the Mill and it was proposed by Mr. Coleman that the premises be purchased for conversion into a depot, storeyard and stabling. The motion was defeated, whereupon Mr. Bide was thanked and his offer declined. Doctor Hayes had drawn attention to a likely yard in South Street, then occupied by Thomas Mitchell and owned by Robert Trimmer, who agreed to sell for £1,500. Mention also was made of Hickley's premises in Castle Street which was soon coming on the market when Hickleys moved to their new place on the corner of South Street and Abbey Street. At a special meeting on 11 September, the advantages of Trimmer's offer and that of Hickleys–£2,000–were considered. Mr. Trimmer was persauded to throw in a little more land, part of Mr. Heath's garden, and it was resolved 'that the land and premises in South Street now offered by Mr. Trimmer to the Council for the sum of £1,500 be purchased conditionally upon the sanction of the Local Government Board being obtained to borrow the purchase money, and that the sale be free from all restrictions ... That the Surveyor be instructed to prepare full particulars of the Council's requirements in regard to Offices, Council Chamber, Fire Brigade Station, Stabling, Storeyard etc. and submit same to the Public Works Committee for consideration and report to the Council'. On receiving the report, it was resolved that architects in the Urban District be invited to submit competitive designs for Council Offices etc., the total cost not to exceed £2,500, in addition to the site. A prize of 15 guineas was offered for the best design. Local Government in Farnham had climbed a long way from the Vestry at the Parish Church.

Cook's son, duke's son, son of a belted earl,
Son of a Lambeth publican–it's all the same today!
Each of 'em doing his country's work
(And who's to look after the girl?),
Pass the hat for your credit's sake
And pay–pay–pay!

Anon.–*Daily Mail,* 31 October 1899.

XXVIII

DEATH OF A QUEEN

ALDERSHOT WAS really taking things seriously now and upwards of 200,000 men had been sent to South Africa, where the victory of the Boers was halted. Farnham felt a special involvement in view of its nearness to the garrison town. The news in February 1900 was good–Kimberley was relieved on the 15th; on the 27th General Cronje surrendered to Lord Roberts and on the following day came the Relief of Ladysmith by Sir Redvers Buller. Before proceeding to the business of the March meeting, the Chairman proposed 'that this Council do invite Lord Wolseley, Commander-in-Chief of the Army, to convey to Lord Roberts, Lord Kitchener, Sir Redvers Buller, Sir George White and General Kekewich the hearty congratulations of the Council upon the recent successes gained by them and the officers and men under their command in South Africa, and to express the Council's appreciation thereof, which appreciation they venture to think is intensified by the close proximity of their District to Aldershot'.

A special Council meeting was held on Friday, 18 May, in anticipation of the last big event of the war, the Relief of Mafeking. News of victory was imminent and Members were told that the meeting had been convened for the purpose of considering what action, if any, should be taken by the Council in the event of the relief of Mafeking. It was resolved 'that the Rector be invited to hold a Public Thanksgiving Service in the Parish Church as near 8 o'clock as the circumstances would permit in the evening of the day on which the news of the Relief is received and that the inhabitants of the District be invited to celebrate the event by decorating their houses and places of business, and by a public half-holiday which, it was suggested, should be given on the following Monday, should the news be received on a Saturday'.

Mafeking was relieved that same day, but the news was not received until the day afterwards, when the Council met again. They resolved to recommend the Postmaster to close the sub-offices in East Street and the Waverley Estate from 1 o'clock on Monday. Mr. Kingham reported that he had engaged the band of the Queens Bays to play in the town on Monday evening from six to nine o'clock and it was decided to ask the Bishop for permission for the band to play in the Park. The Councillors then attended the Public Thanksgiving Service at the Church. At the end of the month, when Roberts took Pretoria, the Council telegraphed the Queen 'offering their loyal congratulations upon the successes of Her Forces in South Africa'. The war was not over, scattered bands of Boers carried on a formidable guerrilla war and peace was not signed until May 1902. The excitement of it was over and there remained the depressing aftermath of battle—the casualties. The dead stayed in South Africa, the wounded were invalided home.

Harmsworth of the *Daily Mail* sponsored a fund-raising campaign to finance the establishment of a convalescent home. Much of the money was collected in music halls in response to the stirring lines of a song, published anonymously in the *Mail* in 1899, and sung to the full-blooded music of Sir Arthur Sullivan in a show called *The Absent Minded Beggar*—Kipling's name for Tommy Atkins. Probably due to its closeness to Aldershot, Farnham was chosen for the site of the proposed Absent Minded Beggars Home and the *Daily Mail's* representative, a Mr. Balch, had made contact with the Council, who recommended a piece of land near the Manor House in Waverley Lane, belonging to Mrs. Hannah Johnston-Forster, who had bought Moor Park from Sir William Rose in 1899. The Council had unfortunately overlooked the fact that, in disposing of the possessions of others, it is important to have their authority beforehand. Normally sticklers for correct etiquette, they had in this unusually provocative situation suffered a severe attack of bad manners and, as a result, the negotiations between Mr. Balch and Mrs. Johnston-Forster never got off the ground. A special meeting on 18 June 1900 was called for the purpose of considering what steps, if any, should be taken to facilitate the establishment of the proposed military convalescent home in the Farnham District. The Chairman reported 'that he had been in communication with Mr. Balch, the gentleman in charge of the negotiations in this District in reference to the Home and had that afternoon received a telegram from him to the effect that there was little hope of the Home now coming to Farnham, and having explained what he knew of the abortive negotiations between Mr. Balch and Mrs. Johnston-Forster in reference to the acquisition of land for the Home at Farnham, a lengthened discussion ensued, in the course of which Mr. Kempson offered to telegraph an offer of a fresh site at Farnham to Mr. Balch, it was on the motion of Mr. Wilcox, seconded by Mr. Smith, resolved that the Clerk do write Mrs. Johnston-Forster:–

> That the Council were unanimously of the opinion that such a Home erected on land near Manor House belonging to her could not fail to have proved an advantage to their District and that it was with much regret that they received an intimation that the negotiations for the sale to the promoters by her of the land in question had fallen through, and the more so as it would appear from the statement of one of their number that that result was said to be in some measure at least owing to the fact that the Council had not approached her on the subject, which they would gladly have done had they not thought such a step savoured of presumption, and to beg that, should the negotiations prove not to be at an end, or should they be reviewed, that she would favour the Council with an interview upon the subject.

The Home went to Alton; it is now Treloars, though sometimes still affectionately called 'The Absent Minded Beggars Home'. What a grand opening ceremony it would have occasioned–Alfred Harmsworth, and certainly some, if not all, of the personalities of the Boer War, Kitchener, Roberts, Buller, Kipling and the rest; not to mention Royalty.

. . . . .

On the home front, Architects A.J. Stedman and A.H. Guyer had written to say that they had found it impossible to keep down to the Council's ceiling of £2,500 for the proposed Council Offices. There were four envelopes of plans on the table. They considered whether to employ an assessor, at 50 guineas, to open them and advise but impatiently decided against this and opened them themsleves, had a quick look and passed them to a committee to study in detail. At a special meeting on 9 January 1900—'Your Committee beg to report that, having very carefully considered the four competitive designs for Council Offices etc. sent in, they found themselves able to dispense with the services of an Expert and, in their opinion, the best design in keeping with the particulars issued by the Council is that marked "Ventilation", and they recommend that the premium of Fifteen guineas be awarded to this Competitor and that such design be adopted by the Council'. The envelope marked 'Ventilation'—it would be interesting to know what prompted the architect in his choice of pseudonym—was thereupon opened and the successful competitor was found to be Paxton Hood Watson. Besides Stedman and Guyer, the fourth entrant was Harold Falkner, whose drawings were subsequently exhibited at the Royal Academy.

Mr. Watson was notified of his success and asked to attend the Local Government Board enquiry on 12 January to support his plan. He produced a builder's quotation for the work, in the sum of £2,496 12s. 7d., which was accepted by the Council—it was not until April that they remembered, or someone reminded them, that they should have advertised for tenders, so they had to start again. In the meantime, they had a second look at the plans and made certain alterations and additions which put another £1,290 on the cost and the estimate now stood as follows:—

Site	£1,500
Buildings—original	2,500
Buildings—additional ...	1,290
Boundary wall	200
Furnishing	200
Costs and Architect's fees ...	250
	£5,940

As readers will have noticed, the cost of projects undertaken by the Council had a way of soaring above the original estimate. They had started off with something like £4,000 in mind, plus a couple of hundred or so for furniture and fees. In June they considered builders' tenders; these were Tompsett & Co., Farnham, £4,285; Herbert Hutchinson, Haslemere, £4,316; J. Harris & Son, Woking, £4,463; A.H. Harris, Mickleham, £4,543 and Musselwhite & Son, Basingstoke, £4,572. Furnishings, too, rose to £300, and architect's fees to £320; in addition, a Clerk of Works materialised at £156. In no time at all, the total had risen to £6,561; before the end it was to rise to something nearer £8,000.

The Market and Fairs Committee recommended that the offer to the Town Hall Company for their tolls should be increased from £300 to £450. Mr. Crundwell insisted, however, that his Directors were not prepared to sell the rights for any less sum than, invested in 2½ per cent Consols, would produce an annual income of £23. Whereupon the Council informed the Company that they were unable to entertain the proposed purchase ... In connection with the proposed improvements in Tilford Road, which in a roundabout way concerned the level-crossing, and Mr. Rupert Anderson of Waverley Abbey, Mr. Bide undertook to wait upon that gentleman; he returned with the message 'that the action of the Council in the matter of the transfer of the Villa of Waverley to the Parish of Farnham Rural quite prevented his offering the Council any favours whatever' ... A licence was granted for the performance of stage plays at the Institute in South Street, on the same terms as those applied to the Town Hall ... Mr. Wells of the Water Company invited the Councillors and Officers to the opening of the new pumping house at the Waterworks on 13 February ... Mr. Cass applied for assistance 'in the shape of a youth' and an office boy was engaged at 5s. a week ... Mr. Warden Stevens asked whether the Council proposed to proceed with the electricity project ... A Mr. Hillkirk sought permission to carry two electric lighting wires over East Street and was discouraged.

At the 1900 Election, George Ransom (255) and R.G. Trimmer (221) lost their seats to Arthur Hart of 117 West Street, who topped the poll with 343 votes, and Samuel Beesley who came back with 270. Samuel Bide (306) and R.D. Kingham (279) were returned. Mr. Kingham became Chairman ... The Medical Officer for the Isolation Hospital was congratulated on the efficient manner in which the hospital was being run ... In view of their important position at the corner of South Street and Abbey Street, Hickleys proposed new premises were a major event in what then passed for town planning–and a potential accident spot on what passes for a by-pass road some sixty years later. In submitting plans, Hickleys' architect John Kingham, requested that a sewer should be laid in South Street to connect the new building. The Council, eager to improve the building line at this point, did a deal with Hickleys for the rounding-off of the corner and two feet of frontage in South Street, in return for a sewer and £40. Hickleys put in a supplementary plan for the Emmanuel Church on part of their plot of land.

Floods, always a nuisance in the low-lying area of the town, had weakened the bridges in South Street and Longbridge by carrying away the ballast from the foundations. Repairs were estimated at £37, but Mr. Cass was encouraged to scout around the neighbourhood and try to recover some of the errant ballast ... Counsel's opinion on damage to highways caused by stall-holders at the fairs was not encouraging. Mr. J.F.P. Rawlinson Q.C., of 5 Crown Office Row, Temple, stated 'I am of the opinion that if from time immemorial the holders of stalls etc. at the Fairs have been accustomed to drive stakes etc. into the highway for the purpose of supporting their stalls, and have never paid the Highway Authority for the repairs thereby occasioned, that a right to do so has been acquired, the presumption being that the highway was dedicated subject to a liability to these obstructions' ... The Farnham Institute Cycling Club wanted to know whether the Council intended any local celebrations on the attainment of peace in South Africa and a public meeting was proposed ... Miss Paget of Lowlands referred to the damage to the drinking troughs in Castle Street and asked the Council's help in tracing the culprit. The matter, together with a complaint about the practice of persons obstructing the highways by standing thereon, was passed to Superintendent Simmonds to deal with ... The Surveyor was instructed to clear up wrappers from Sunday papers thrown about the streets.

At an average monthly meeting they dealt with some two dozen minor breaches of bye-laws, mainly over sanitation. Although drainage had been installed for ten years, there were still many properties without adequate water-closets ... The wages of Adams, driver of the large water cart, were increased from 17s. to 19s. per week ... Ashbourne Rural District Council advocated the taxation of cyclists and Mr. Bide proposed, with Mr. Smith seconding, 'that, as cyclists and others have now the great advantage of improved highways, this Council is of the opinion that it is desirable that a tax should be imposed upon cycles, motor-cars and motor-cycles, such tax to be applied towards the repair and improvement of highways'. The motion was defeated by four votes to five, but, with the exception of cycles, the idea soon caught on ... Doctor Hayes called attention to the nuisance arising from music upon certain land in South Street.

At the meeting in September 1900, Mr. Wright acted as Clerk. The Chairman stated 'that it was with great regret that he had to inform the Council of the sudden death of their Clerk's son, Mr. Alfred E. Mason, within the last half-hour, and moved that, as a mark of respect to the Clerk, the meeting do stand adjourned until this day week'. As on a previous occasion, death struck thrice at the Council that autumn. In October they expressed their sympathy to Daniel Goddard in his long illness–his last attendance had been at the May meeting. Goddard died soon afterwards. He can claim a place among Farnham's great men of the 19th century. His name, in faded signwriting, still identifies the vast derelict premises in East Street that were once the workshops of his craftsmen; more indelibly, his mark is on many Farnham buildings, for it is the privilege of a builder to erect his own monuments; Daniel Goddard even took a part in building his own cemetery. Charles Smith, the saddler of 72 Castle Street, who died an hour before the meeting on 6 November, was one of those plodding, less resolute members, a good seconder, shy of making proposals but ever ready to support the motions of others.

Death struck, too, that winter at one-quarter of the world. Queen Victoria died on Tuesday, 22 January 1901. The event was acknowledged by the Farnham Urban District Council at a special meeting on the following Monday, attended by all ten living members. It was proposed by the Chairman, seconded by Mr. Bide and unanimously resolved:–

> This this Council do record their heartfelt sorrow on the death of Her Most Gracious Majesty Queen Victoria, and offer their loyal and sincere devotion to His Majesty King Edward VII.

The Clerk was directed to send a copy of such Resolution to the Home Secretary. A notice was issued, inviting the inhabitants of the District to suspend all business during the whole of Saturday, 2 February, the day fixed for the funeral of the Queen. The Councillors accepted an invitation of the Rector and Churchwardens to attend in their official capacity the service to be held at the Parish Church on the following Saturday in memory of the beloved Queen.

My experience of the past, and I think it will be of the future, is that as soon as a gentleman comes upon the Council, he is bound to show himself to be what he is–a representative of the town, and is bound to prove himself to be a gentleman.

Richard Mason, *1907.*

EPILOGUE

IT IS the duty of every writer to round off his narrative with some sort of conclusion; it is difficult to do this when the plot has no ending. The Queen had died; the Council paused in their stride to pay their official respects and to join the townspeople in their's. Then they returned to their agenda, for, notwithstanding people's deaths, the business of the Council continued, uninterrupted by anything more than briefly minuted acceptances of death. At the time of the Queen's death the Council were engaged in various unfinished matters of some importance. In order to provide some semblance of an ending to this history, therefore, it is necessary to peep summarily into its future, not only in reference to those particular matters but as regards the fortunes of the Council generally.

The Councillors first met in their new home in South Street on 2 December 1902. The building of it had been beset with difficulties and mounting costs. They had terminated their tenancy of the Council Chamber at the Town Hall with effect from 30 June 1902 in the anticipation of getting possession of the new building by that date. The key was handed over in the following September, and there remained the matter of furnishings. That the official opening was conducted by no less a person than the Archbishop of Canterbury is easier to understand when one recalls that the invitation had initially been issued to and accepted by Bishop Randall Davidson at the castle, and that before the offices were ready for the ceremony his Lordship had been promoted to Canterbury, thus enabling a delighted Council to print his new title on the programmes.

Their excursion into the realms of gas and electricity, on the other hand, were doomed to failure. Having obtained at considerable expense a Provisional Order for the supply of electricity, they felt in duty bound to pursue their hasty decision. To cut a long story short, they became enmeshed in a tangled web of transactions with a London firm of consultants, Messrs. Preece & Cardew, who for a fat fee advised them to accept the tender of some contractors named the Edmundson Electricity Corporation. They had got completely out of their depth, not knowing whether to go ahead or to cut their mounting losses, when the townspeople took a hand. A memorial signed by 435 residents demanded a poll of the inhabitants; the 1902 Election was bitterly fought on the electric lighting issue and three complete strangers headed the poll. 'I take my stand upon electric light', canvassed one candidate, 'I declare it to be unnecessary, it will involve a heavily increased rate and it is open to ratepayers to vote against it'. A month later, the new Council told Edmundsons that the deal was off. Meanwhile a nicely timed move by the Gas Company, together with the offer of a contract with more conciliatory terms, relieved the disillusioned Council of any remaining thought of buying out the Company. A final blow to prestige–when electricity eventually came to Farnham, it was not the Council, or Mr. A.J. Nash, who obtained the Order, but the 'Farnham Gas and Electricity Company Limited'.

In April 1902 the boundaries were extended in accordance with Mr. Cass' recommendations to take in the housing developments up Firgrove Hill and Tilford Road, as far as Great Austins and the Ridgway, thus bringing sewerage to those new residents ... That year also Farnham's first houses for the working classes were built, by Kemp, the Aldershot builder, in Adams Park Road ... At the meeting on 3 June 1902 they celebrated the news that peace had been restored in South Africa by rising to their feet and singing 'God Save the King'. The Local Volunteers began arriving home and a public welcome was arranged for them; for those who did not come home a brass tablet was placed inside the Church. They had great things lined up for the return of General Herbert Plumer, who lived at Leigh House in West Street (where the G.P.O. came), but Lady Plumer tactfully averted this forbidding prospect.

Basically, over the years, the business of the Council changed but little, though it grew in volume as the area of the District was increased by boundary extensions. As already mentioned orders came into force which in 1914 included the villages of Hale, Heath End, Weybourne and Badshot Lea and, in 1924, the areas of Boundstone, Rowledge, Wrecclesham, Bourne, Waverley and Dippenhall. Thus, with the exception of Tilford, the Council won back the territory of the old Parish of Farnham which the Local Board had abandoned in 1866. Now twenty-one in number, the Councillors needed a larger staff. Richard Mason died in May 1910, after forty-five years as Clerk to the Local Board and Council, and his successor, Mr. J.W. Wright, took as an assistant in 1920 Arthur Minns, who in his turn became Clerk in 1928. Mr. Cass now had a staff of three and was so busy that he relinquished his duties as Sanitary and Building Inspector to Mr. R.M. Sargent. In 1922 Richard Watson was appointed Accountancy Assistant and later rose to Chief Financial Officer. By 1929 when the writer joined Alfred Thorp and his assistant, Frederic Holloway (later Rating and Valuation Officer) in the Collector's Office, the staff had spread beyond the confines of Paxton Watson's office building into an adjoining annexe, formerly Mr. Arthur Rose's house, Montrose. On the retirement of Mr. Cass in 1925, Leonard Starling was appointed Surveyor; Cass' son, George, was his assistant. Doctor Sloman's long service ended and Doctor F. Bedo Hobbs was appointed Medical Officer of Health. Gradually, with the residential development of the District, the paper work increased and the number of junior staff with it. Then one by one these men, too, went and others took their places.

The changing concepts of the 20th century in the life and structure of the town have necessarily had their effect, though the old leisurely pattern is discernible through the quickened tempo of modern Farnham. One notices, for instance, the same tendency of the street-sweepers to lean upon their brooms and the old buildings of the town, jealously guarded from vandalism, are framed rather than overshadowed by the Woolmead shopping centre. The smells have diminished, also the infectious diseases, but the same close watch is maintained; the streets are still congested by traffic, though the horses have disappeared. The present population figure of over 30,000 might suggest a town full of strangers, but this is not strictly true for in that figure are included most of the families who have lived in the town for generations. The old names survive–Mason, Patrick, Crosby, Borelli, Kingham, Falkner, Robins, Goddard, Bide, Simmonds; one could keep on.

Although the business of the Council has not altered much in essential matters, one notices here and there signs of different things to come, or things that have come. At the meeting held on 5 August 1969 it was reported that the Southern Gas Board had been consulted regarding the removal of that last bulwark of the Farnham Gas Company, the gas-holder. The cost of demolition being prohibitive, it was decided to camouflage it instead. A working party recommended the preservation, on historical or architectural grounds, of the *Jolly Farmer* and houses in Bridge Square and Abbey Street and of the Emmanuel Church in South Street. The redevelopment of Goddard's Yard in East Street was considered. There was opposition from residents to the proposed improvement of Upper Hale Road. Notice served on the owner of cottages in Mead Lane to repair a defective drain having been disregarded, further action under the Public Health Acts was considered. Proceedings were recommended against the purveyor of a pork pie found to be infested with maggots. The Thames Conservancy Board were reviewing the existing consent to the discharge of treated sewage effluent. The modernisation of Council houses in Adams Park Road was put in hand. A report was studied on the findings of Redcliffe-Maud's Royal Commission for the reorganisation of local government, tolling the knell of Urban District Councils and all other existing local authorities. The Chairman reported the text of a telegram he had addressed to the American Ambassador on the occasion of the landing of man on the Moon.

INDEX